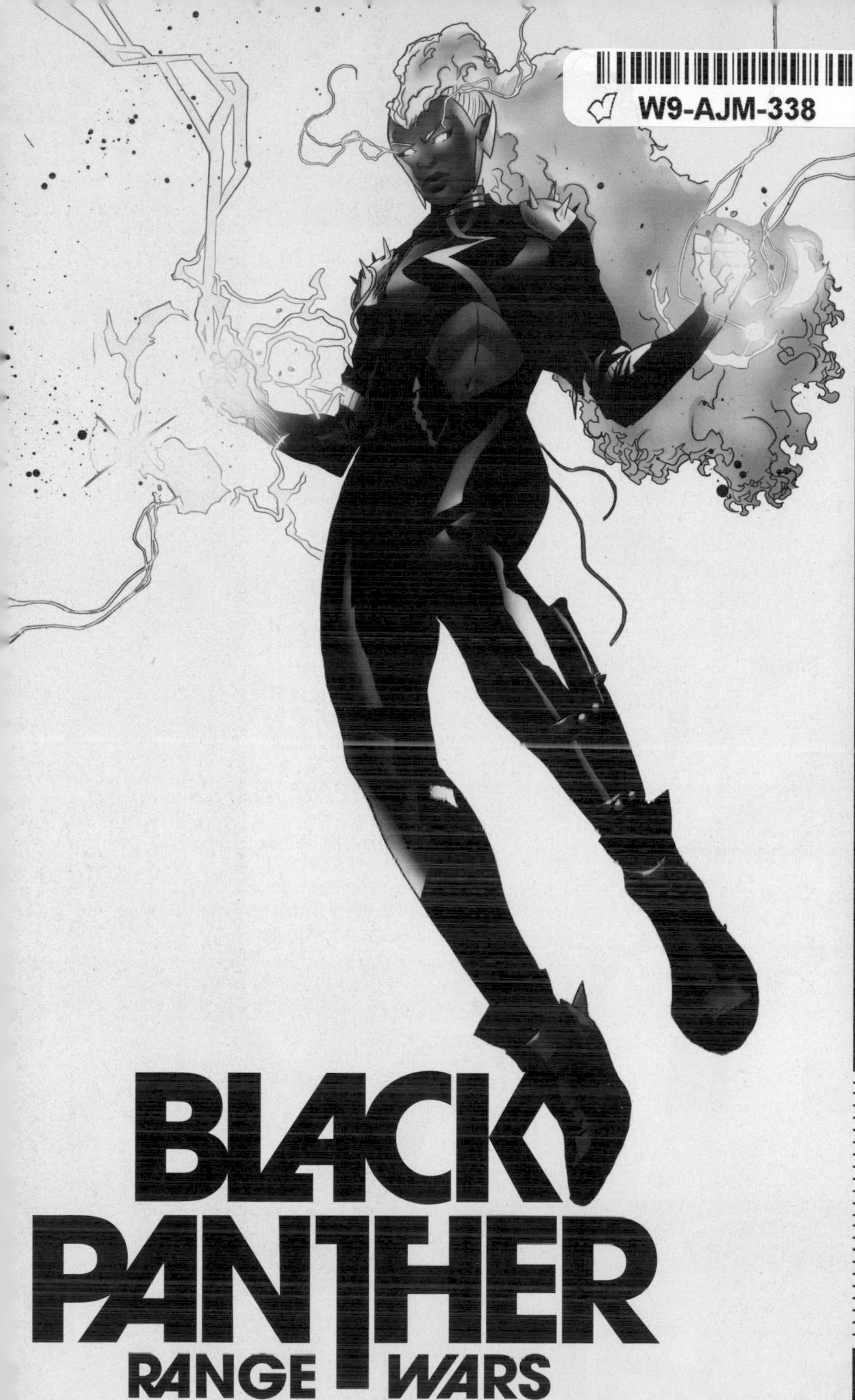

BLACK PANTHER
RANGE WARS

PREVIOUSLY:

While **King T'Challa** was off-planet, **Wakanda** transformed into a parliamentary democracy. T'Challa reluctantly accepted the new governance — until a mysterious group started targeting his personal network of sleeper agents, starting with the murder of his best friend, **Jhai**. Now, with the help of **Shuri** and Jhai's partner, **Omolola**, T'Challa is racing to uncover the assassins before he loses anyone else.

But after Omolola's deceptions made her the primary suspect and led to her arrest, the investigation was thrown into chaos. Omolola convinced Shuri of her innocence, and so Shuri found a new suspect: Who had more to gain from a destabilized Wakanda than **Akili**, the leader of Wakanda's secret police, the **Hatut Zeraze**? However, Akili had a suspect of his own — T'Challa himself. T'Challa escaped **Birnin Zana**, but after relinquishing the mantle of Black Panther, he must now rely on his own skills to fight off the Hatut Zeraze and prove his innocence, knowing he will soon have to reckon with the fallout of his own lies…

RANGE WARS

Writer | | | | | | | | | **JOHN RIDLEY**

Artists | | | | | | | | | | **STEFANO LANDINI** (#6-8) &
| | | | | | | | | | | | | **GERMÁN PERALTA** (#9-10)

Color Artists | | | | **MATT MILLA** (#6-8) &
| | | | | | | | | | | | **JESUS ABURTOV** (#9-10)

Letterer | | | | | | | VC's **JOE SABINO**

Cover Art | | | | | | | **ALEX ROSS**

Logo | | | | | | | | | | | **JAY BOWEN**

Wakandan Flag | | **BRIAN STELFREEZE**

Assistant Editors | | **MICHELLE MARCHESE**
| | | | | | | | | | | | | | | & **KAITLYN LINDTVEDT**

Editors | | | | | | | | | | **WIL MOSS** with **ALANNA SMITH**

Collection Editor | | | | | | | | | | | | | | | | | | | | | **DANIEL KIRCHHOFFER**

Assistant Managing Editor | | | | | | | | | | | | | **MAIA LOY**

Associate Manager, Talent Relations | | | | **LISA MONTALBANO**

Director, Production & Special Projects | | **JENNIFER GRÜNWALD**

VP Production & Special Projects | | | | | | | **JEFF YOUNGQUIST**

SVP Print, Sales & Marketing | | | | | | | | | | | **DAVID GABRIEL**

Book Designer | | | | | | | | | | | | | | | | | | | | **JAY BOWEN**

Editor in Chief | | | | | | | | | | | | | | | | | | | | | | | | **C.B. CEBULSKI**

BLACK PANTHER CREATED BY STAN LEE & JACK KIRBY

BLACK PANTHER BY JOHN RIDLEY VOL. 2: RANGE WARS. Contains material originally published in magazine form as BLACK PANTHER (2021) #6-10. First printing 2022 ISBN 978-1-302-92883-4. Published by MARVEL WORLDWIDE, INC., a subsidiary of MARVEL ENTERTAINMENT, LLC. OFFICE OF PUBLICATION: 1290 Avenue of the Americas, New York, NY 10104. © 2022 MARVEL No similarity between any of the names, characters, persons, and/or institutions in this book with those of any living or dead person or institution is intended, and any such similarity which may exist is purely coincidental. **Printed in Canada.** KEVIN FEIGE, Chief Creative Officer; DAN BUCKLEY, President, Marvel Entertainment; DAVID BOGART, Associate Publisher & SVP of Talent Affairs; TOM BREVOORT, VP, Executive Editor; NICK LOWE, Executive Editor, VP of Content, Digital Publishing; DAVID GABRIEL, VP of Print & Digital Publishing; SVEN LARSEN, VP of Licensed Publishing; MARK ANNUNZIATO, VP of Planning & Forecasting; JEFF YOUNGQUIST, VP of Production & Special Projects; ALEX MORALES, Director of Publishing Operations; DAN EDINGTON, Director of Editorial Operations; RICKEY PURDIN, Director of Talent Relations; JENNIFER GRÜNWALD, Director of Production & Special Projects; SUSAN CRESPI, Production Manager; STAN LEE, Chairman Emeritus. For information regarding advertising in Marvel Comics or on Marvel.com, please contact Vit DeBellis, Custom Solutions & Integrated Advertising Manager, at vdebellis@marvel.com. For Marvel subscription inquiries, please call 888-511-5480. **Manufactured between 8/26/2022 and 9/27/2022** by SOLISCO PRINTERS, SCOTT, QC, CANADA.

10 9 8 7 6 5 4 3 2 1

6

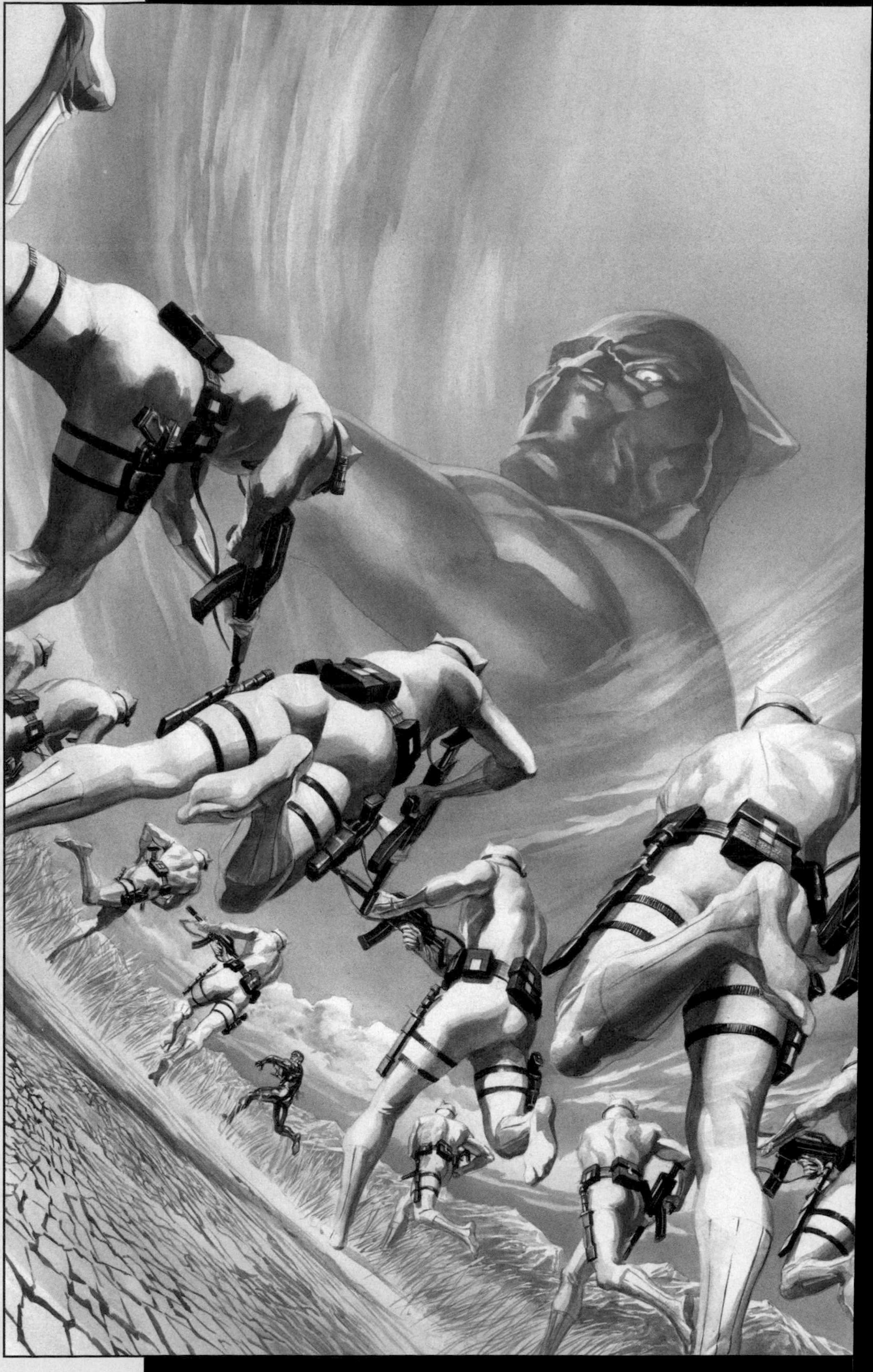

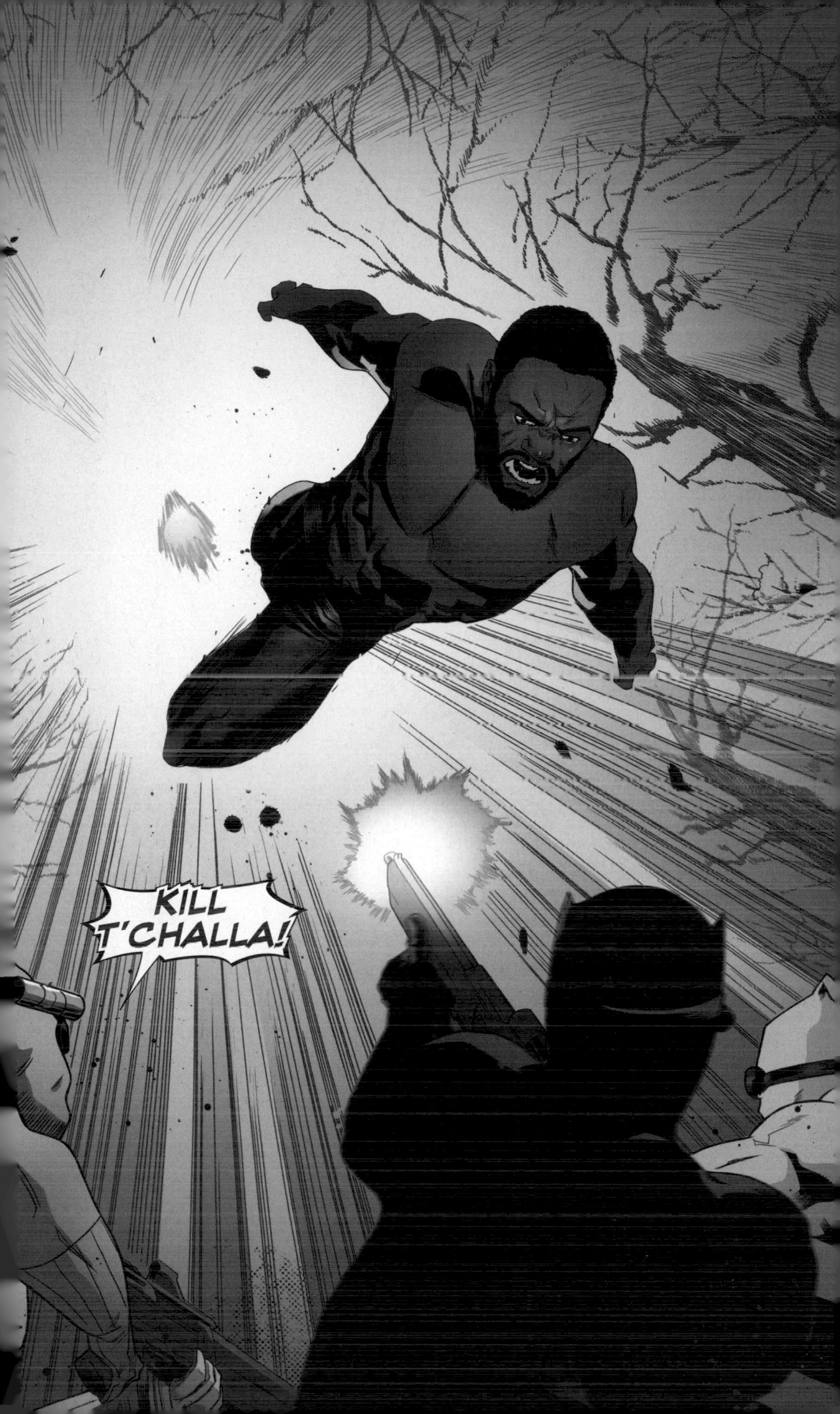
KILL T'CHALLA!

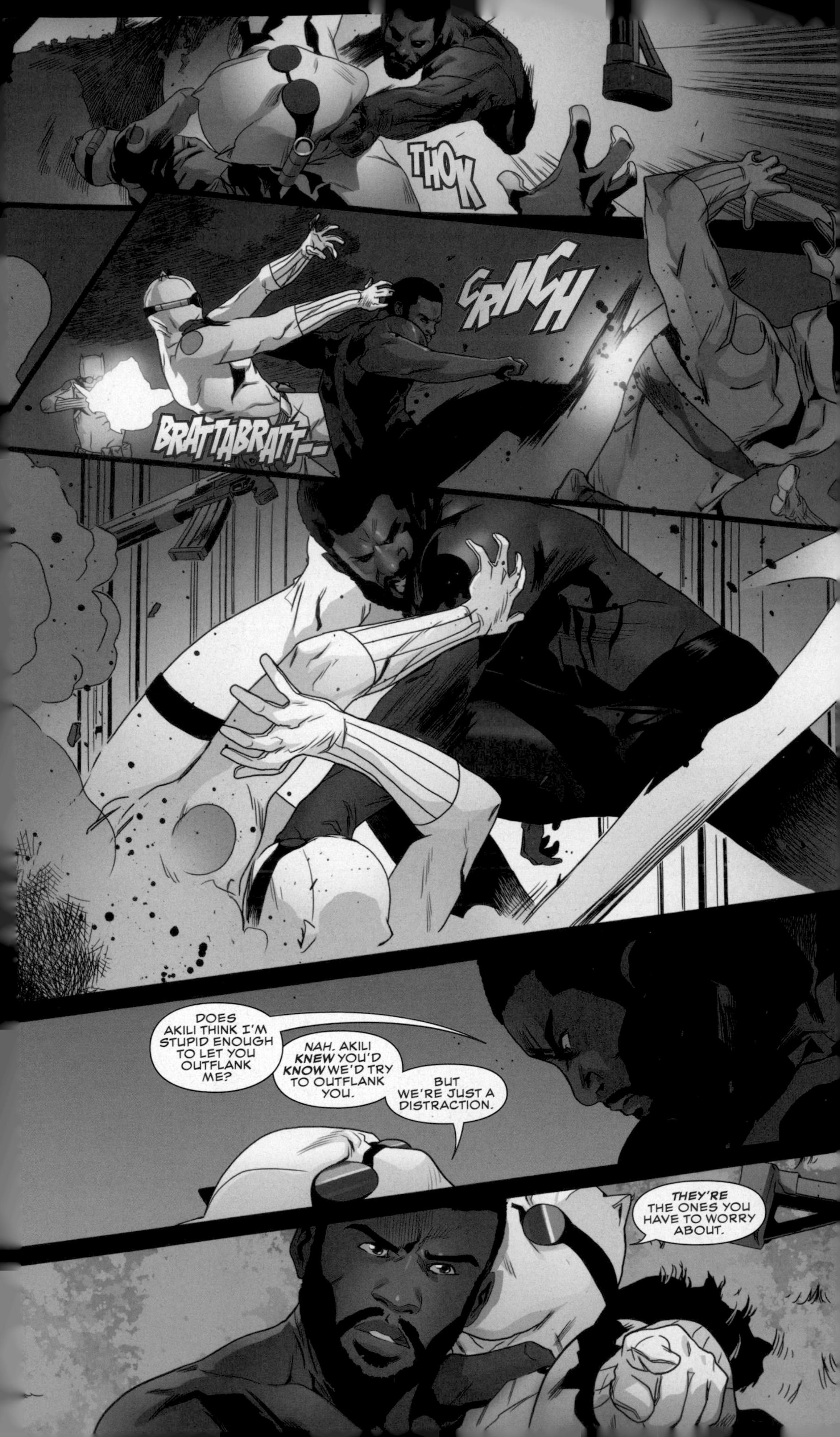

THOK
CRNCH
BRATTABRATT--
DOES AKILI THINK I'M STUPID ENOUGH TO LET YOU OUTFLANK ME?
NAH. AKILI KNEW YOU'D KNOW WE'D TRY TO OUTFLANK YOU.
BUT WE'RE JUST A DISTRACTION.
THEY'RE THE ONES YOU HAVE TO WORRY ABOUT.

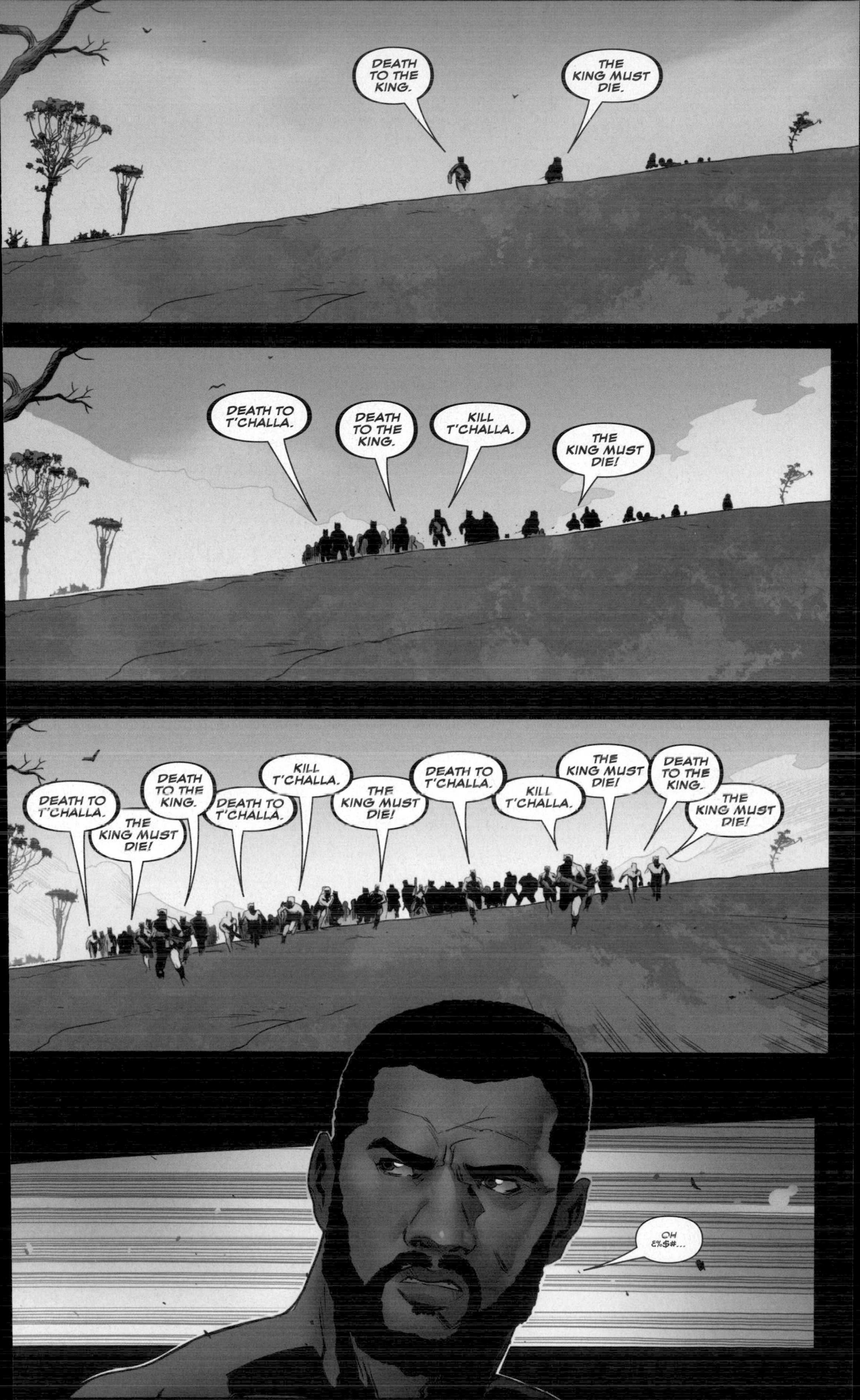
DEATH TO THE KING.
THE KING MUST DIE.
DEATH TO T'CHALLA.
DEATH TO THE KING.
KILL T'CHALLA.
THE KING MUST DIE!
DEATH TO T'CHALLA.
THE KING MUST DIE!
DEATH TO THE KING.
DEATH TO T'CHALLA.
KILL T'CHALLA.
THE KING MUST DIE!
DEATH TO T'CHALLA.
KILL T'CHALLA.
THE KING MUST DIE!
DEATH TO THE KING.
THE KING MUST DIE!
OH &%$#...

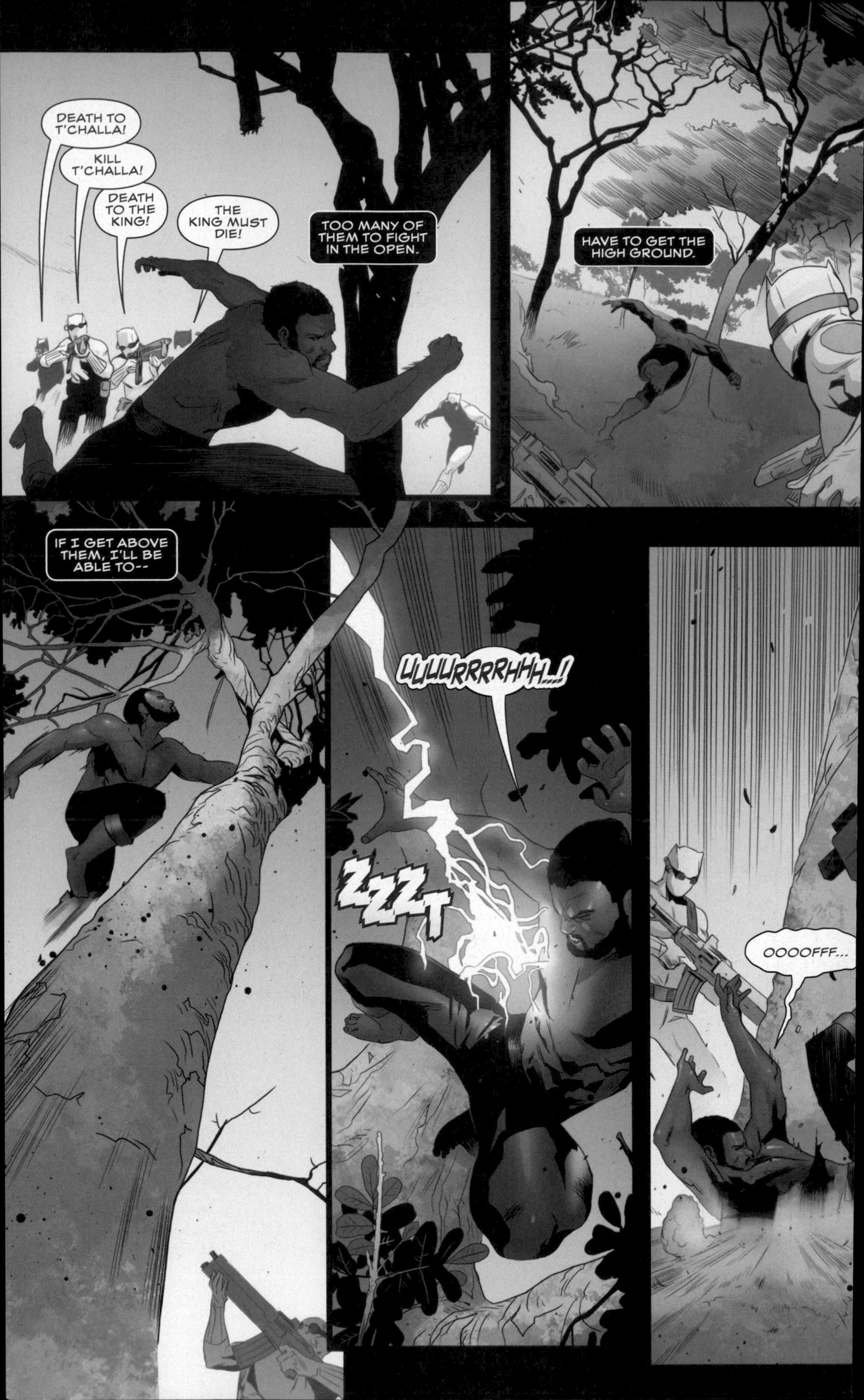
DEATH TO T'CHALLA!
KILL T'CHALLA!
DEATH TO THE KING!
THE KING MUST DIE!
TOO MANY OF THEM TO FIGHT IN THE OPEN.
HAVE TO GET THE HIGH GROUND.
IF I GET ABOVE THEM, I'LL BE ABLE TO--
UUUURRRRHHH...!
ZZZT
OOOOFFF...

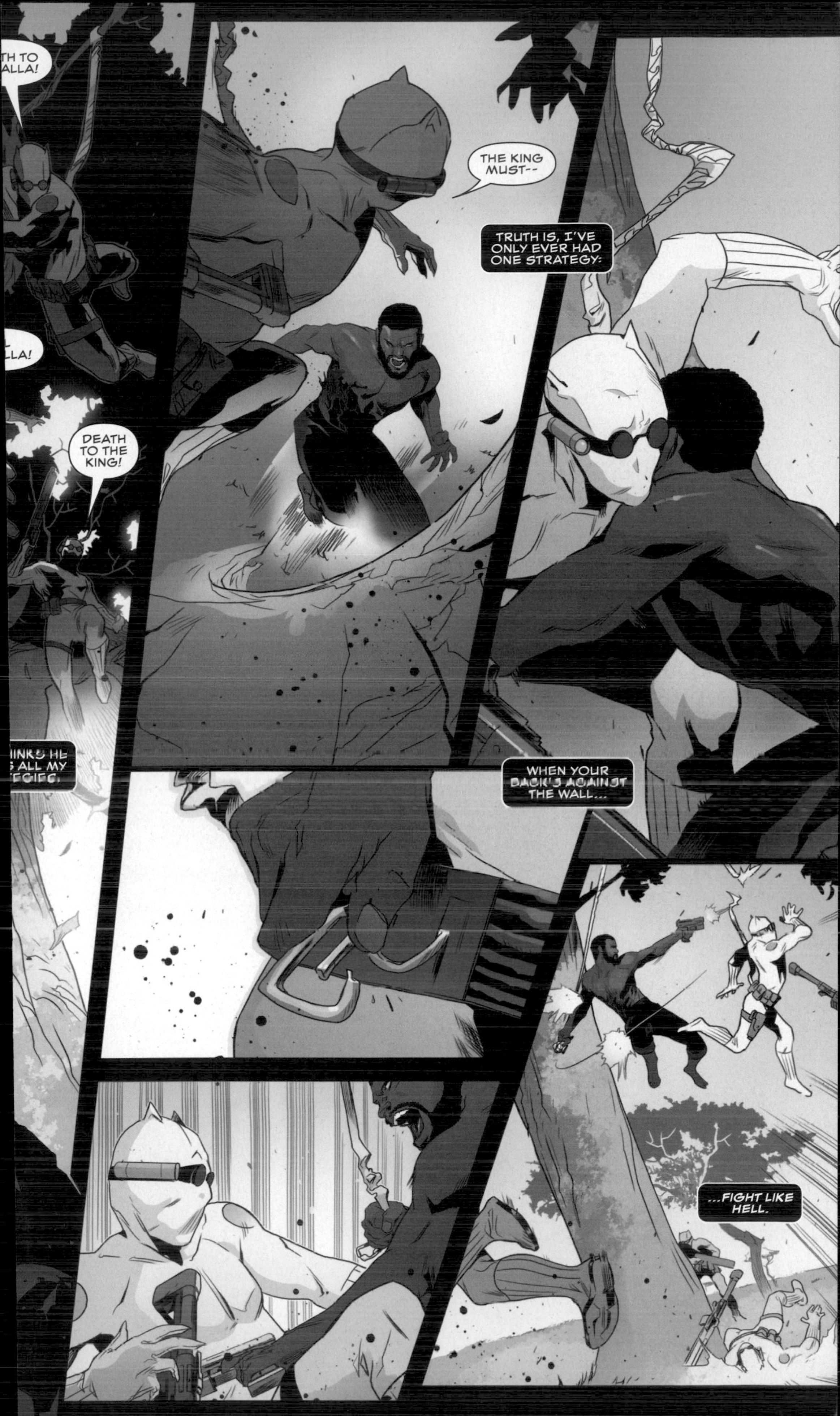
DEATH TO THE KING!
THE KING MUST--
TRUTH IS, I'VE ONLY EVER HAD ONE STRATEGY:
WHEN YOUR BACK'S AGAINST THE WALL...
...FIGHT LIKE HELL.

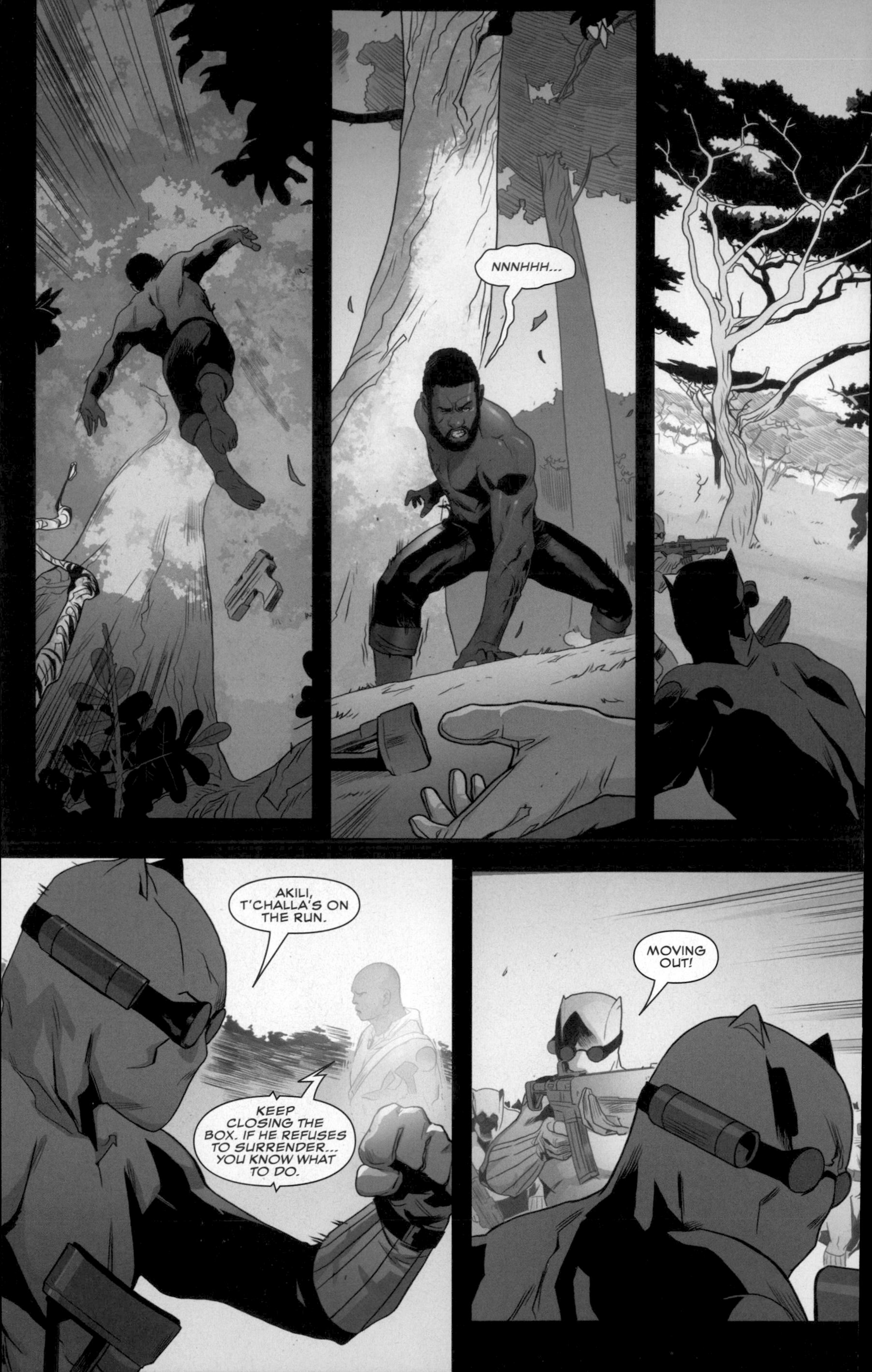
NNNHHH...
AKILI, T'CHALLA'S ON THE RUN.
KEEP CLOSING THE BOX. IF HE REFUSES TO SURRENDER... YOU KNOW WHAT TO DO.
MOVING OUT!

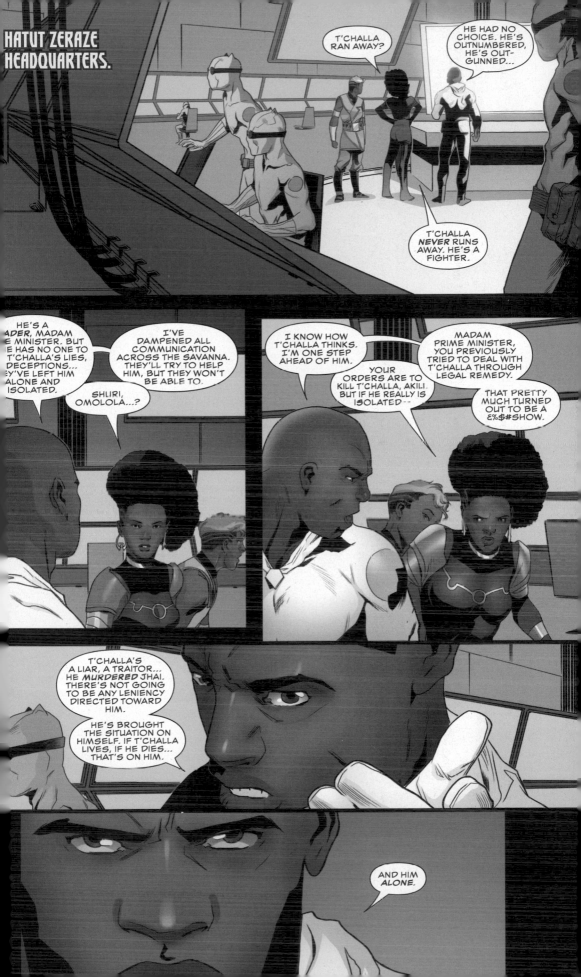

T'CHALLA RAN AWAY?

HE HAD NO CHOICE. HE'S OUTNUMBERED, HE'S OUT-GUNNED...

T'CHALLA *NEVER* RUNS AWAY. HE'S A FIGHTER.

HE'S A LEADER, MADAM PRIME MINISTER. BUT HE HAS NO ONE TO COUNTER T'CHALLA'S LIES, HIS DECEPTIONS... THEY'VE LEFT HIM ALONE AND ISOLATED.

I'VE DAMPENED ALL COMMUNICATION ACROSS THE SAVANNA. THEY'LL TRY TO HELP HIM, BUT THEY WON'T BE ABLE TO.

SHURI, OMOLOLA...?

I KNOW HOW T'CHALLA THINKS. I'M ONE STEP AHEAD OF HIM.

YOUR ORDERS ARE TO KILL T'CHALLA, AKILI. BUT IF HE REALLY IS ISOLATED--

MADAM PRIME MINISTER, YOU PREVIOUSLY TRIED TO DEAL WITH T'CHALLA THROUGH LEGAL REMEDY.

THAT PRETTY MUCH TURNED OUT TO BE A &%$#SHOW.

T'CHALLA'S A LIAR, A TRAITOR... HE *MURDERED* JHAI. THERE'S NOT GOING TO BE ANY LENIENCY DIRECTED TOWARD HIM.

HE'S BROUGHT THE SITUATION ON HIMSELF. IF T'CHALLA LIVES, IF HE DIES... THAT'S ON HIM.

AND HIM ALONE.

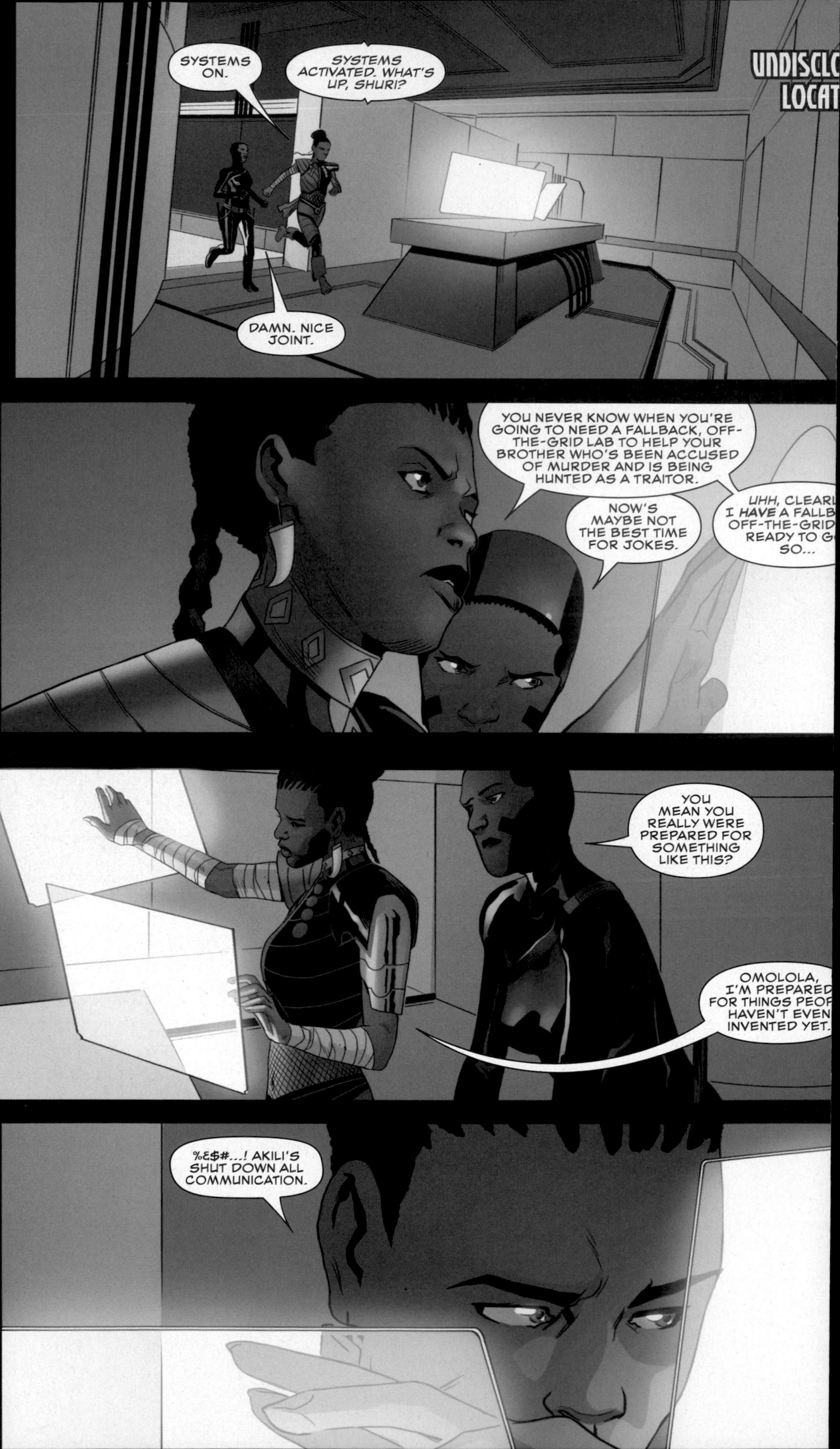
UNDISCLO
LOCAT
SYSTEMS ON.
SYSTEMS ACTIVATED. WHAT'S UP, SHURI?
DAMN. NICE JOINT.
YOU NEVER KNOW WHEN YOU'RE GOING TO NEED A FALLBACK, OFF-THE-GRID LAB TO HELP YOUR BROTHER WHO'S BEEN ACCUSED OF MURDER AND IS BEING HUNTED AS A TRAITOR.
NOW'S MAYBE NOT THE BEST TIME FOR JOKES.
UHH, CLEARL I *HAVE* A FALLB OFF-THE-GRID READY TO G SO...
YOU MEAN YOU REALLY WERE PREPARED FOR SOMETHING LIKE THIS?
OMOLOLA, I'M PREPARED FOR THINGS PEOP HAVEN'T EVEN INVENTED YET.
%&$#...! AKILI'S SHUT DOWN ALL COMMUNICATION.

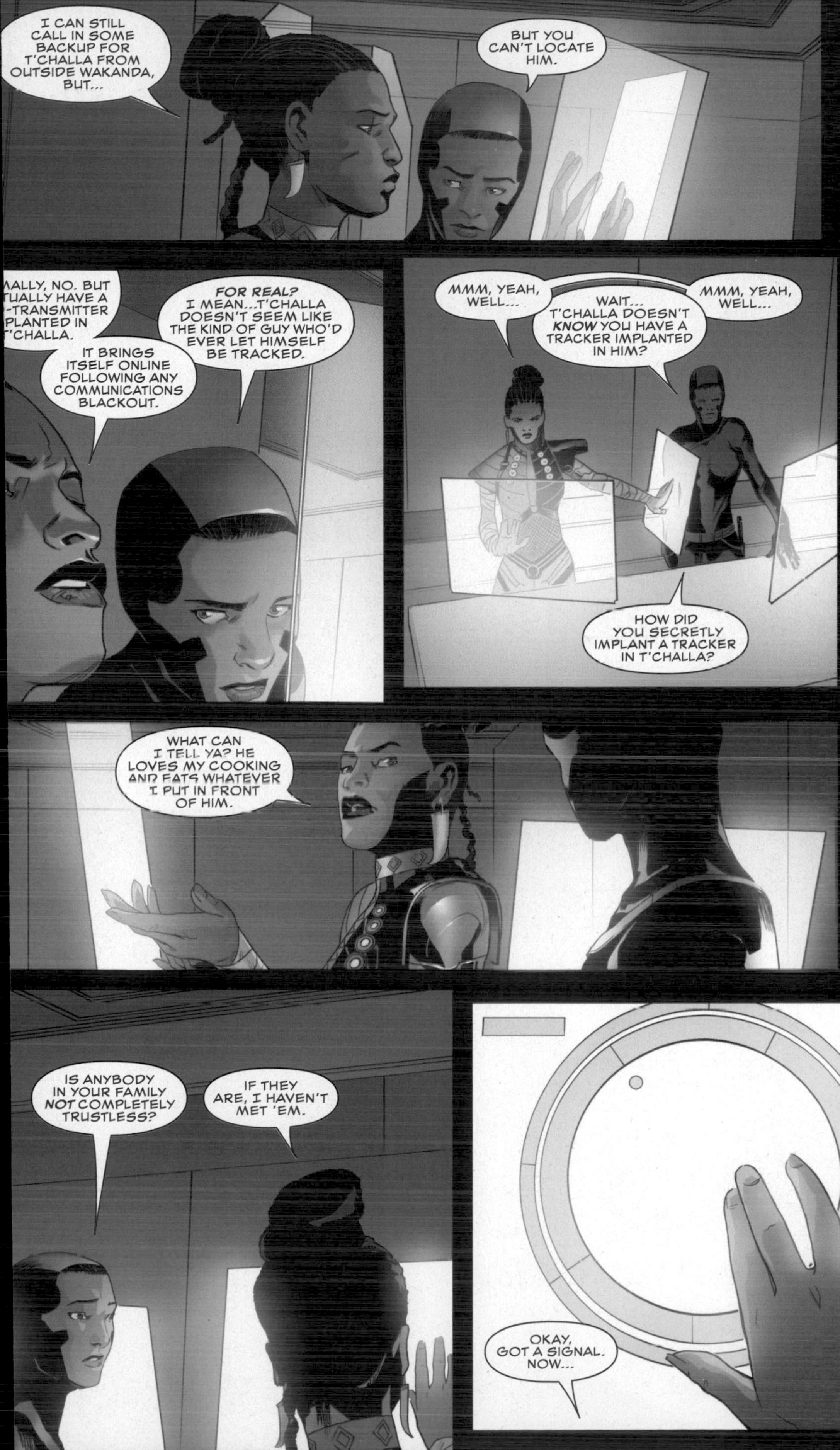
I CAN STILL CALL IN SOME BACKUP FOR T'CHALLA FROM OUTSIDE WAKANDA, BUT...
BUT YOU CAN'T LOCATE HIM.
ALLY, NO. BUT TUALLY HAVE A -TRANSMITTER PLANTED IN T'CHALLA.
IT BRINGS ITSELF ONLINE FOLLOWING ANY COMMUNICATIONS BLACKOUT.
FOR REAL? I MEAN...T'CHALLA DOESN'T SEEM LIKE THE KIND OF GUY WHO'D EVER LET HIMSELF BE TRACKED.
MMM, YEAH, WELL...
MMM, YEAH, WELL...
WAIT... T'CHALLA DOESN'T *KNOW* YOU HAVE A TRACKER IMPLANTED IN HIM?
HOW DID YOU SECRETLY IMPLANT A TRACKER IN T'CHALLA?
WHAT CAN I TELL YA? HE LOVES MY COOKING AND EATS WHATEVER I PUT IN FRONT OF HIM.
IS ANYBODY IN YOUR FAMILY *NOT* COMPLETELY TRUSTLESS?
IF THEY ARE, I HAVEN'T MET 'EM.
OKAY, GOT A SIGNAL. NOW...

"...LET'S GET T'CHALLA SOME HELP."

KILL T'CHALLA!

THE KING MUST DIE!

DEATH TO T'CHALLA!

DEATH TO THE KING!

NOT...

DEATH TO T'CHALLA!

KILL T'CHALLA!

DEATH TO THE KING!

THE KING MUST DIE!

...GOO

...AT ALL.

BUT THEN...

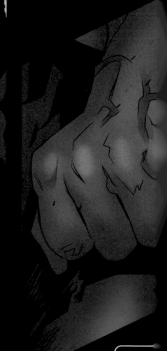

...NEITH AM I

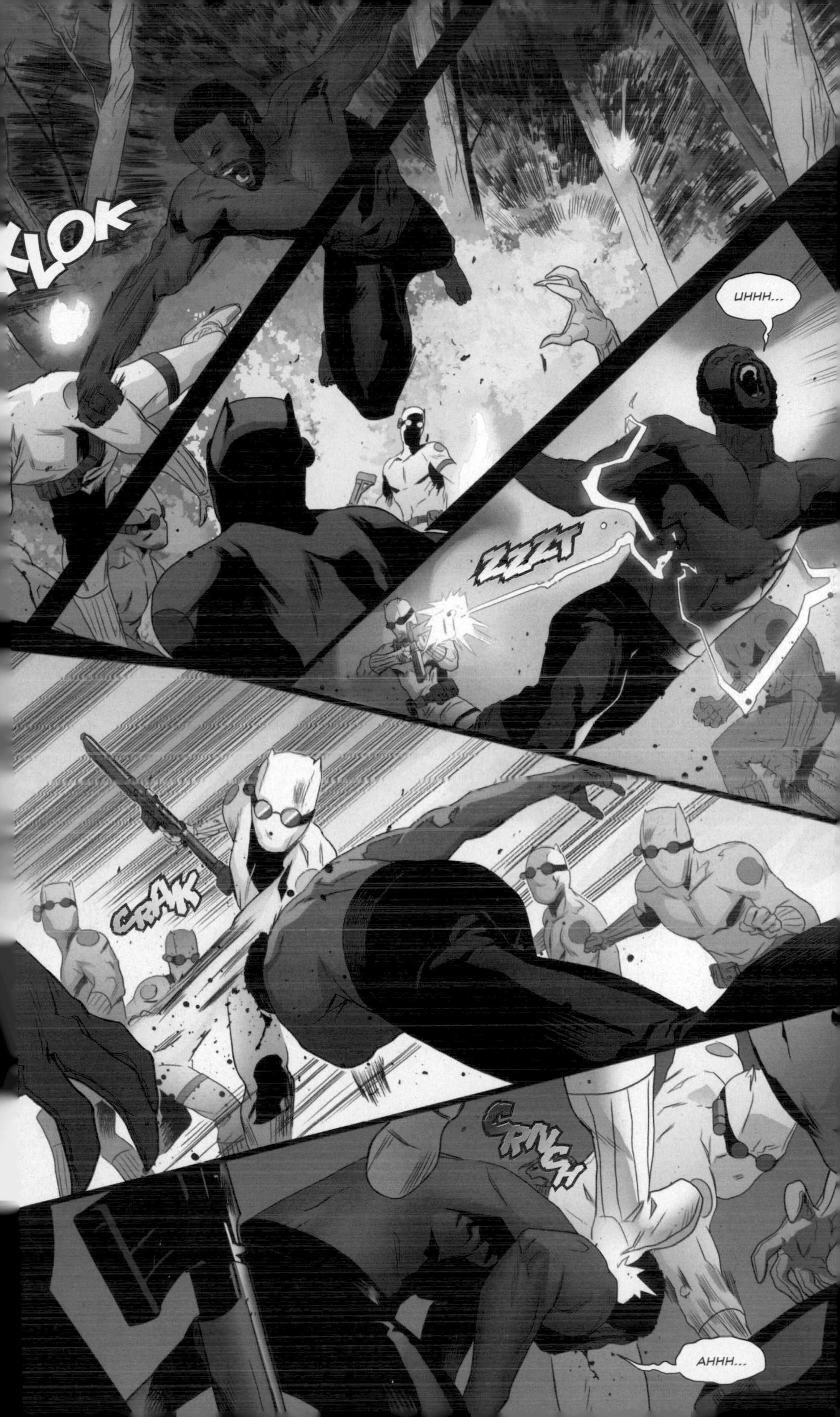
KLOK
UHHH...
ZZZT
CRAK
CRNCH
AHHH...

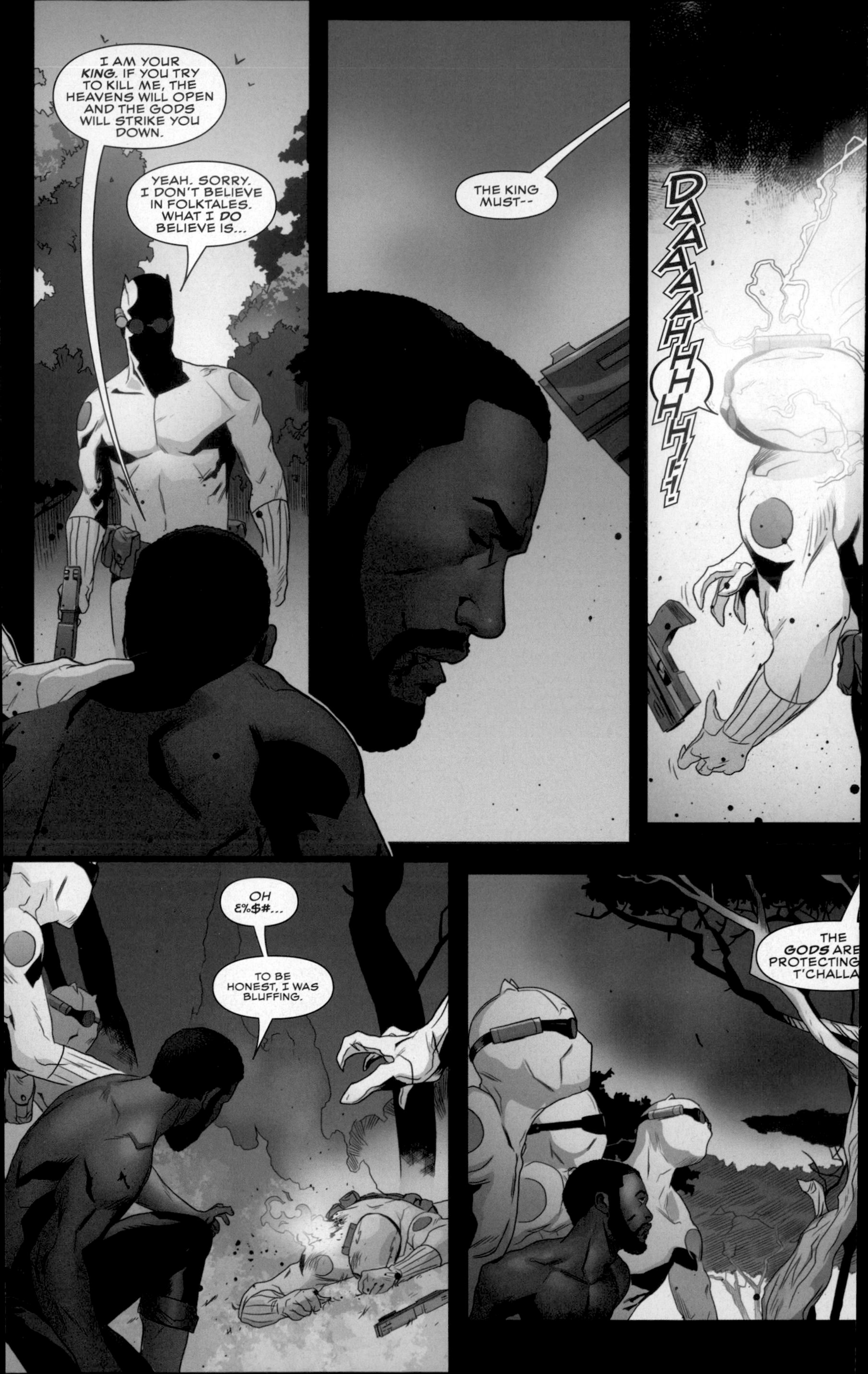
I AM YOUR KING. IF YOU TRY TO KILL ME, THE HEAVENS WILL OPEN AND THE GODS WILL STRIKE YOU DOWN.
YEAH. SORRY. I DON'T BELIEVE IN FOLKTALES. WHAT I DO BELIEVE IS...
THE KING MUST--
DAAAAAHHHHH!!
OH &%$#...
TO BE HONEST, I WAS BLUFFING.
THE GODS ARE PROTECTING T'CHALLA

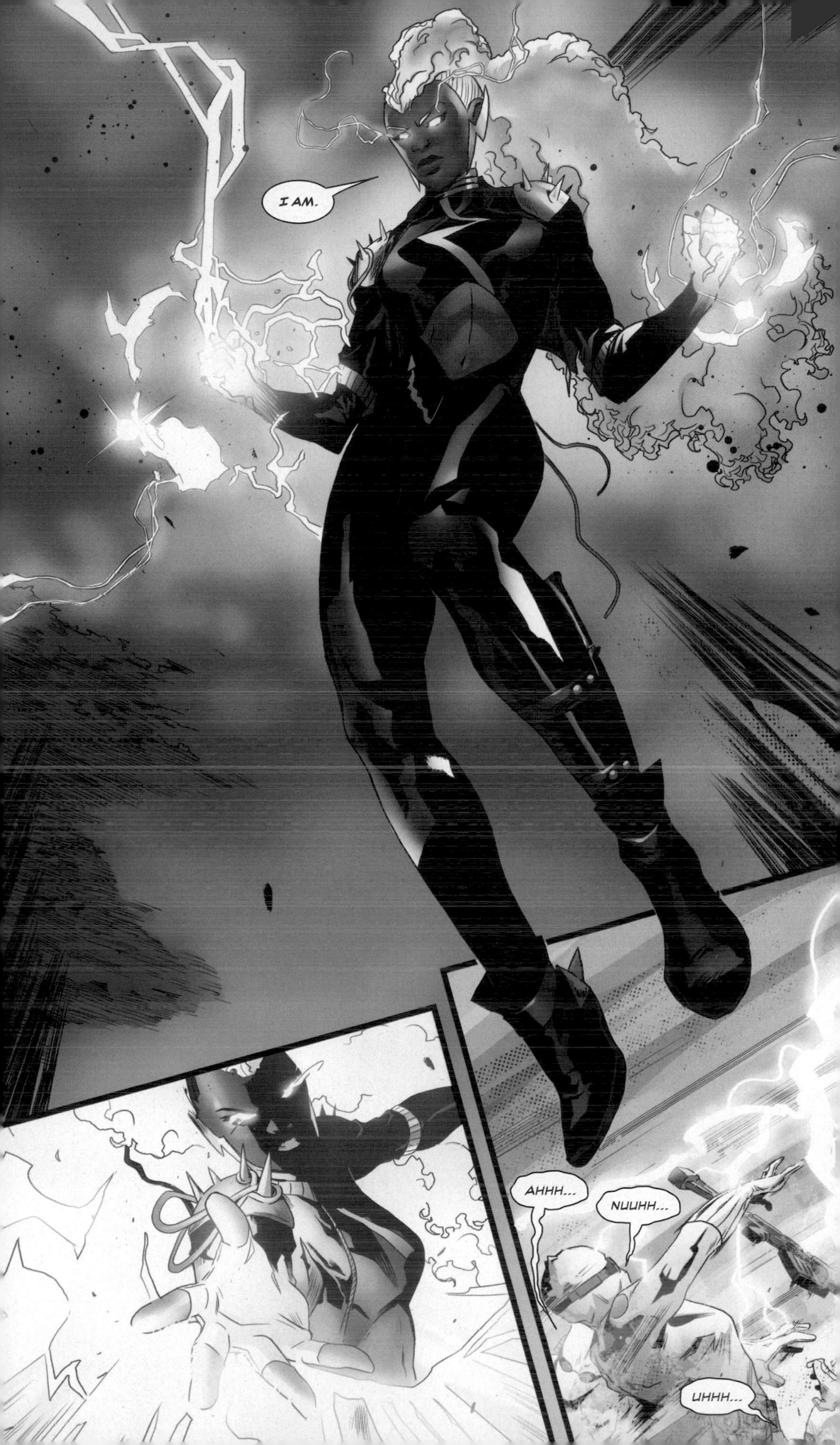
I AM.
AHHH...
NUUHH...
UHHH...

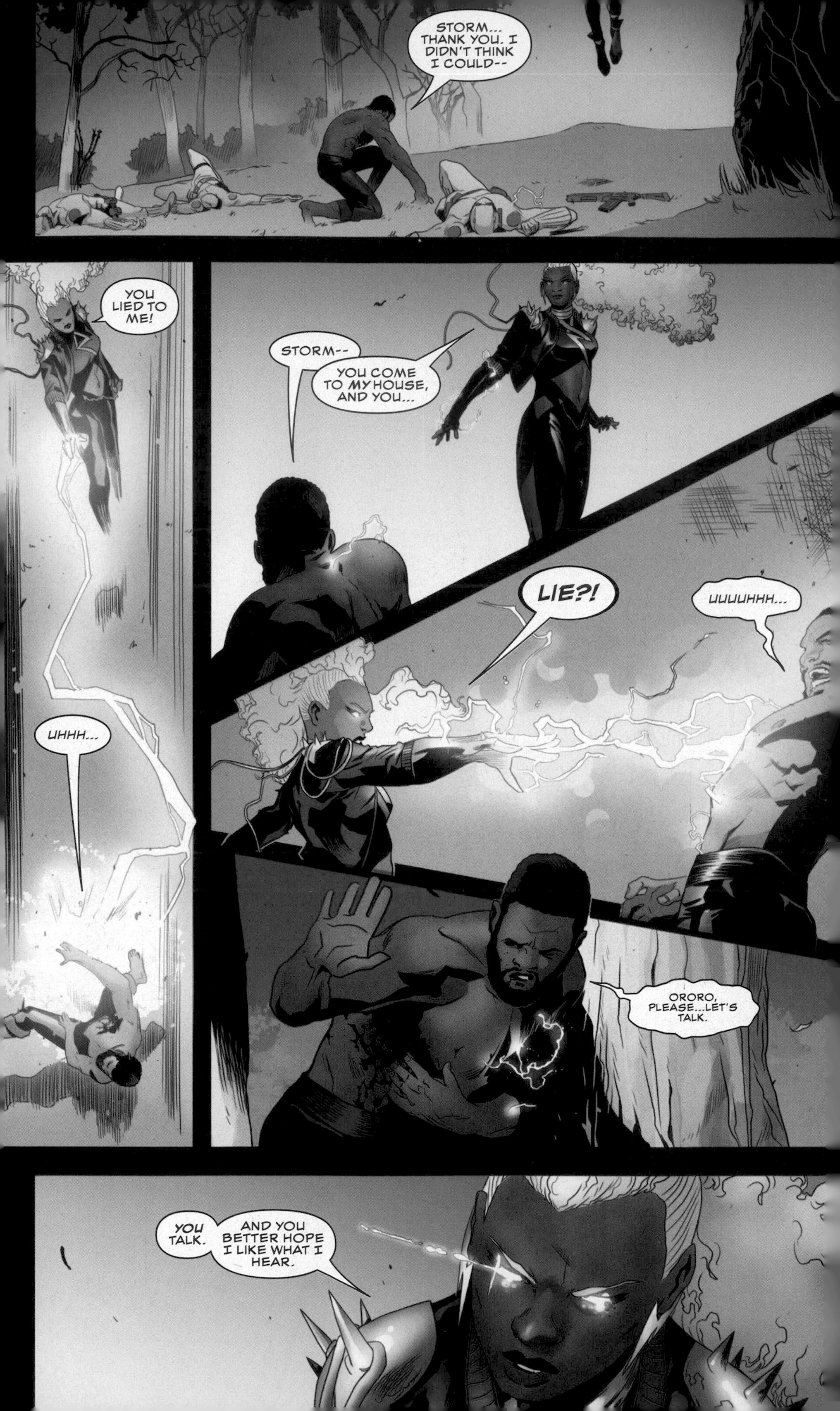
STORM... THANK YOU. I DIDN'T THINK I COULD--
YOU LIED TO ME!
STORM--
YOU COME TO MY HOUSE, AND YOU...
LIE?!
UUUUHHH...
UHHH...
ORORO, PLEASE...LET'S TALK.
YOU TALK.
AND YOU BETTER HOPE I LIKE WHAT I HEAR.

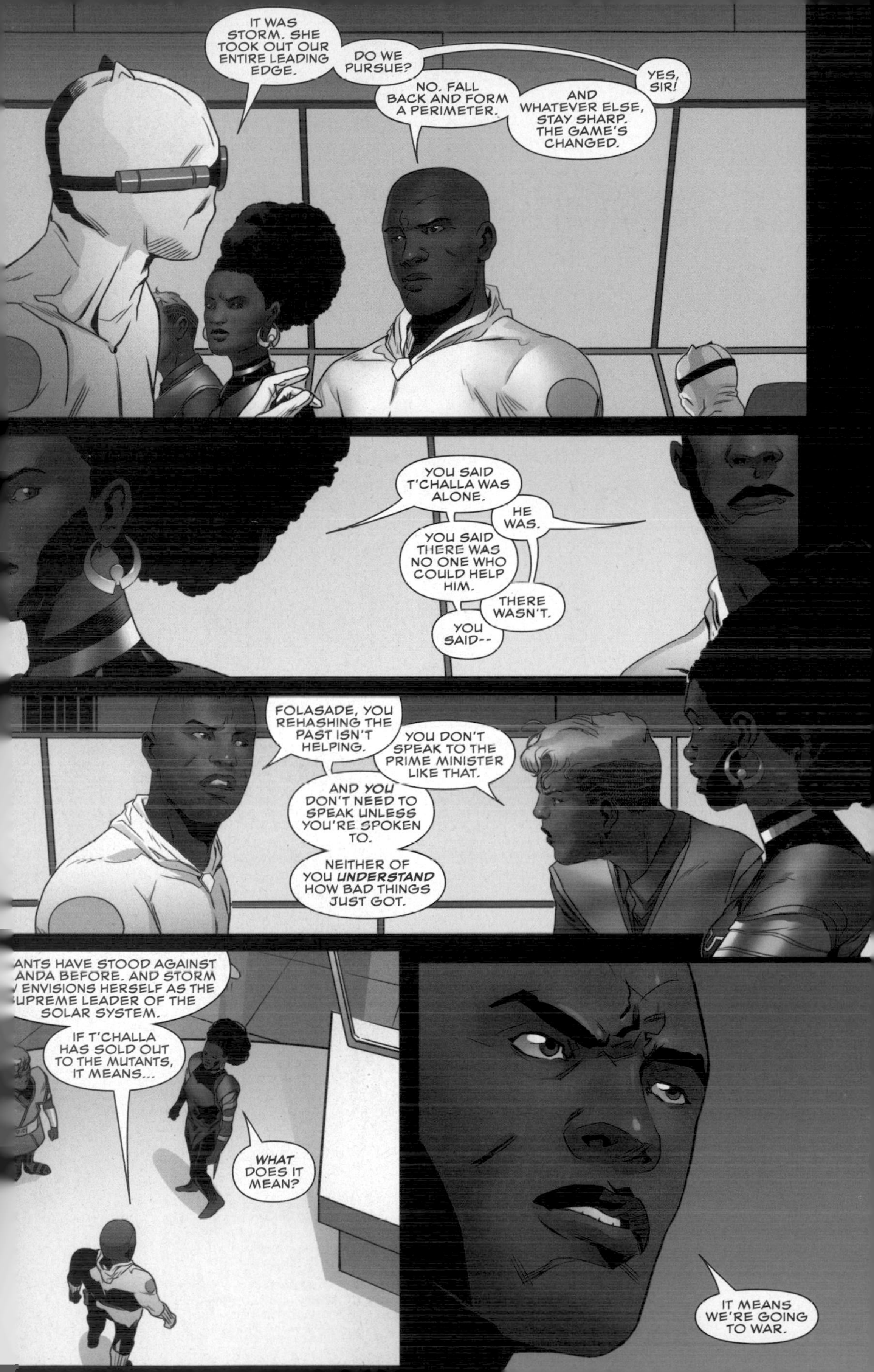
IT WAS STORM. SHE TOOK OUT OUR ENTIRE LEADING EDGE.
DO WE PURSUE?
NO. FALL BACK AND FORM A PERIMETER.
YES, SIR!
AND WHATEVER ELSE, STAY SHARP. THE GAME'S CHANGED.
YOU SAID T'CHALLA WAS ALONE.
HE WAS.
YOU SAID THERE WAS NO ONE WHO COULD HELP HIM.
THERE WASN'T.
YOU SAID--
FOLASADE, YOU REHASHING THE PAST ISN'T HELPING.
YOU DON'T SPEAK TO THE PRIME MINISTER LIKE THAT.
AND *YOU* DON'T NEED TO SPEAK UNLESS YOU'RE SPOKEN TO.
NEITHER OF YOU ***UNDERSTAND*** HOW BAD THINGS JUST GOT.
ANTS HAVE STOOD AGAINST ANDA BEFORE. AND STORM V ENVISIONS HERSELF AS THE UPREME LEADER OF THE SOLAR SYSTEM.
IF T'CHALLA HAS SOLD OUT TO THE MUTANTS, IT MEANS...
WHAT DOES IT MEAN?
IT MEANS WE'RE GOING TO WAR.

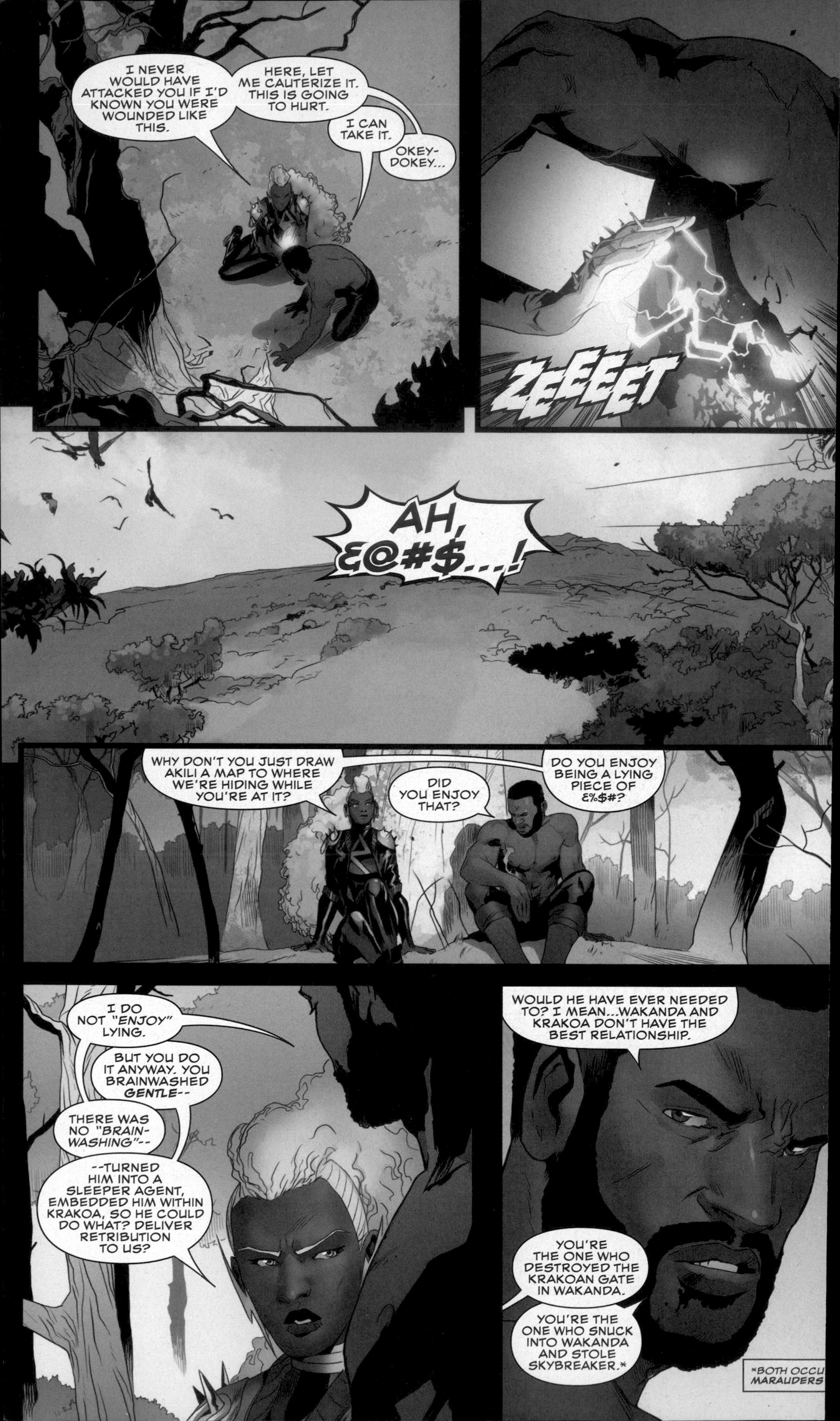
I NEVER WOULD HAVE ATTACKED YOU IF I'D KNOWN YOU WERE WOUNDED LIKE THIS.
HERE, LET ME CAUTERIZE IT. THIS IS GOING TO HURT.
I CAN TAKE IT.
OKEY-DOKEY...
ZEEEET
AH, &@#$...!
WHY DON'T YOU JUST DRAW AKILI A MAP TO WHERE WE'RE HIDING WHILE YOU'RE AT IT?
DID YOU ENJOY THAT?
DO YOU ENJOY BEING A LYING PIECE OF &%$#?
I DO NOT "ENJOY" LYING.
BUT YOU DO IT ANYWAY. YOU BRAINWASHED GENTLE--
THERE WAS NO "BRAIN-WASHING"--
--TURNED HIM INTO A SLEEPER AGENT, EMBEDDED HIM WITHIN KRAKOA, SO HE COULD DO WHAT? DELIVER RETRIBUTION TO US?
WOULD HE HAVE EVER NEEDED TO? I MEAN...WAKANDA AND KRAKOA DON'T HAVE THE BEST RELATIONSHIP.
YOU'RE THE ONE WHO DESTROYED THE KRAKOAN GATE IN WAKANDA.
YOU'RE THE ONE WHO SNUCK INTO WAKANDA AND STOLE SKYBREAKER.*
*BOTH OCCU
MARAUDERS

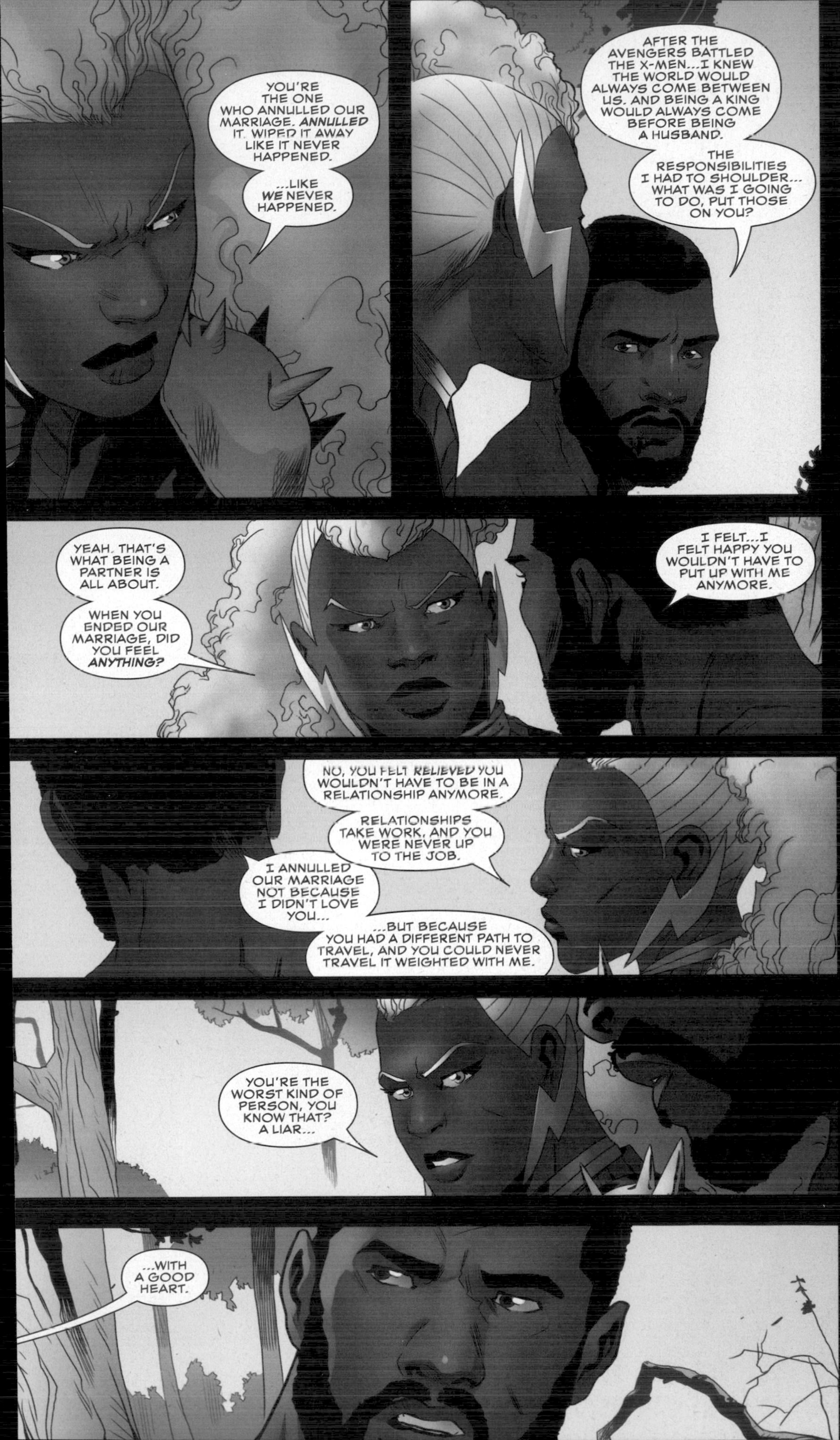
YOU'RE THE ONE WHO ANNULLED OUR MARRIAGE. *ANNULLED* IT. WIPED IT AWAY LIKE IT NEVER HAPPENED.
...LIKE *WE* NEVER HAPPENED.
AFTER THE AVENGERS BATTLED THE X-MEN...I KNEW THE WORLD WOULD ALWAYS COME BETWEEN US. AND BEING A KING WOULD ALWAYS COME BEFORE BEING A HUSBAND.
THE RESPONSIBILITIES I HAD TO SHOULDER... WHAT WAS I GOING TO DO, PUT THOSE ON YOU?
YEAH. THAT'S WHAT BEING A PARTNER IS ALL ABOUT.
WHEN YOU ENDED OUR MARRIAGE, DID YOU FEEL *ANYTHING?*
I FELT...I FELT HAPPY YOU WOULDN'T HAVE TO PUT UP WITH ME ANYMORE.
NO, YOU FELT *RELIEVED* YOU WOULDN'T HAVE TO BE IN A RELATIONSHIP ANYMORE.
RELATIONSHIPS TAKE WORK, AND YOU WERE NEVER UP TO THE JOB.
I ANNULLED OUR MARRIAGE NOT BECAUSE I DIDN'T LOVE YOU...
...BUT BECAUSE YOU HAD A DIFFERENT PATH TO TRAVEL, AND YOU COULD NEVER TRAVEL IT WEIGHTED WITH ME.
YOU'RE THE WORST KIND OF PERSON, YOU KNOW THAT? A LIAR...
...WITH A GOOD HEART.

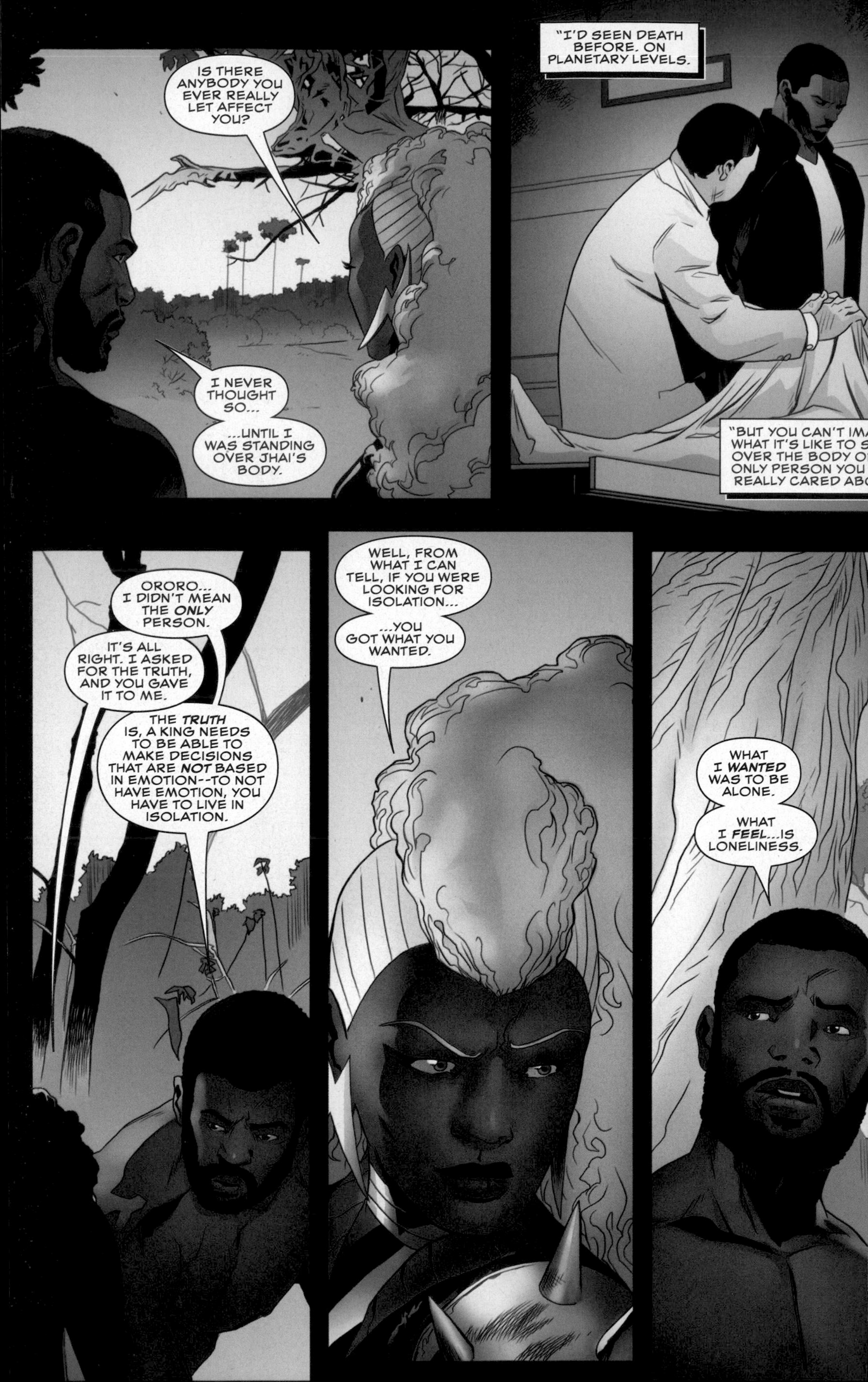

IS THERE ANYBODY YOU EVER REALLY LET AFFECT YOU?
I NEVER THOUGHT SO...
...UNTIL I WAS STANDING OVER JHAI'S BODY.
"I'D SEEN DEATH BEFORE. ON PLANETARY LEVELS.
"BUT YOU CAN'T IMA WHAT IT'S LIKE TO S OVER THE BODY O ONLY PERSON YOU REALLY CARED ABO
ORORO... I DIDN'T MEAN THE *ONLY* PERSON.
IT'S ALL RIGHT. I ASKED FOR THE TRUTH, AND YOU GAVE IT TO ME.
THE *TRUTH* IS, A KING NEEDS TO BE ABLE TO MAKE DECISIONS THAT ARE *NOT* BASED IN EMOTION--TO NOT HAVE EMOTION, YOU HAVE TO LIVE IN ISOLATION.
WELL, FROM WHAT I CAN TELL, IF YOU WERE LOOKING FOR ISOLATION...
...YOU GOT WHAT YOU WANTED.
WHAT I *WANTED* WAS TO BE ALONE.
WHAT I *FEEL*...IS LONELINESS.

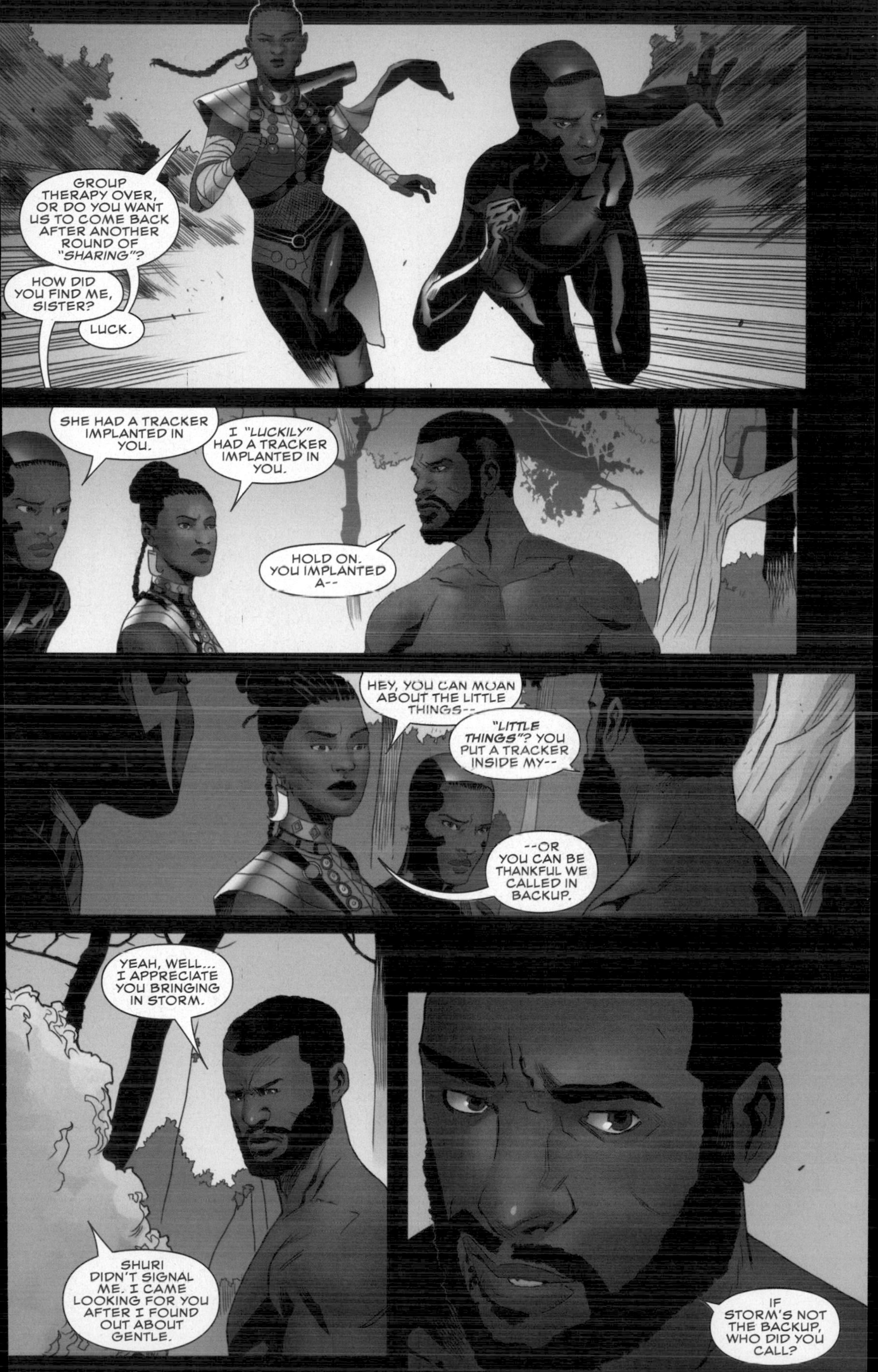
GROUP THERAPY OVER, OR DO YOU WANT US TO COME BACK AFTER ANOTHER ROUND OF "SHARING"?
HOW DID YOU FIND ME, SISTER?
LUCK.
SHE HAD A TRACKER IMPLANTED IN YOU.
I "LUCKILY" HAD A TRACKER IMPLANTED IN YOU.
HOLD ON. YOU IMPLANTED A--
HEY, YOU CAN MOAN ABOUT THE LITTLE THINGS--
"LITTLE THINGS"? YOU PUT A TRACKER INSIDE MY--
--OR YOU CAN BE THANKFUL WE CALLED IN BACKUP.
YEAH, WELL... I APPRECIATE YOU BRINGING IN STORM.
SHURI DIDN'T SIGNAL ME. I CAME LOOKING FOR YOU AFTER I FOUND OUT ABOUT GENTLE.
IF STORM'S NOT THE BACKUP, WHO DID YOU CALL?

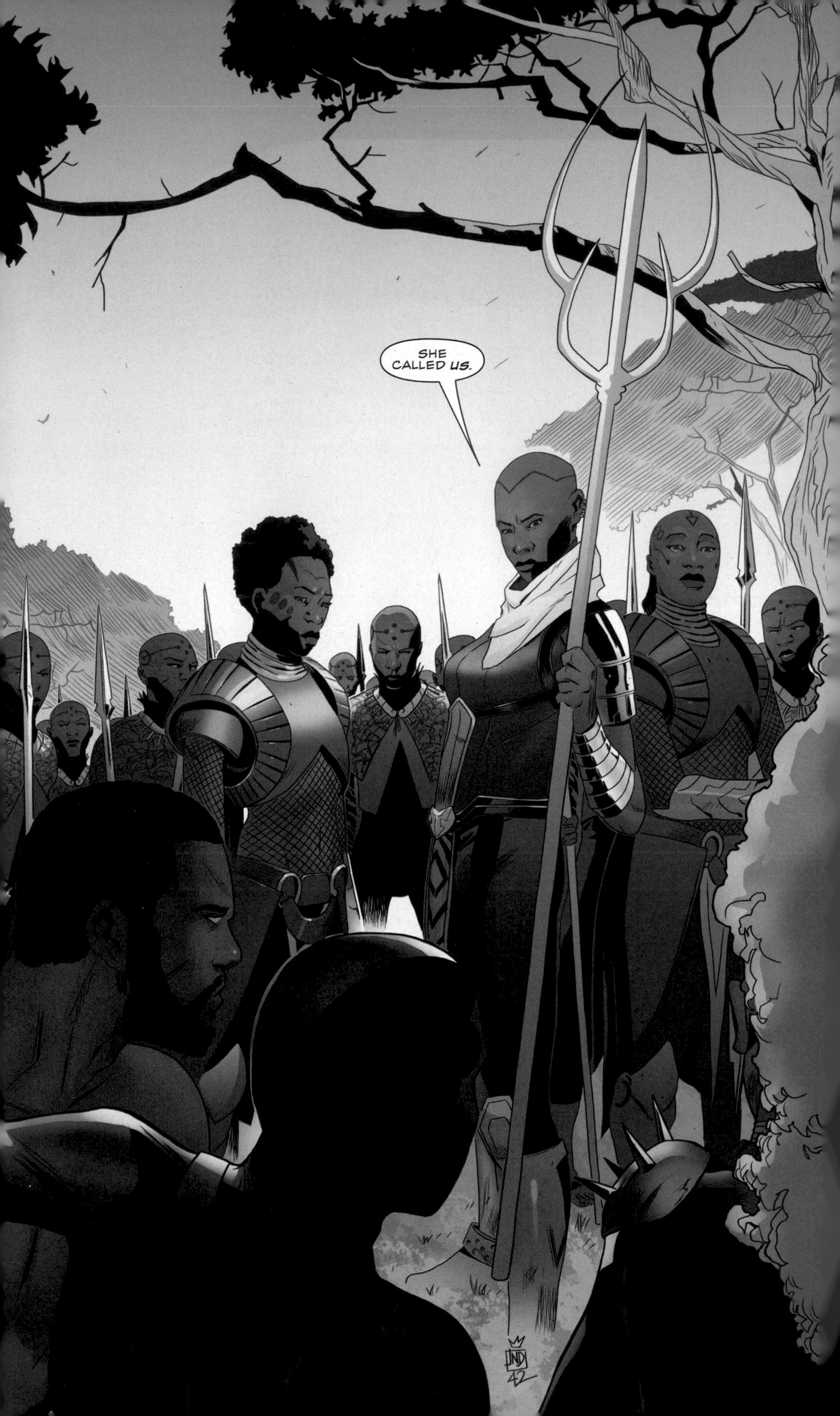
SHE CALLED US.

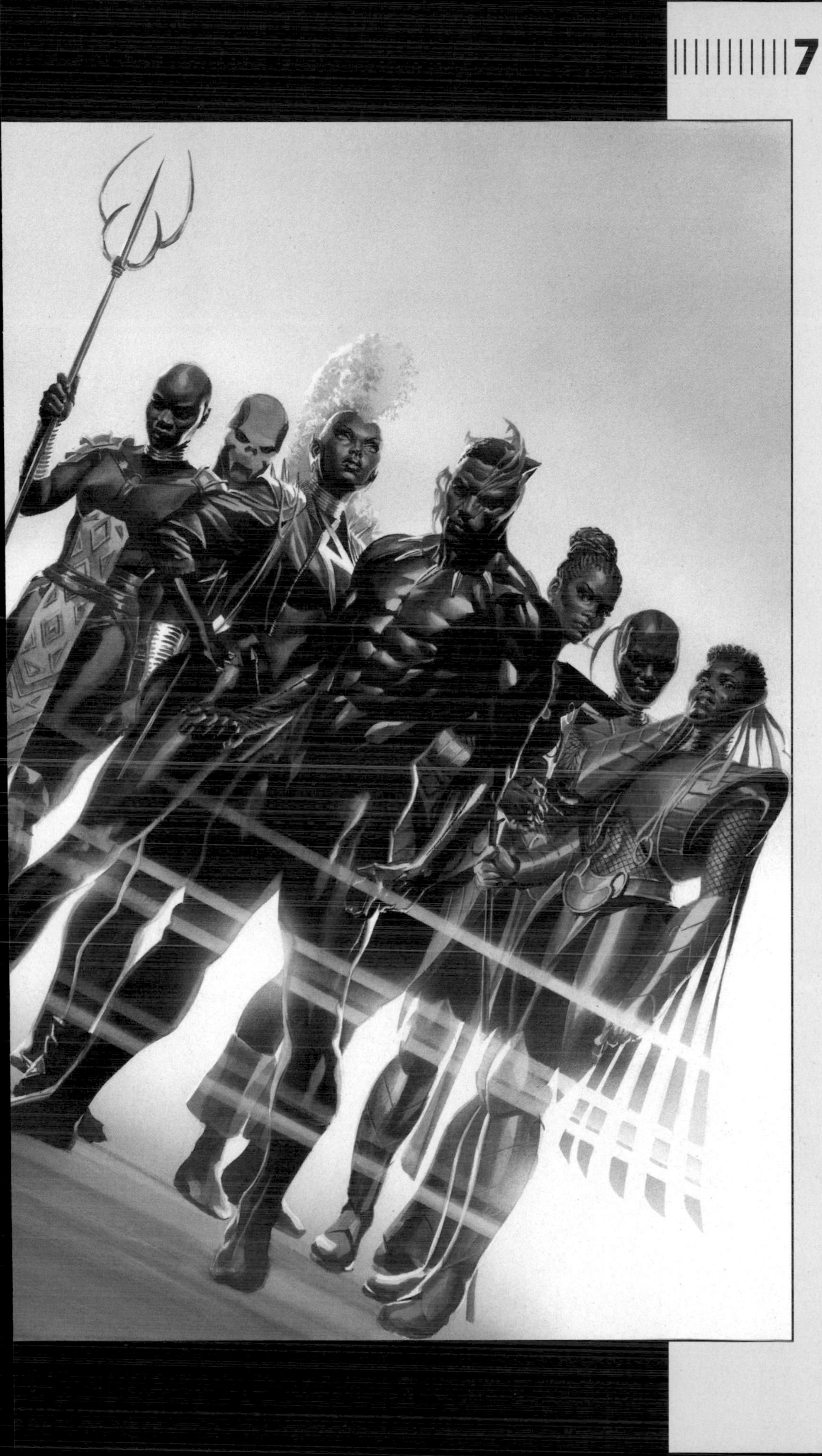

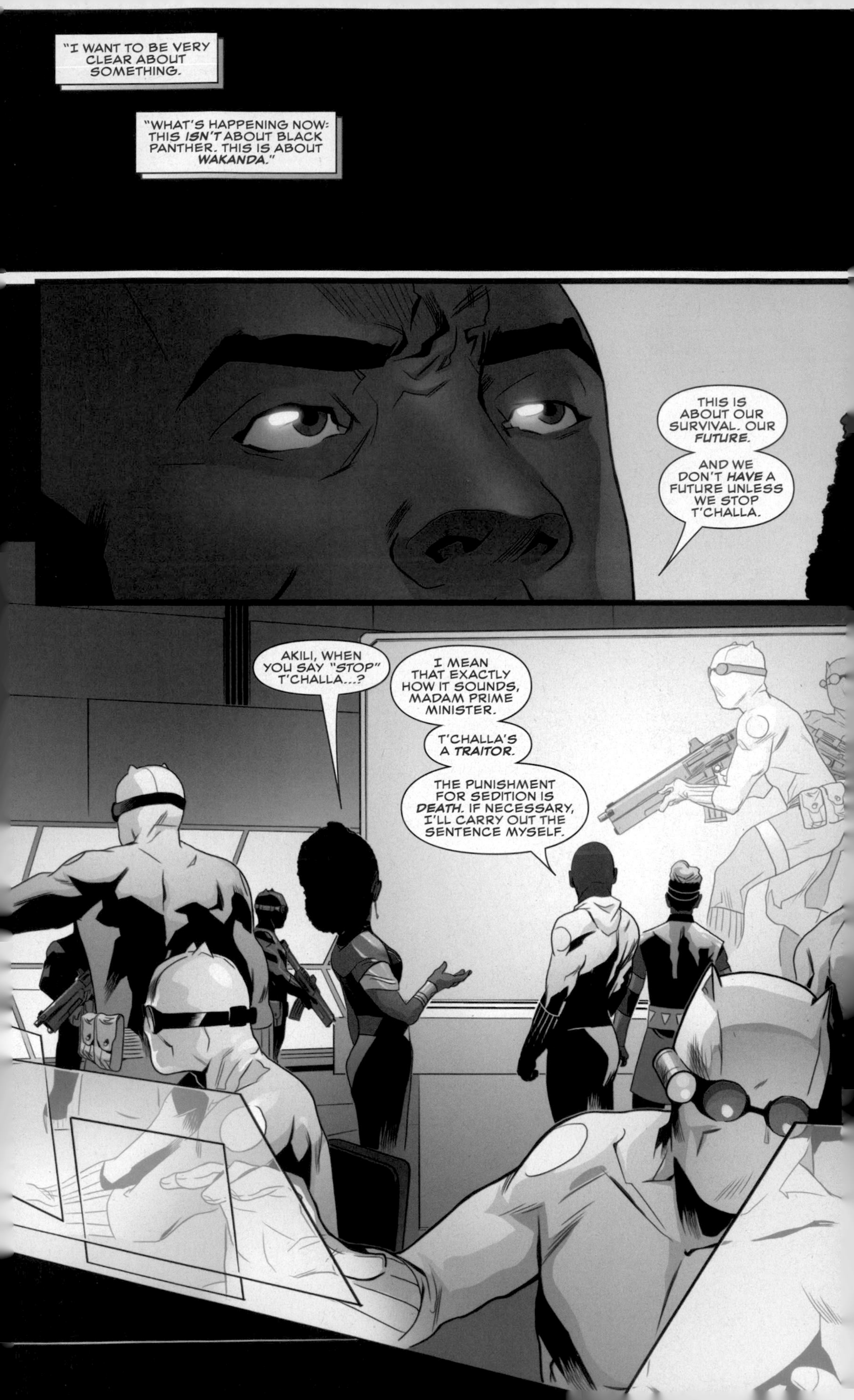
"I WANT TO BE VERY CLEAR ABOUT SOMETHING.
"WHAT'S HAPPENING NOW: THIS *ISN'T* ABOUT BLACK PANTHER. THIS IS ABOUT *WAKANDA*."
THIS IS ABOUT OUR SURVIVAL. OUR *FUTURE*.
AND WE DON'T *HAVE* A FUTURE UNLESS WE STOP T'CHALLA.
AKILI, WHEN YOU SAY "*STOP*" T'CHALLA...?
I MEAN THAT EXACTLY HOW IT SOUNDS, MADAM PRIME MINISTER.
T'CHALLA'S A *TRAITOR*.
THE PUNISHMENT FOR SEDITION IS *DEATH*. IF NECESSARY, I'LL CARRY OUT THE SENTENCE MYSELF.

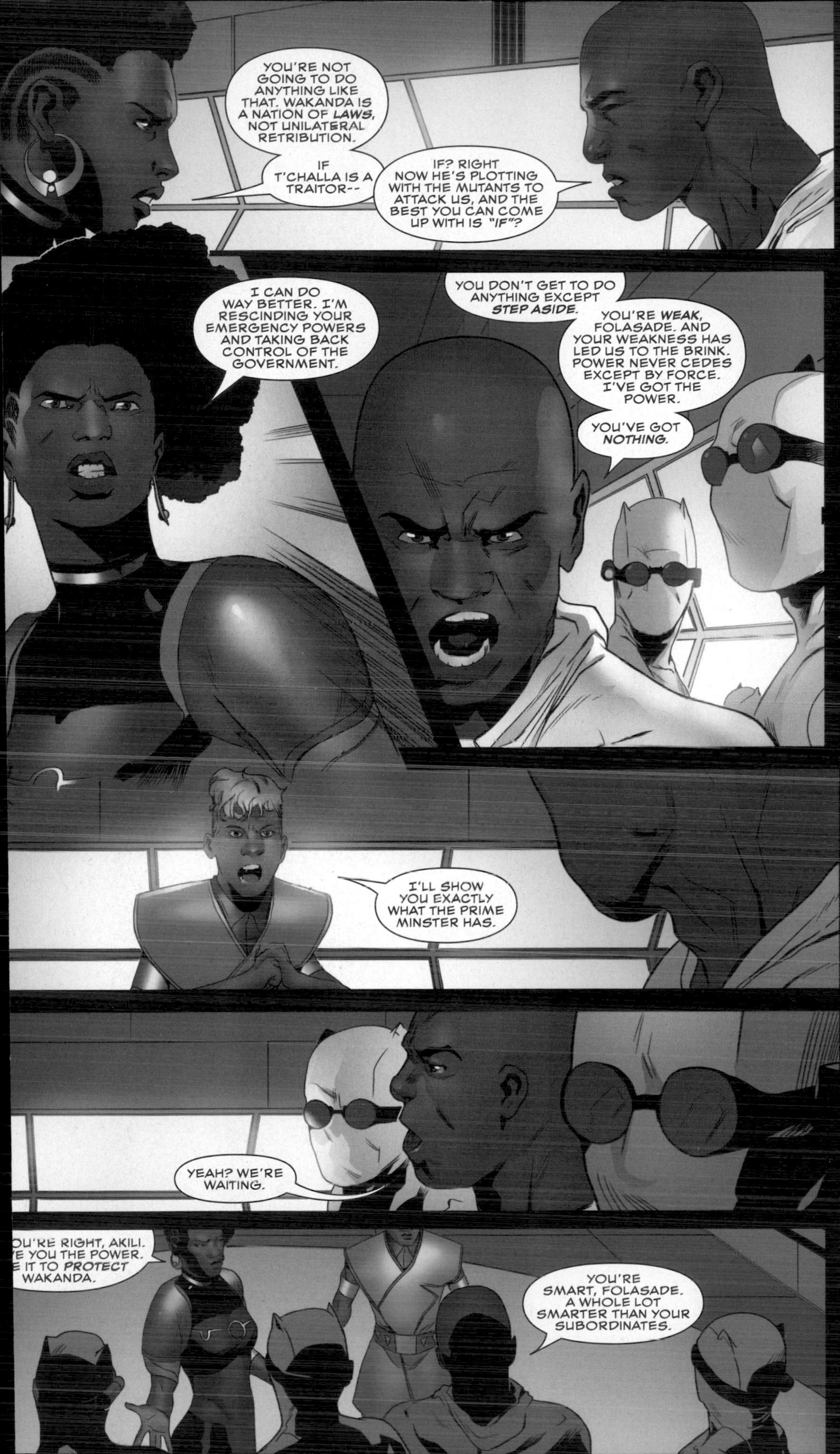
YOU'RE NOT GOING TO DO ANYTHING LIKE THAT. WAKANDA IS A NATION OF *LAWS*, NOT UNILATERAL RETRIBUTION.
IF T'CHALLA IS A TRAITOR--
IF? RIGHT NOW HE'S PLOTTING WITH THE MUTANTS TO ATTACK US, AND THE BEST YOU CAN COME UP WITH IS *"IF"*?
I CAN DO WAY BETTER. I'M RESCINDING YOUR EMERGENCY POWERS AND TAKING BACK CONTROL OF THE GOVERNMENT.
YOU DON'T GET TO DO ANYTHING EXCEPT *STEP ASIDE.*
YOU'RE *WEAK*, FOLASADE. AND YOUR WEAKNESS HAS LED US TO THE BRINK. POWER NEVER CEDES EXCEPT BY FORCE. I'VE GOT THE POWER.
YOU'VE GOT *NOTHING.*
I'LL SHOW YOU EXACTLY WHAT THE PRIME MINSTER HAS.
YEAH? WE'RE WAITING.
OU'RE RIGHT, AKILI. VE YOU THE POWER. E IT TO *PROTECT* WAKANDA.
YOU'RE SMART, FOLASADE. A WHOLE LOT SMARTER THAN YOUR SUBORDINATES.

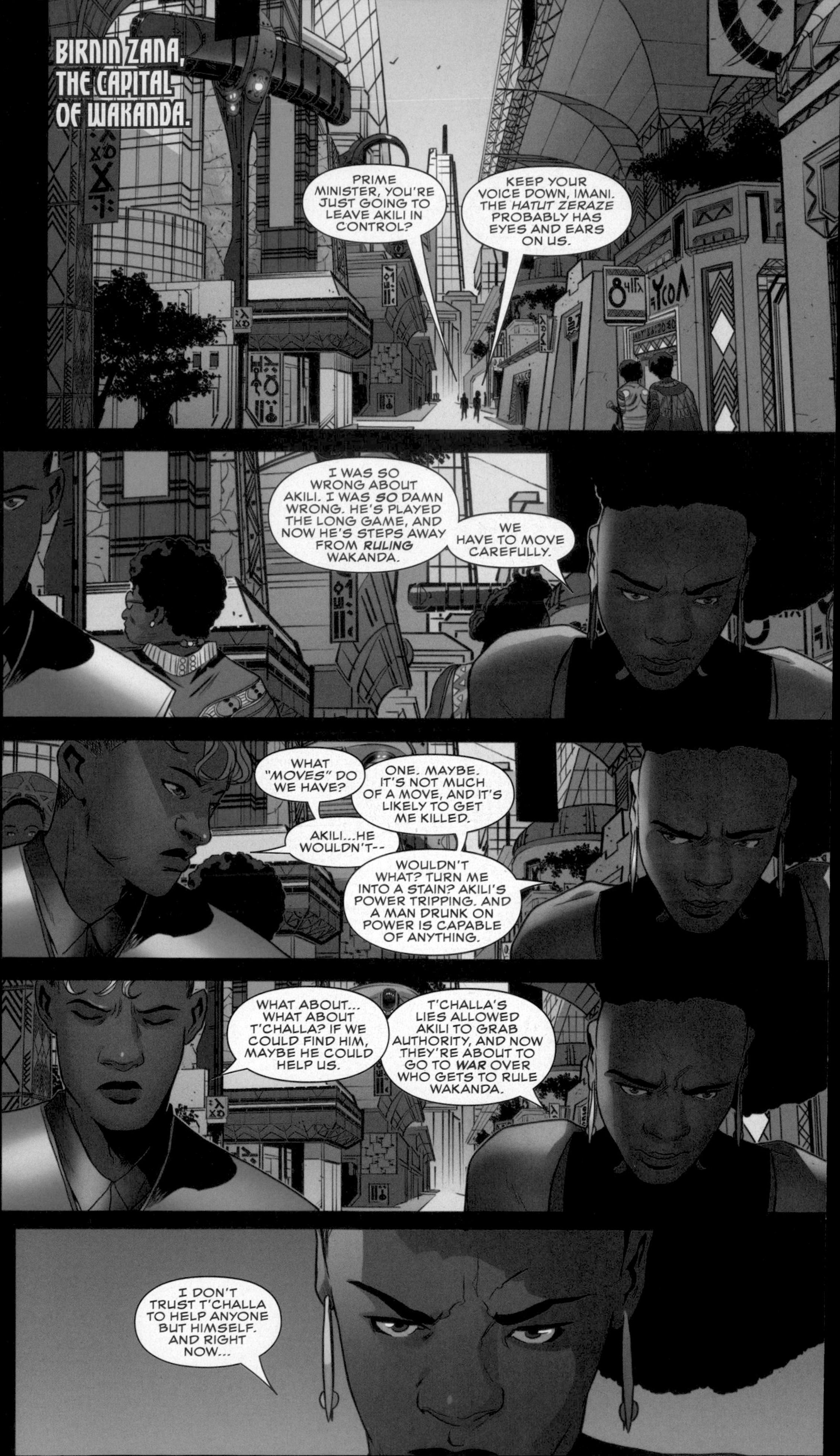

BIRNIN ZANA, THE CAPITAL OF WAKANDA.
PRIME MINISTER, YOU'RE JUST GOING TO LEAVE AKILI IN CONTROL?
KEEP YOUR VOICE DOWN, IMANI. THE HATUT ZERAZE PROBABLY HAS EYES AND EARS ON US.
I WAS SO WRONG ABOUT AKILI. I WAS SO DAMN WRONG. HE'S PLAYED THE LONG GAME, AND NOW HE'S STEPS AWAY FROM RULING WAKANDA.
WE HAVE TO MOVE CAREFULLY.
WHAT "MOVES" DO WE HAVE?
ONE. MAYBE. IT'S NOT MUCH OF A MOVE, AND IT'S LIKELY TO GET ME KILLED.
AKILI...HE WOULDN'T--
WOULDN'T WHAT? TURN ME INTO A STAIN? AKILI'S POWER TRIPPING. AND A MAN DRUNK ON POWER IS CAPABLE OF ANYTHING.
WHAT ABOUT... WHAT ABOUT T'CHALLA? IF WE COULD FIND HIM, MAYBE HE COULD HELP US.
T'CHALLA'S LIES ALLOWED AKILI TO GRAB AUTHORITY, AND NOW THEY'RE ABOUT TO GO TO WAR OVER WHO GETS TO RULE WAKANDA.
I DON'T TRUST T'CHALLA TO HELP ANYONE BUT HIMSELF. AND RIGHT NOW...

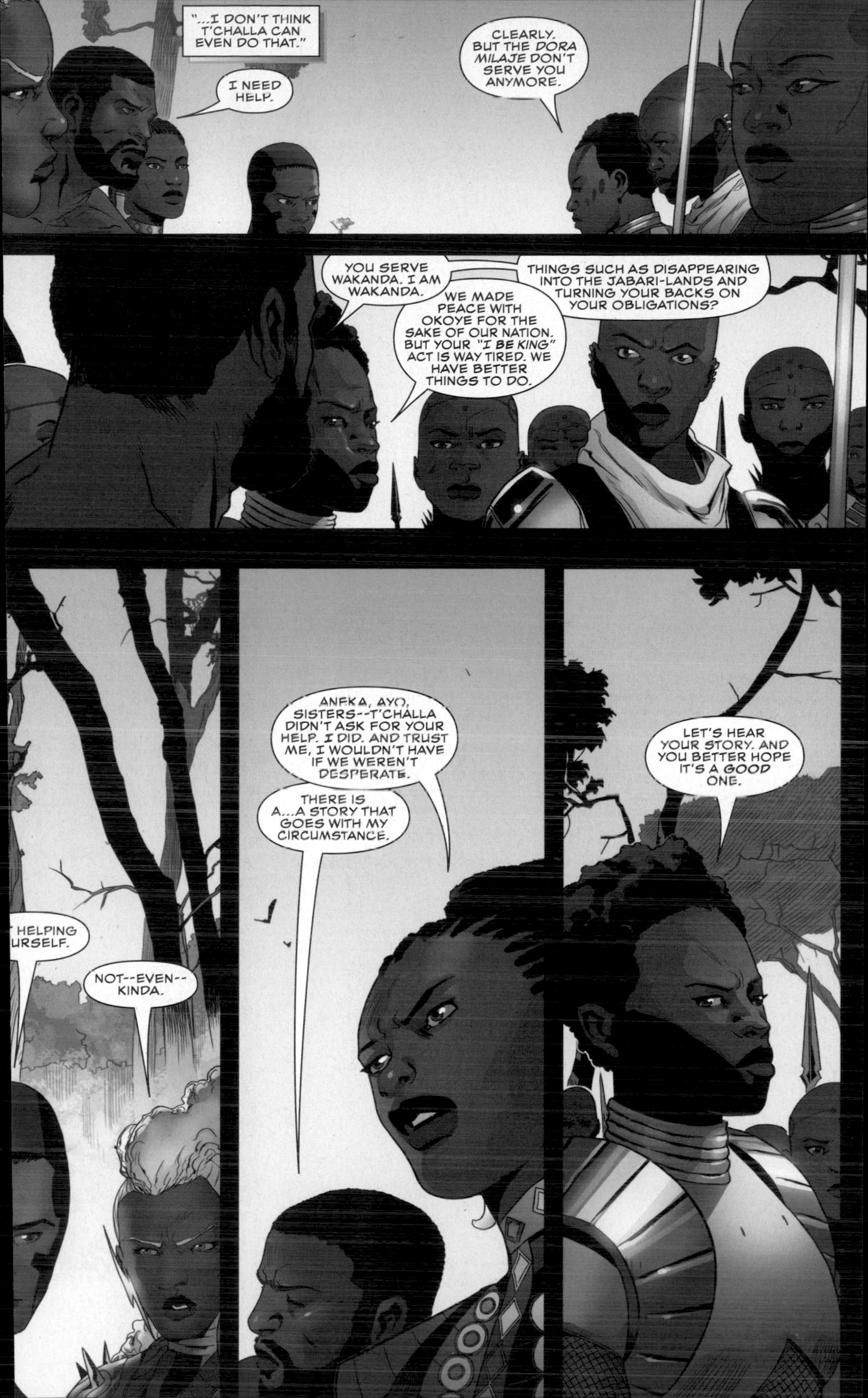
"...I DON'T THINK T'CHALLA CAN EVEN DO THAT."
I NEED HELP.
CLEARLY. BUT THE DORA MILAJE DON'T SERVE YOU ANYMORE.
YOU SERVE WAKANDA. I AM WAKANDA.
WE MADE PEACE WITH OKOYE FOR THE SAKE OF OUR NATION. BUT YOUR "I BE KING" ACT IS WAY TIRED. WE HAVE BETTER THINGS TO DO.
THINGS SUCH AS DISAPPEARING INTO THE JABARI-LANDS AND TURNING YOUR BACKS ON YOUR OBLIGATIONS?
HELPING URSELF.
NOT--EVEN--KINDA.
ANEKA, AYO, SISTERS--T'CHALLA DIDN'T ASK FOR YOUR HELP. I DID. AND TRUST ME, I WOULDN'T HAVE IF WE WEREN'T DESPERATE.
THERE IS A...A STORY THAT GOES WITH MY CIRCUMSTANCE.
LET'S HEAR YOUR STORY. AND YOU BETTER HOPE IT'S A GOOD ONE.

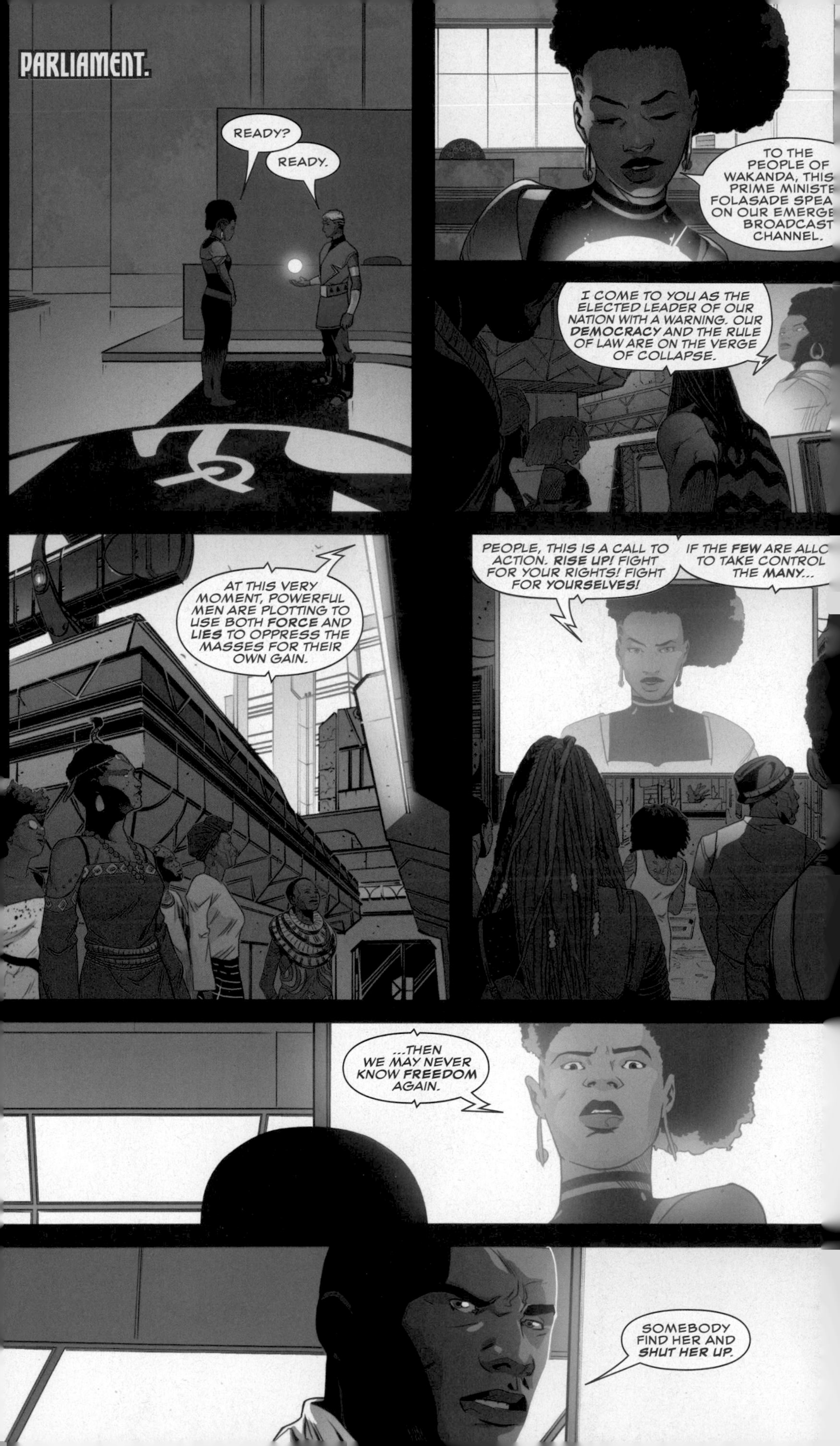
PARLIAMENT.
READY?
READY.
TO THE PEOPLE OF WAKANDA, THIS PRIME MINISTE FOLASADE SPEA ON OUR EMERGE BROADCAST CHANNEL.
I COME TO YOU AS THE ELECTED LEADER OF OUR NATION WITH A WARNING. OUR DEMOCRACY AND THE RULE OF LAW ARE ON THE VERGE OF COLLAPSE.
AT THIS VERY MOMENT, POWERFUL MEN ARE PLOTTING TO USE BOTH FORCE AND LIES TO OPPRESS THE MASSES FOR THEIR OWN GAIN.
PEOPLE, THIS IS A CALL TO ACTION. RISE UP! FIGHT FOR YOUR RIGHTS! FIGHT FOR YOURSELVES!
IF THE FEW ARE ALLO TO TAKE CONTROL THE MANY...
...THEN WE MAY NEVER KNOW FREEDOM AGAIN.
SOMEBODY FIND HER AND SHUT HER UP.

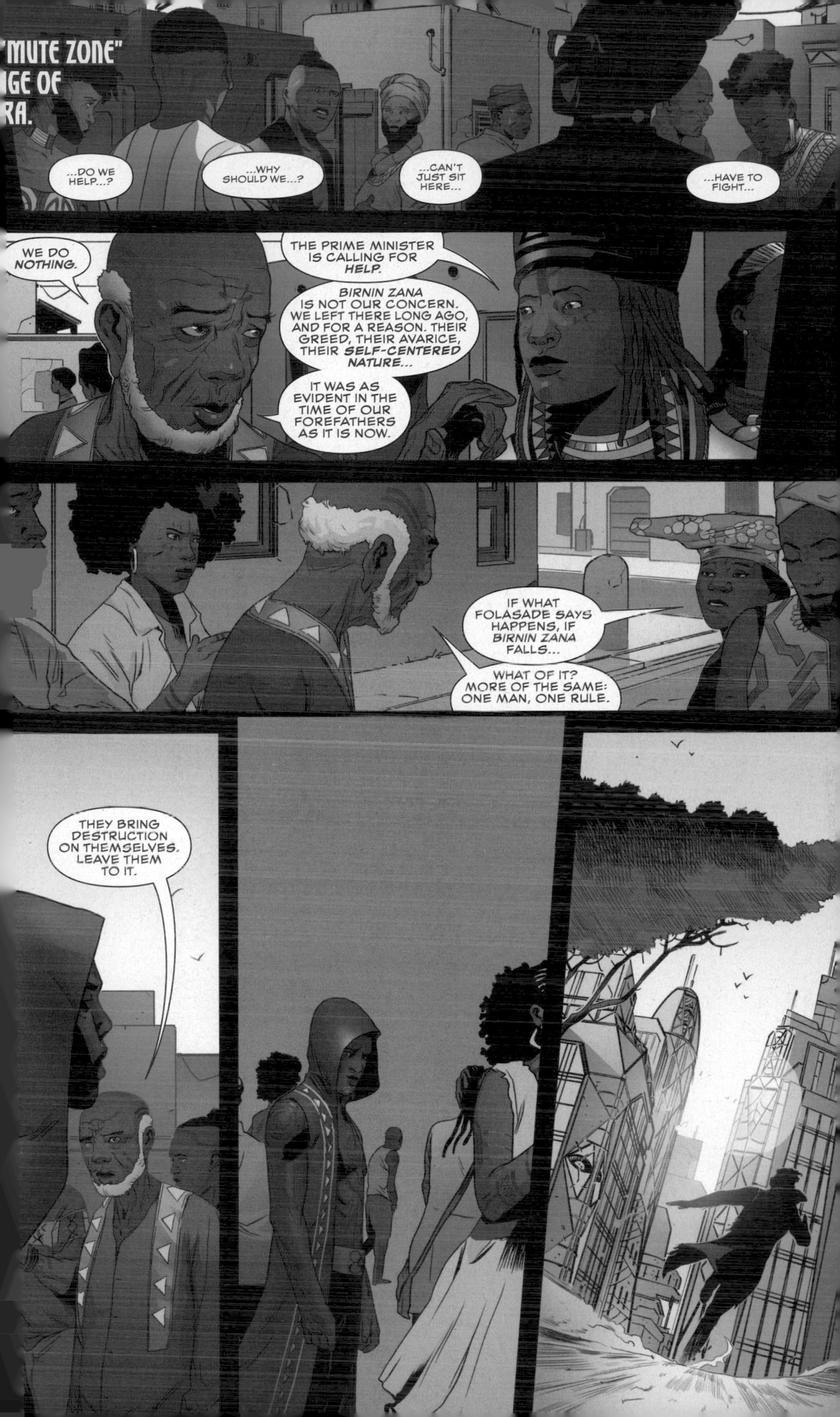
"MUTE ZONE"
IGE OF
RA.
...DO WE HELP...?
...WHY SHOULD WE...?
...CAN'T JUST SIT HERE...
...HAVE TO FIGHT...
WE DO *NOTHING.*
THE PRIME MINISTER IS CALLING FOR *HELP.*
BIRNIN ZANA IS NOT OUR CONCERN. WE LEFT THERE LONG AGO, AND FOR A REASON. THEIR GREED, THEIR AVARICE, THEIR ***SELF-CENTERED NATURE...***
IT WAS AS EVIDENT IN THE TIME OF OUR FOREFATHERS AS IT IS NOW.
IF WHAT FOLASADE SAYS HAPPENS, IF *BIRNIN ZANA* FALLS...
WHAT OF IT? MORE OF THE SAME: ONE MAN, ONE RULE.
THEY BRING DESTRUCTION ON THEMSELVES. LEAVE THEM TO IT.

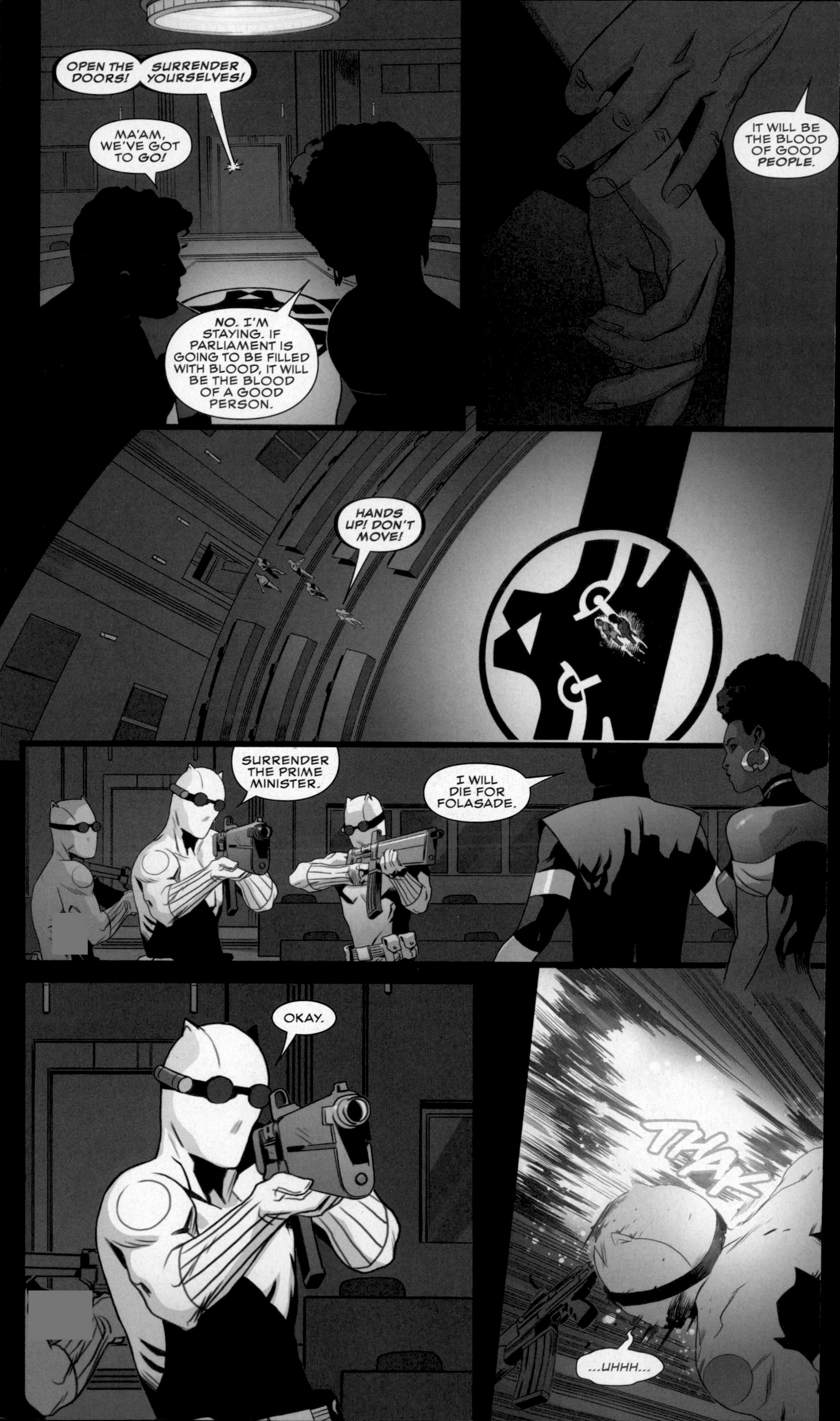
OPEN THE DOORS!
SURRENDER YOURSELVES!
MA'AM, WE'VE GOT TO GO!
NO. I'M STAYING. IF PARLIAMENT IS GOING TO BE FILLED WITH BLOOD, IT WILL BE THE BLOOD OF A GOOD PERSON.
IT WILL BE THE BLOOD OF GOOD PEOPLE.
HANDS UP! DON'T MOVE!
SURRENDER THE PRIME MINISTER.
I WILL DIE FOR FOLASADE.
OKAY.
THAK
...UHHH...

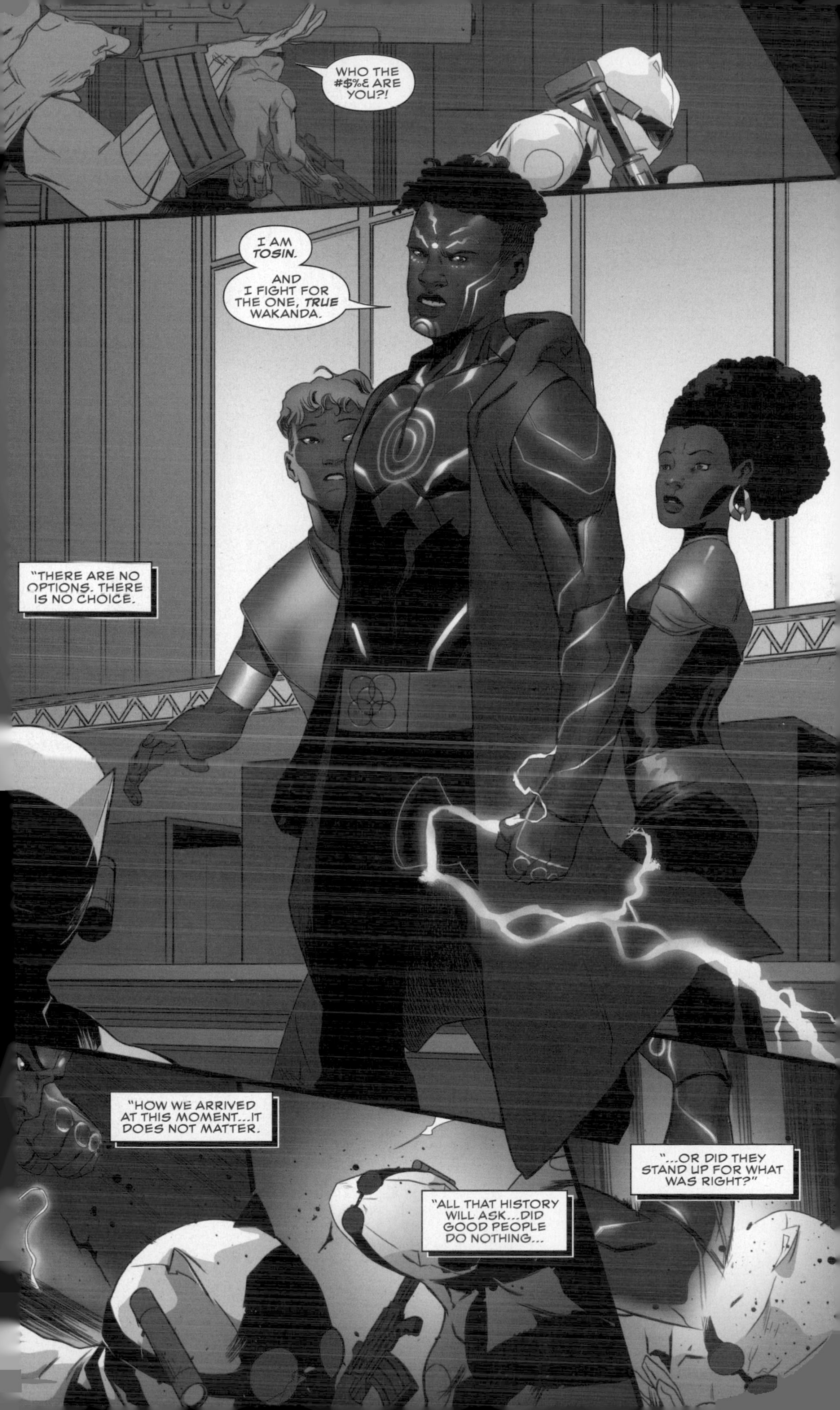
WHO THE #$%& ARE YOU?!
I AM TOSIN.
AND I FIGHT FOR THE ONE, TRUE WAKANDA.
"THERE ARE NO OPTIONS. THERE IS NO CHOICE.
"HOW WE ARRIVED AT THIS MOMENT...IT DOES NOT MATTER.
"ALL THAT HISTORY WILL ASK...DID GOOD PEOPLE DO NOTHING...
"...OR DID THEY STAND UP FOR WHAT WAS RIGHT?"

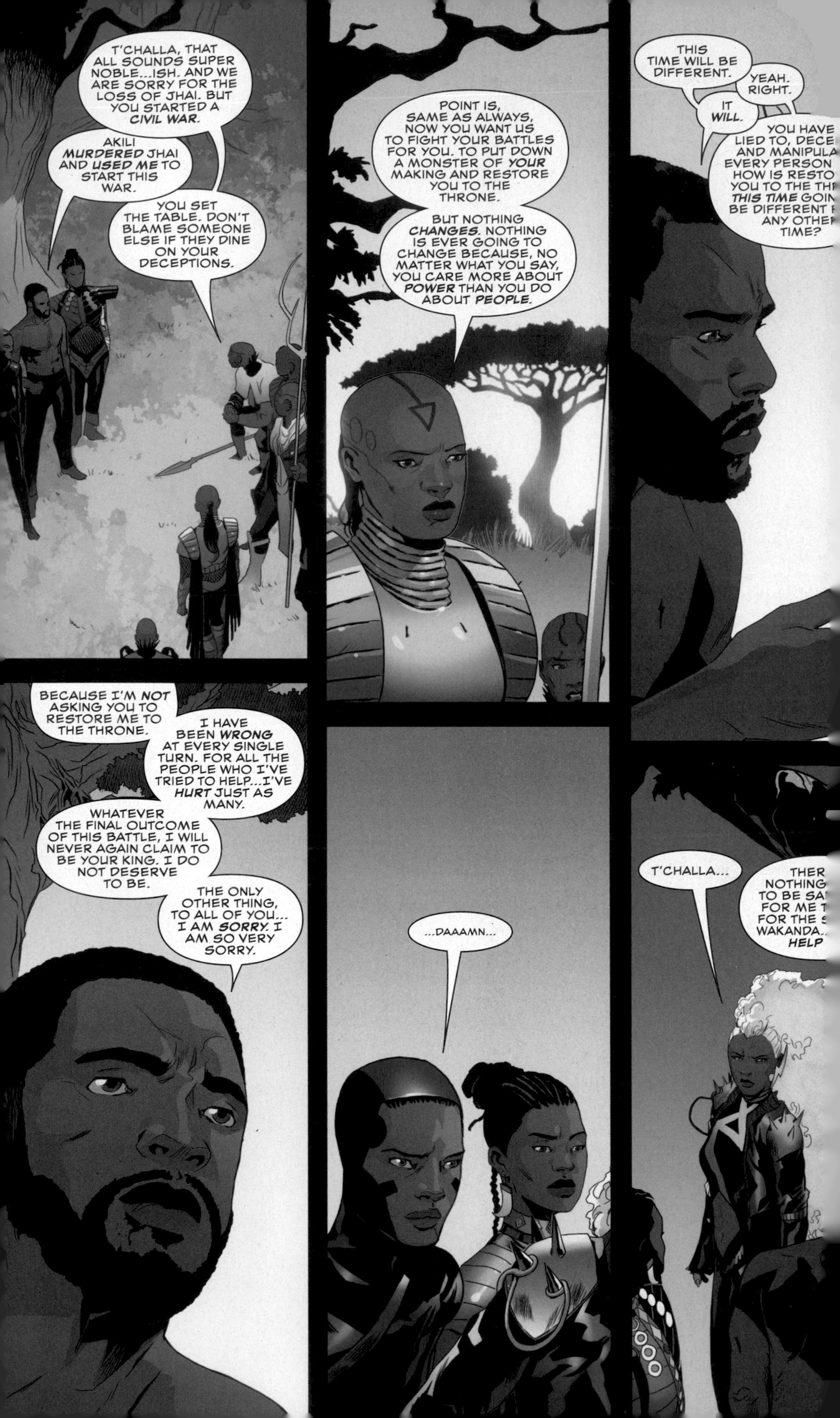
T'CHALLA, THAT ALL SOUNDS SUPER NOBLE...ISH. AND WE ARE SORRY FOR THE LOSS OF JHAI. BUT YOU STARTED A CIVIL WAR.
AKILI MURDERED JHAI AND USED ME TO START THIS WAR.
YOU SET THE TABLE. DON'T BLAME SOMEONE ELSE IF THEY DINE ON YOUR DECEPTIONS.
POINT IS, SAME AS ALWAYS, NOW YOU WANT US TO FIGHT YOUR BATTLES FOR YOU. TO PUT DOWN A MONSTER OF YOUR MAKING AND RESTORE YOU TO THE THRONE.
BUT NOTHING CHANGES. NOTHING IS EVER GOING TO CHANGE BECAUSE, NO MATTER WHAT YOU SAY, YOU CARE MORE ABOUT POWER THAN YOU DO ABOUT PEOPLE.
THIS TIME WILL BE DIFFERENT.
YEAH. RIGHT.
IT WILL.
BECAUSE I'M NOT ASKING YOU TO RESTORE ME TO THE THRONE.
I HAVE BEEN WRONG AT EVERY SINGLE TURN. FOR ALL THE PEOPLE WHO I'VE TRIED TO HELP...I'VE HURT JUST AS MANY.
WHATEVER THE FINAL OUTCOME OF THIS BATTLE, I WILL NEVER AGAIN CLAIM TO BE YOUR KING. I DO NOT DESERVE TO BE.
THE ONLY OTHER THING, TO ALL OF YOU... I AM SORRY. I AM SO VERY SORRY.
...DAAAMN...
T'CHALLA...

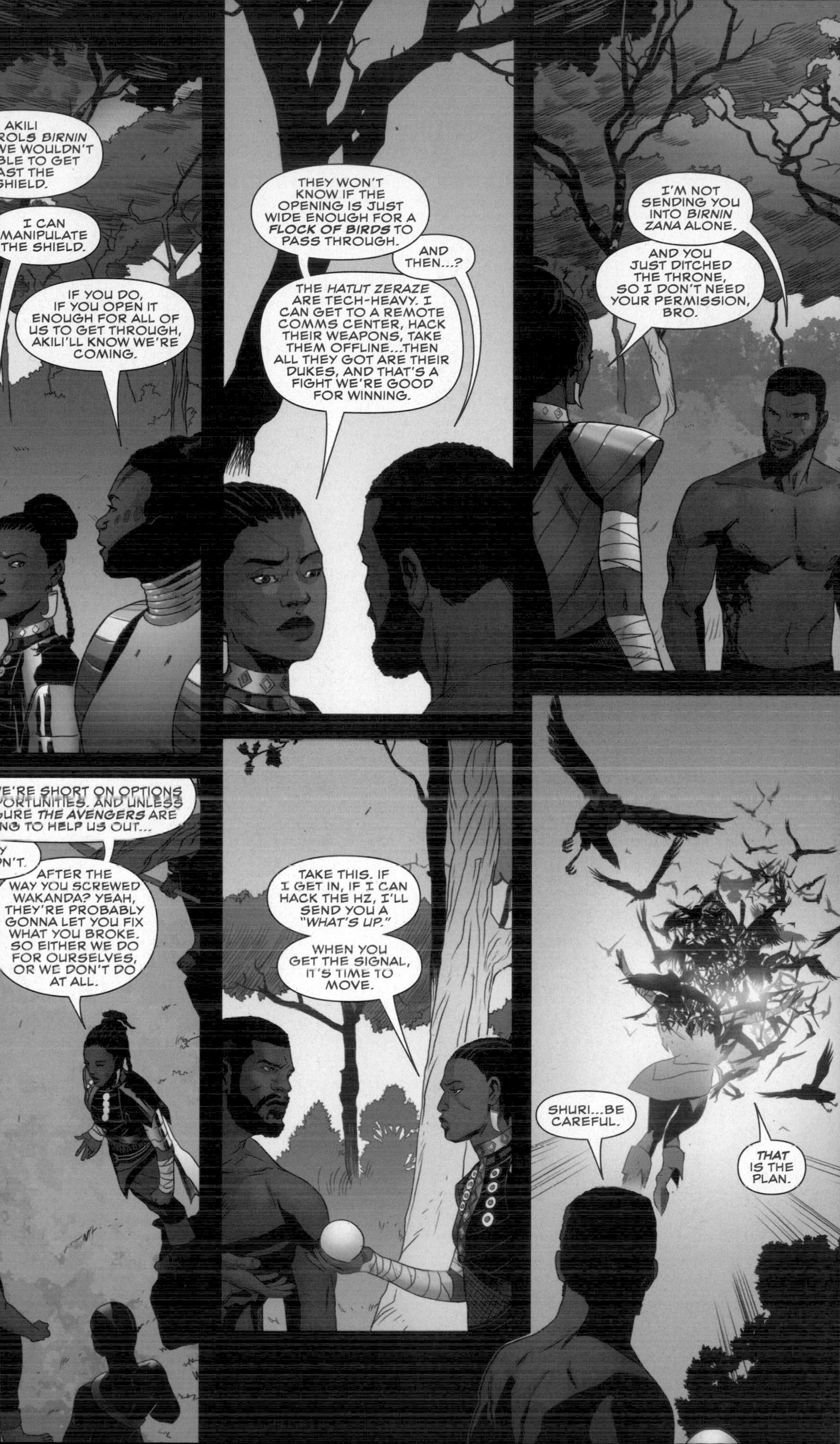
AKILI
ROLS BIRNIN
WE WOULDN'T
BLE TO GET
AST THE
SHIELD.
I CAN MANIPULATE THE SHIELD.
IF YOU DO, IF YOU OPEN IT ENOUGH FOR ALL OF US TO GET THROUGH, AKILI'LL KNOW WE'RE COMING.
THEY WON'T KNOW IF THE OPENING IS JUST WIDE ENOUGH FOR A FLOCK OF BIRDS TO PASS THROUGH.
AND THEN...?
THE HATUT ZERAZE ARE TECH-HEAVY. I CAN GET TO A REMOTE COMMS CENTER, HACK THEIR WEAPONS, TAKE THEM OFFLINE...THEN ALL THEY GOT ARE THEIR DUKES, AND THAT'S A FIGHT WE'RE GOOD FOR WINNING.
I'M NOT SENDING YOU INTO BIRNIN ZANA ALONE.
AND YOU JUST DITCHED THE THRONE, SO I DON'T NEED YOUR PERMISSION, BRO.
E'RE SHORT ON OPTIONS
PORTUNITIES. AND UNLESS
GURE THE AVENGERS ARE
NG TO HELP US OUT...
Y
N'T.
AFTER THE WAY YOU SCREWED WAKANDA? YEAH, THEY'RE PROBABLY GONNA LET YOU FIX WHAT YOU BROKE. SO EITHER WE DO FOR OURSELVES, OR WE DON'T DO AT ALL.
TAKE THIS. IF I GET IN, IF I CAN HACK THE HZ, I'LL SEND YOU A "WHAT'S UP."
WHEN YOU GET THE SIGNAL, IT'S TIME TO MOVE.
SHURI...BE CAREFUL.
THAT IS THE PLAN.

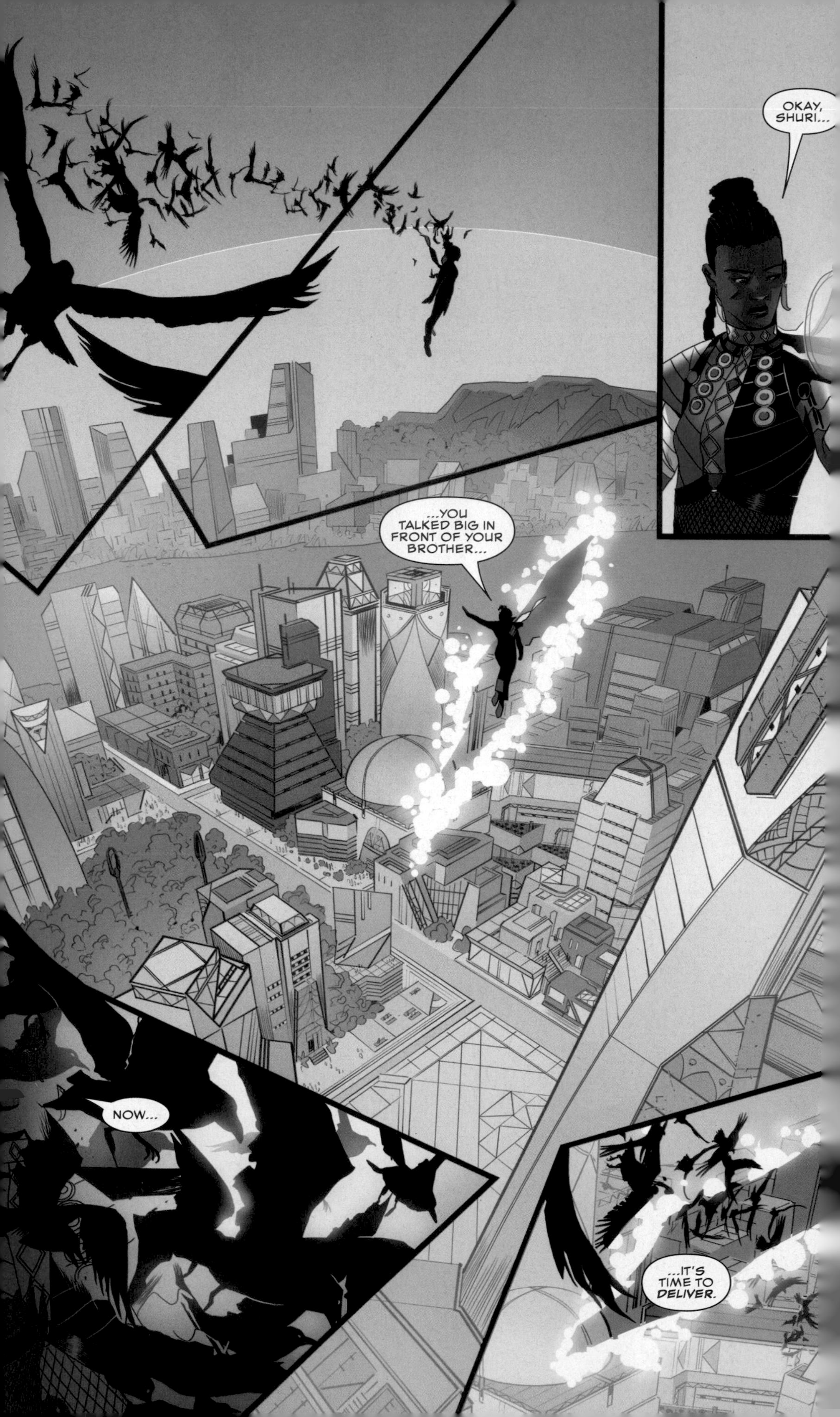
OKAY, SHURI...
...YOU TALKED BIG IN FRONT OF YOUR BROTHER...
NOW...
...IT'S TIME TO DELIVER.

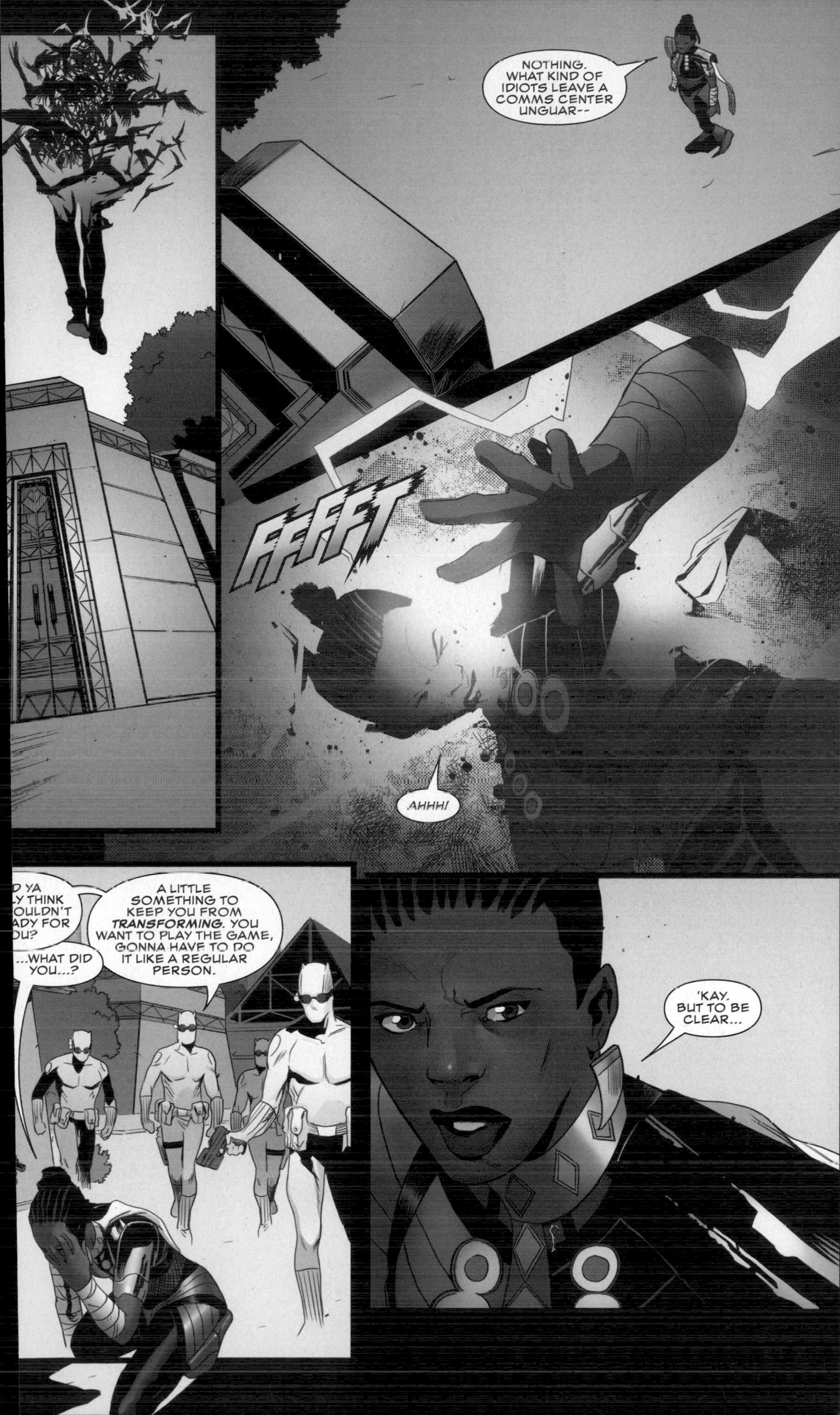
NOTHING. WHAT KIND OF IDIOTS LEAVE A COMMS CENTER UNGUAR--
FFFFT
AHHH!
D YA LY THINK OULDN'T ADY FOR OU?
...WHAT DID YOU...?
A LITTLE SOMETHING TO KEEP YOU FROM TRANSFORMING. YOU WANT TO PLAY THE GAME, GONNA HAVE TO DO IT LIKE A REGULAR PERSON.
'KAY. BUT TO BE CLEAR...

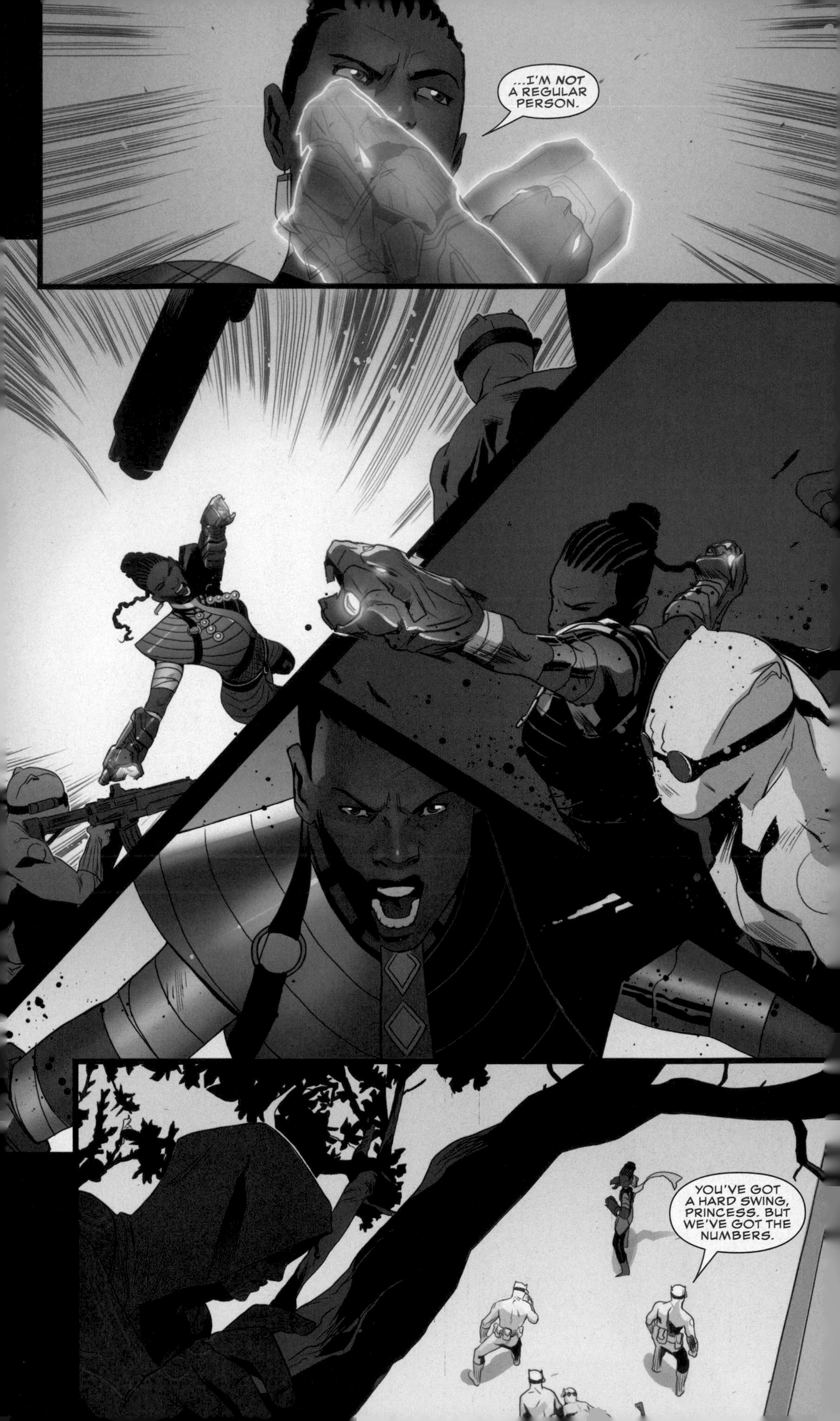
...I'M NOT A REGULAR PERSON.
YOU'VE GOT A HARD SWING, PRINCESS. BUT WE'VE GOT THE NUMBERS.

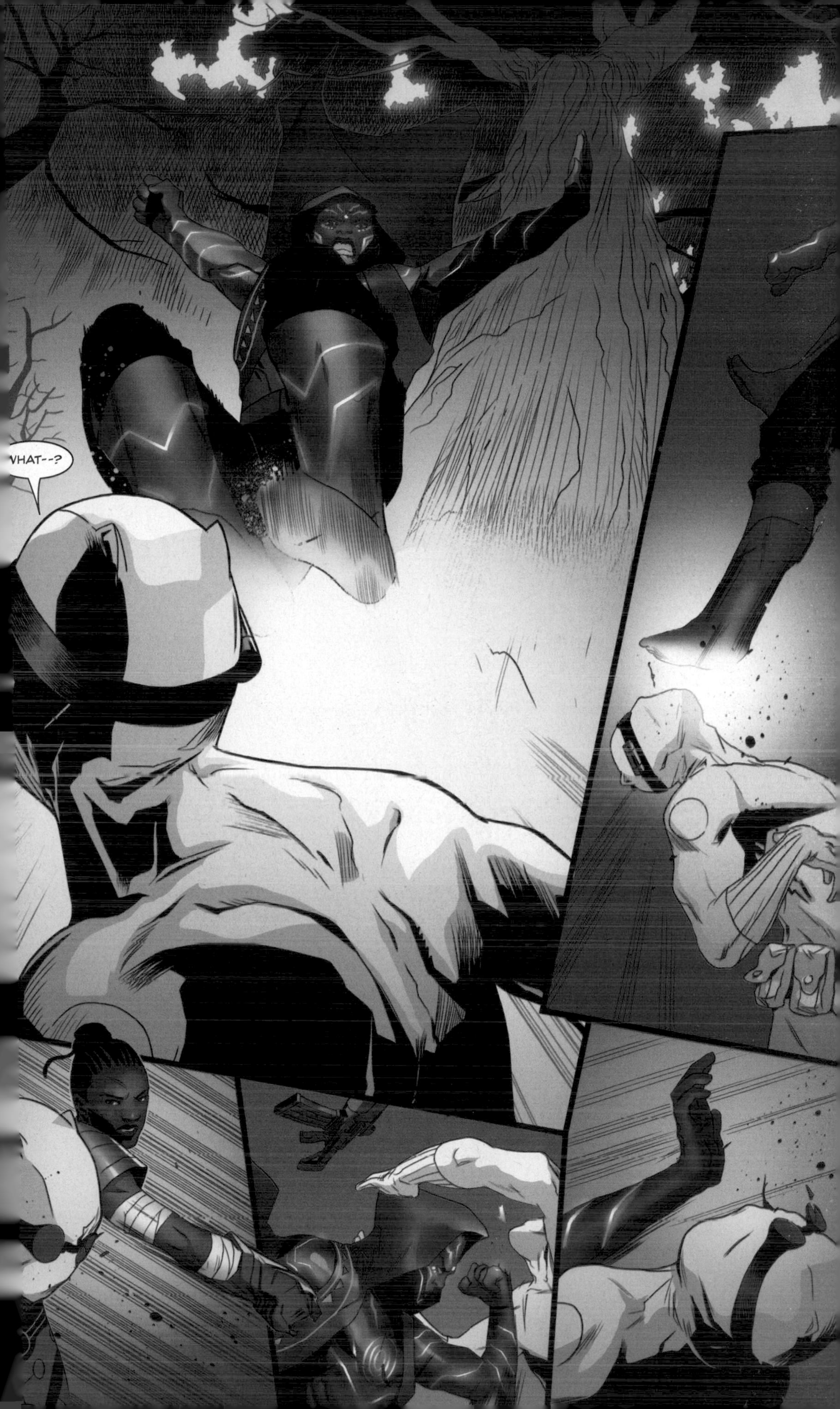
WHAT--?

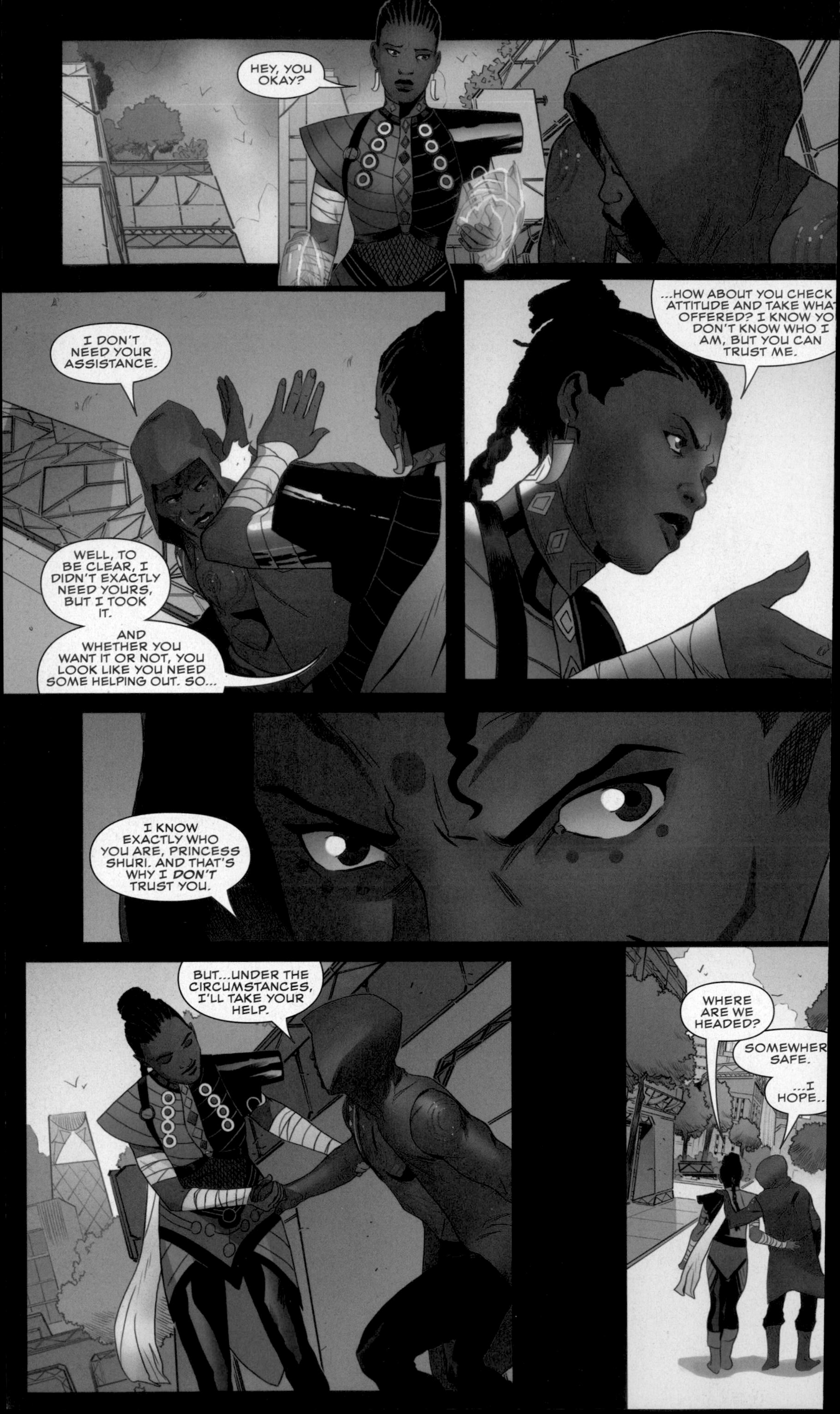
HEY, YOU OKAY?
I DON'T NEED YOUR ASSISTANCE.
WELL, TO BE CLEAR, I DIDN'T EXACTLY NEED YOURS, BUT I TOOK IT.
AND WHETHER YOU WANT IT OR NOT, YOU LOOK LIKE YOU NEED SOME HELPING OUT. SO...
...HOW ABOUT YOU CHECK ATTITUDE AND TAKE WHAT OFFERED? I KNOW YO DON'T KNOW WHO I AM, BUT YOU CAN TRUST ME.
I KNOW EXACTLY WHO YOU ARE, PRINCESS SHURI. AND THAT'S WHY I *DON'T* TRUST YOU.
BUT...UNDER THE CIRCUMSTANCES, I'LL TAKE YOUR HELP.
WHERE ARE WE HEADED?
SOMEWHER SAFE.
...I HOPE..

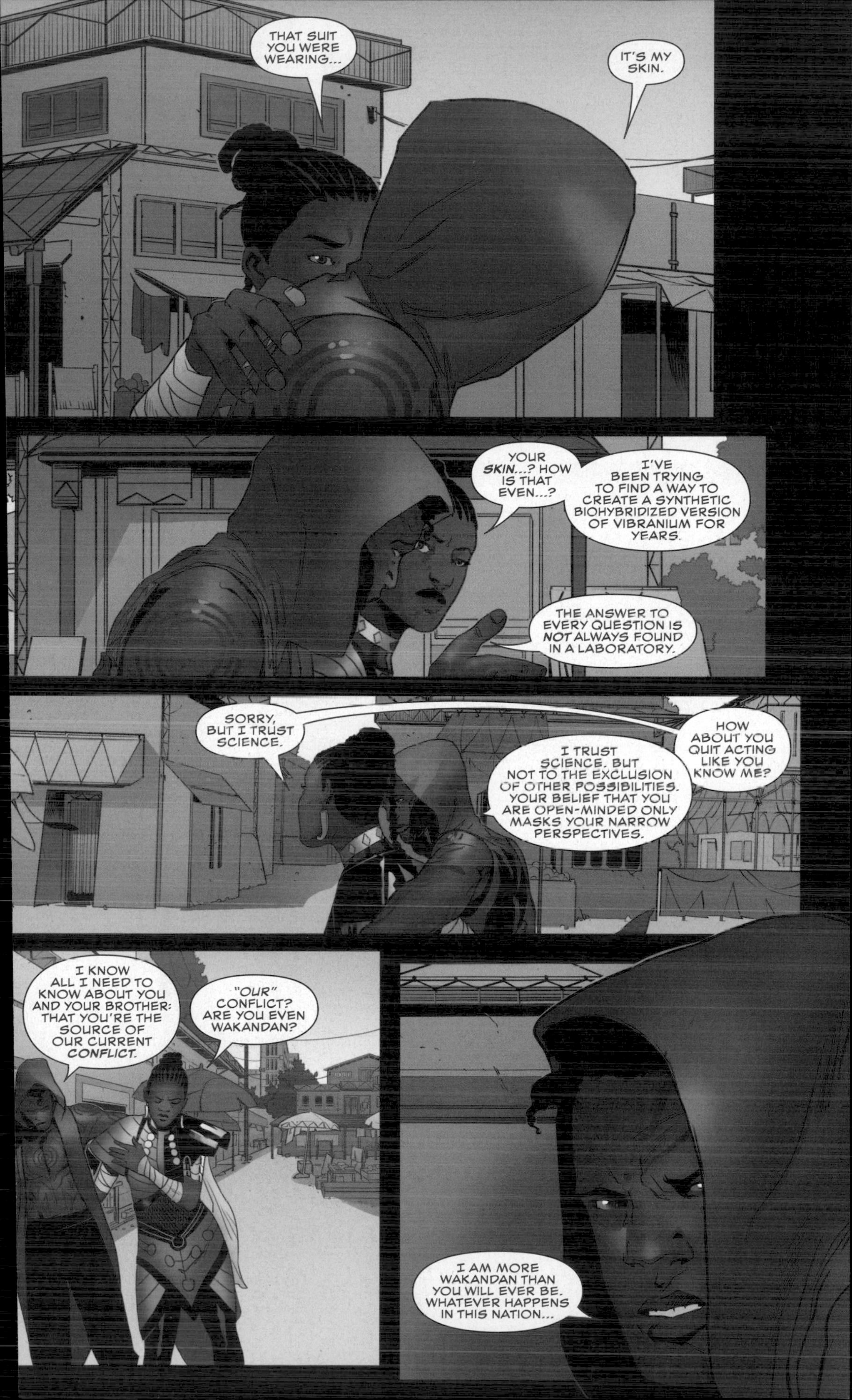

THAT SUIT YOU WERE WEARING...
IT'S MY SKIN.
YOUR SKIN...? HOW IS THAT EVEN...?
I'VE BEEN TRYING TO FIND A WAY TO CREATE A SYNTHETIC BIOHYBRIDIZED VERSION OF VIBRANIUM FOR YEARS.
THE ANSWER TO EVERY QUESTION IS NOT ALWAYS FOUND IN A LABORATORY.
SORRY, BUT I TRUST SCIENCE.
I TRUST SCIENCE. BUT NOT TO THE EXCLUSION OF OTHER POSSIBILITIES. YOUR BELIEF THAT YOU ARE OPEN-MINDED ONLY MASKS YOUR NARROW PERSPECTIVES.
HOW ABOUT YOU QUIT ACTING LIKE YOU KNOW ME?
I KNOW ALL I NEED TO KNOW ABOUT YOU AND YOUR BROTHER: THAT YOU'RE THE SOURCE OF OUR CURRENT CONFLICT.
"OUR" CONFLICT? ARE YOU EVEN WAKANDAN?
I AM MORE WAKANDAN THAN YOU WILL EVER BE. WHATEVER HAPPENS IN THIS NATION...

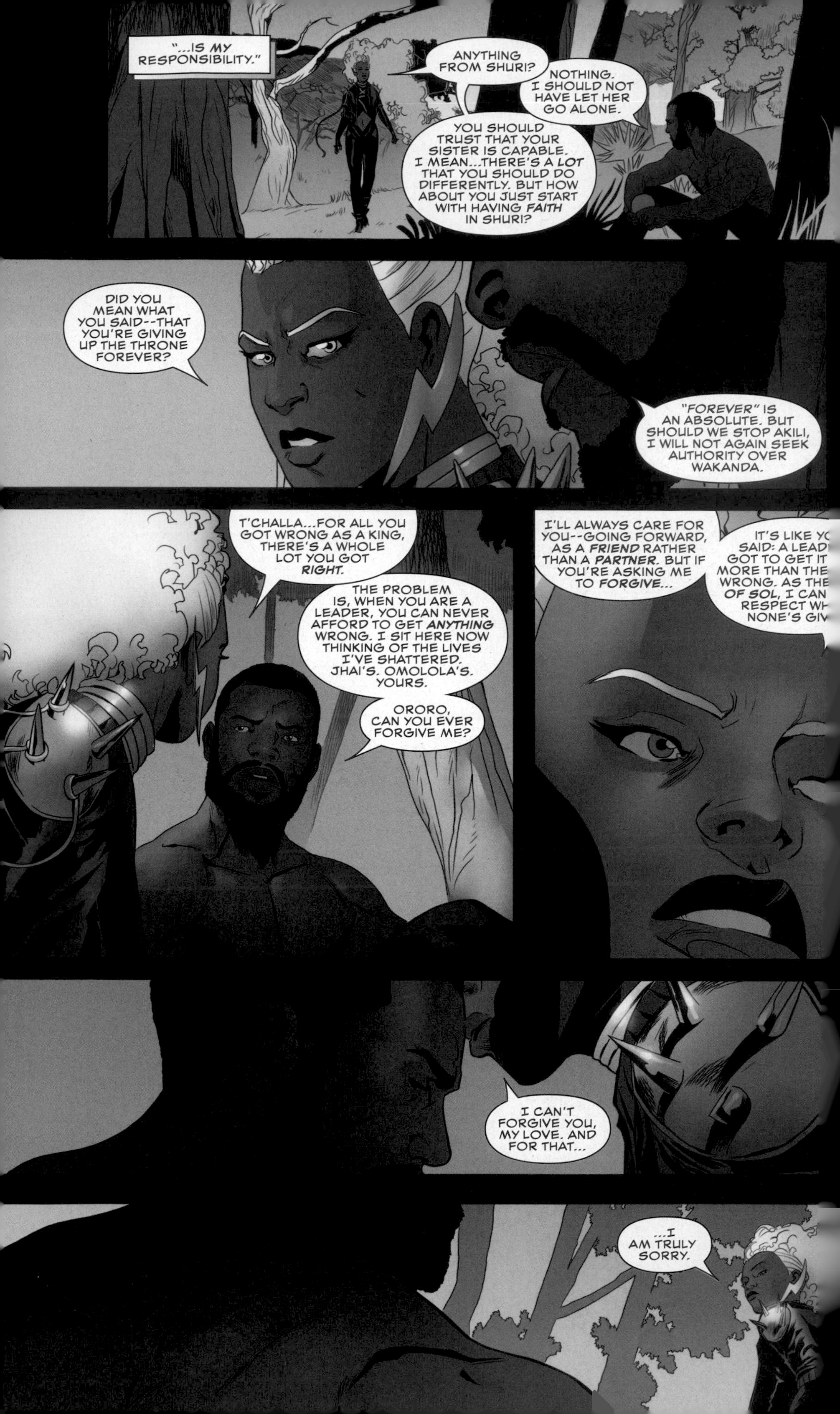
"...IS MY RESPONSIBILITY."
ANYTHING FROM SHURI?
NOTHING. I SHOULD NOT HAVE LET HER GO ALONE.
YOU SHOULD TRUST THAT YOUR SISTER IS CAPABLE. I MEAN...THERE'S A LOT THAT YOU SHOULD DO DIFFERENTLY. BUT HOW ABOUT YOU JUST START WITH HAVING FAITH IN SHURI?
DID YOU MEAN WHAT YOU SAID--THAT YOU'RE GIVING UP THE THRONE FOREVER?
"FOREVER" IS AN ABSOLUTE. BUT SHOULD WE STOP AKILI, I WILL NOT AGAIN SEEK AUTHORITY OVER WAKANDA.
T'CHALLA...FOR ALL YOU GOT WRONG AS A KING, THERE'S A WHOLE LOT YOU GOT RIGHT.
THE PROBLEM IS, WHEN YOU ARE A LEADER, YOU CAN NEVER AFFORD TO GET ANYTHING WRONG. I SIT HERE NOW THINKING OF THE LIVES I'VE SHATTERED. JHAI'S. OMOLOLA'S. YOURS.
ORORO, CAN YOU EVER FORGIVE ME?
I'LL ALWAYS CARE FOR YOU--GOING FORWARD, AS A FRIEND RATHER THAN A PARTNER. BUT IF YOU'RE ASKING ME TO FORGIVE...
IT'S LIKE YO SAID: A LEAD GOT TO GET IT MORE THAN THE WRONG. AS THE OF SOL, I CAN RESPECT WH NONE'S GIV
I CAN'T FORGIVE YOU, MY LOVE. AND FOR THAT...
...I AM TRULY SORRY.

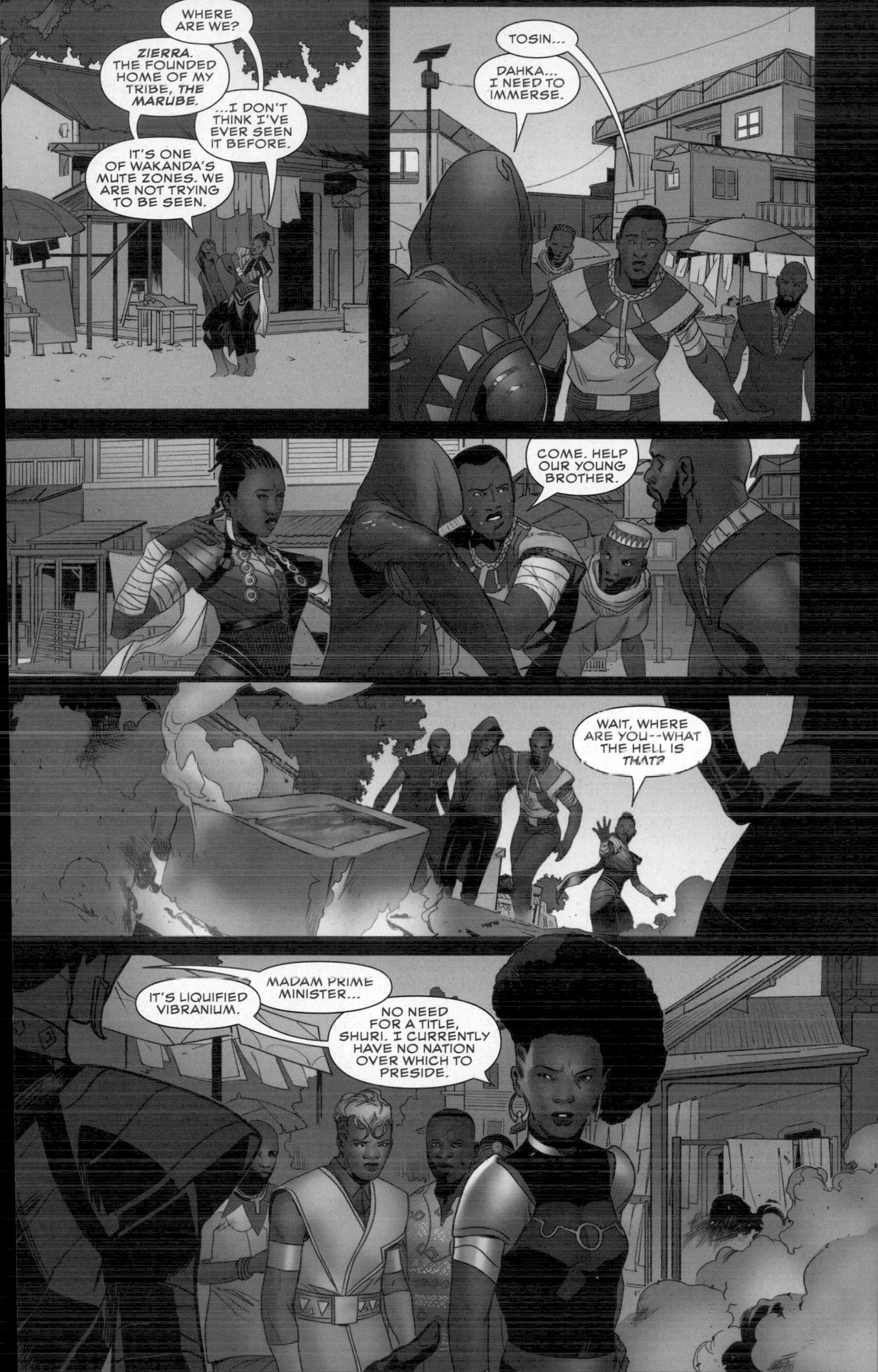

WHERE ARE WE?
ZIERRA. THE FOUNDED HOME OF MY TRIBE, *THE MARUBE.*
...I DON'T THINK I'VE EVER SEEN IT BEFORE.
IT'S ONE OF WAKANDA'S MUTE ZONES. WE ARE NOT TRYING TO BE SEEN.
TOSIN...
DAHKA... I NEED TO IMMERSE.
COME. HELP OUR YOUNG BROTHER.
WAIT, WHERE ARE YOU--WHAT THE HELL IS *THAT?*
IT'S LIQUIFIED VIBRANIUM.
MADAM PRIME MINISTER...
NO NEED FOR A TITLE, SHURI. I CURRENTLY HAVE NO NATION OVER WHICH TO PRESIDE.

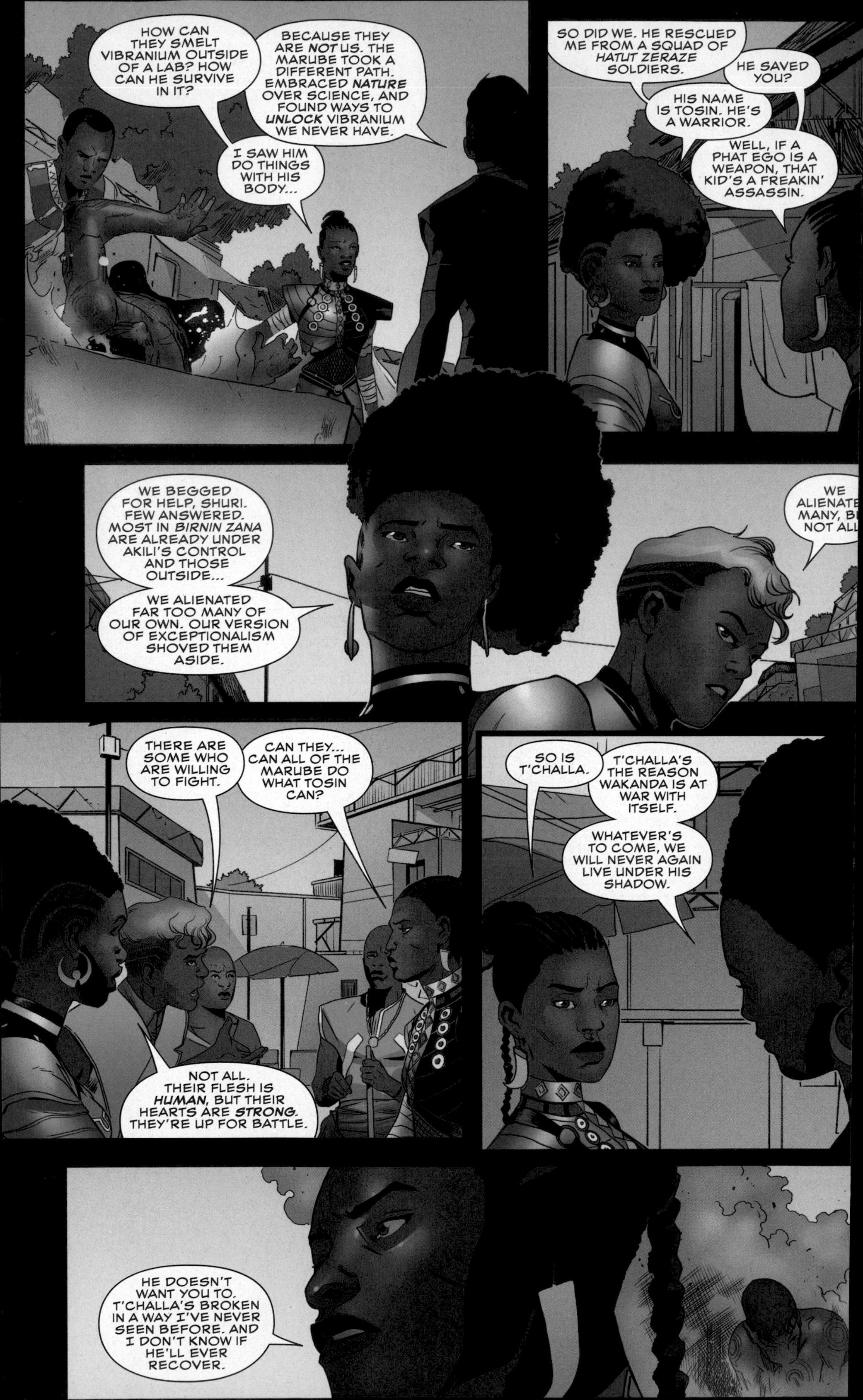
HOW CAN THEY SMELT VIBRANIUM OUTSIDE OF A LAB? HOW CAN HE SURVIVE IN IT?
BECAUSE THEY ARE NOT US. THE MARUBE TOOK A DIFFERENT PATH. EMBRACED NATURE OVER SCIENCE, AND FOUND WAYS TO UNLOCK VIBRANIUM WE NEVER HAVE.
I SAW HIM DO THINGS WITH HIS BODY...
SO DID WE. HE RESCUED ME FROM A SQUAD OF HATUT ZERAZE SOLDIERS.
HE SAVED YOU?
HIS NAME IS TOSIN. HE'S A WARRIOR.
WELL, IF A PHAT EGO IS A WEAPON, THAT KID'S A FREAKIN' ASSASSIN.
WE BEGGED FOR HELP, SHURI. FEW ANSWERED. MOST IN BIRNIN ZANA ARE ALREADY UNDER AKILI'S CONTROL AND THOSE OUTSIDE...
WE ALIENATED FAR TOO MANY OF OUR OWN. OUR VERSION OF EXCEPTIONALISM SHOVED THEM ASIDE.
THERE ARE SOME WHO ARE WILLING TO FIGHT.
CAN THEY... CAN ALL OF THE MARUBE DO WHAT TOSIN CAN?
NOT ALL. THEIR FLESH IS HUMAN, BUT THEIR HEARTS ARE STRONG. THEY'RE UP FOR BATTLE.
SO IS T'CHALLA.
T'CHALLA'S THE REASON WAKANDA IS AT WAR WITH ITSELF.
WHATEVER'S TO COME, WE WILL NEVER AGAIN LIVE UNDER HIS SHADOW.
HE DOESN'T WANT YOU TO. T'CHALLA'S BROKEN IN A WAY I'VE NEVER SEEN BEFORE. AND I DON'T KNOW IF HE'LL EVER RECOVER.

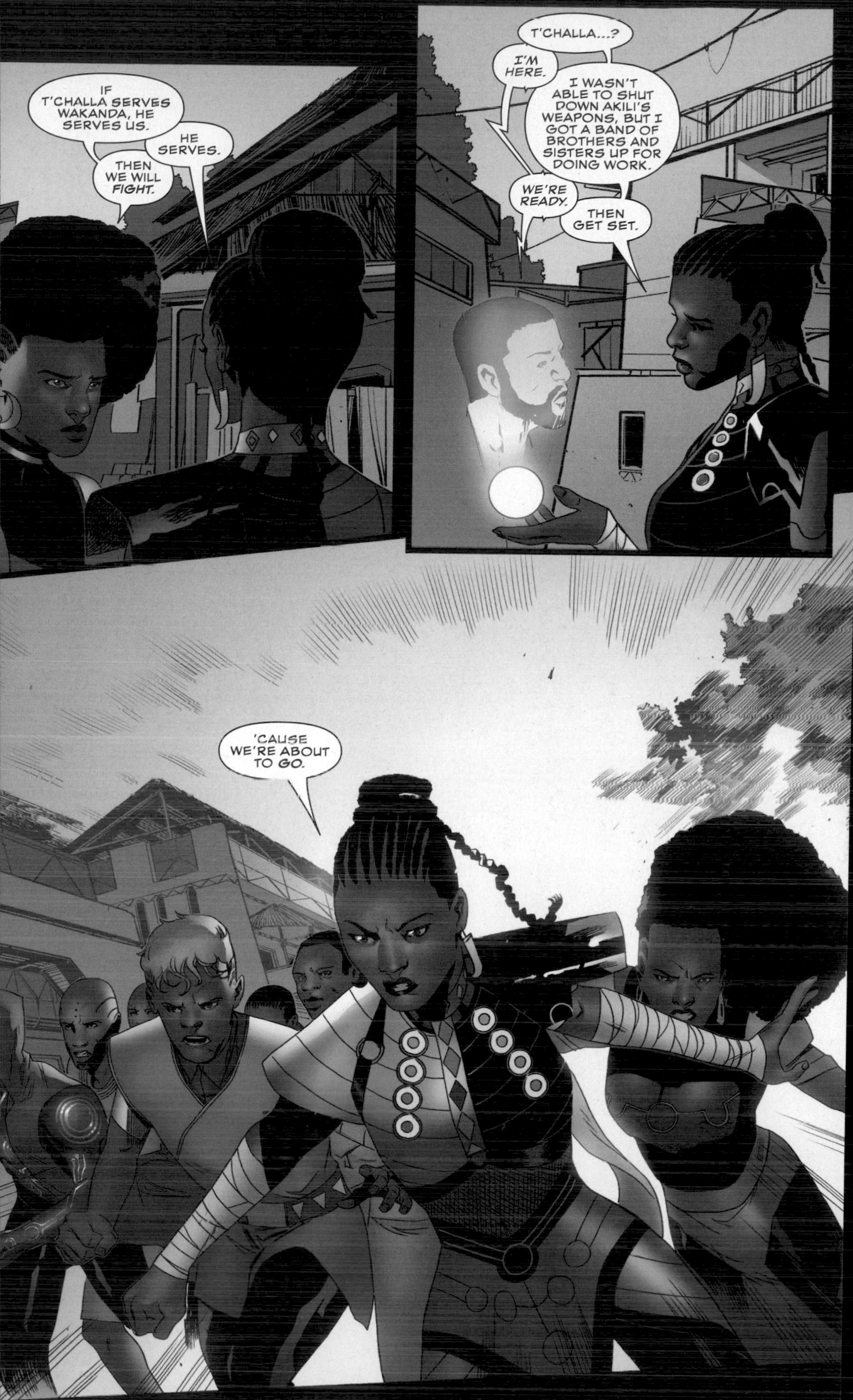
IF T'CHALLA SERVES WAKANDA, HE SERVES US.
HE SERVES.
THEN WE WILL FIGHT.
T'CHALLA...?
I'M HERE.
I WASN'T ABLE TO SHUT DOWN AKILI'S WEAPONS, BUT I GOT A BAND OF BROTHERS AND SISTERS UP FOR DOING WORK.
WE'RE READY.
THEN GET SET.
'CAUSE WE'RE ABOUT TO GO.

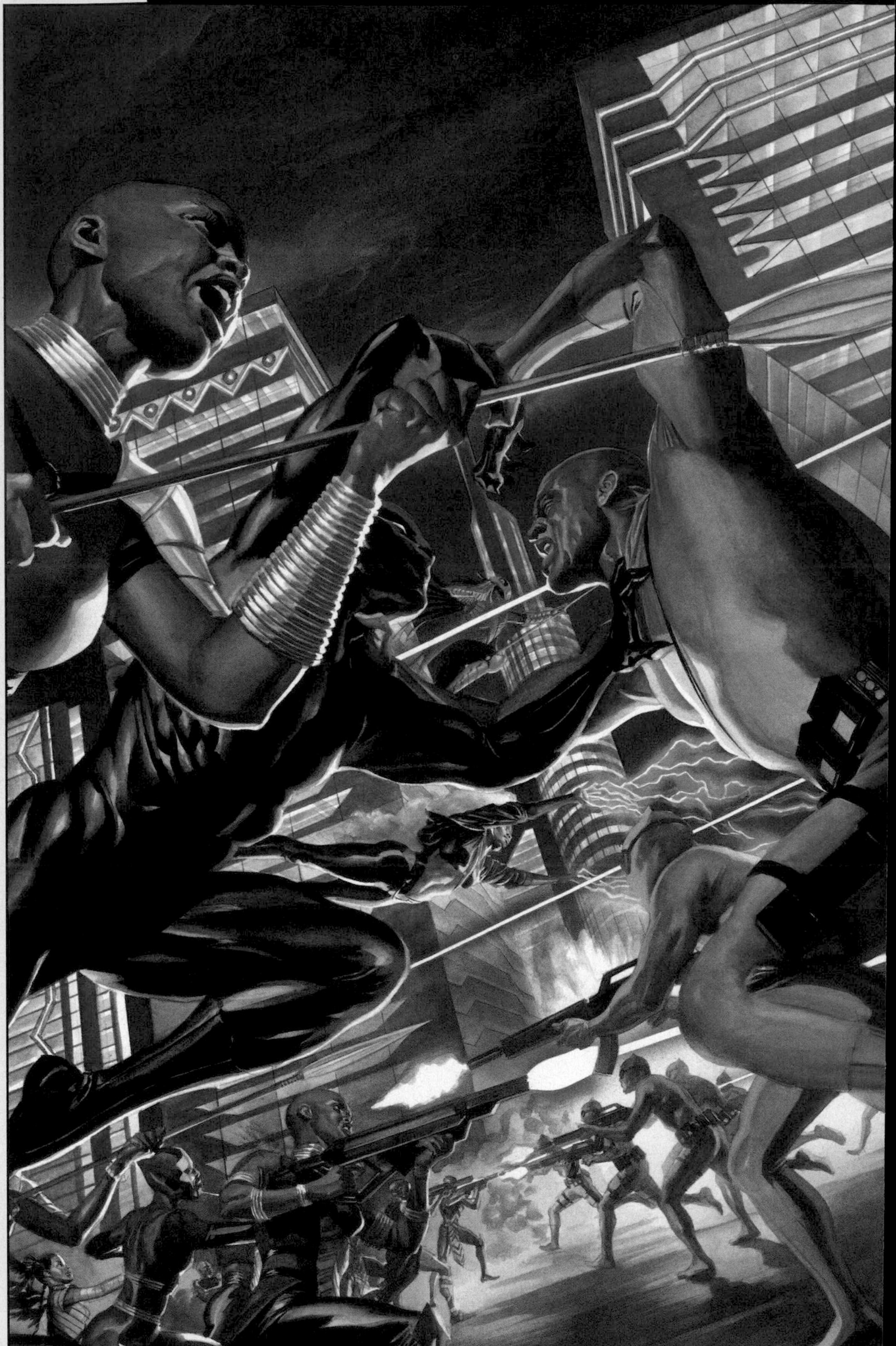

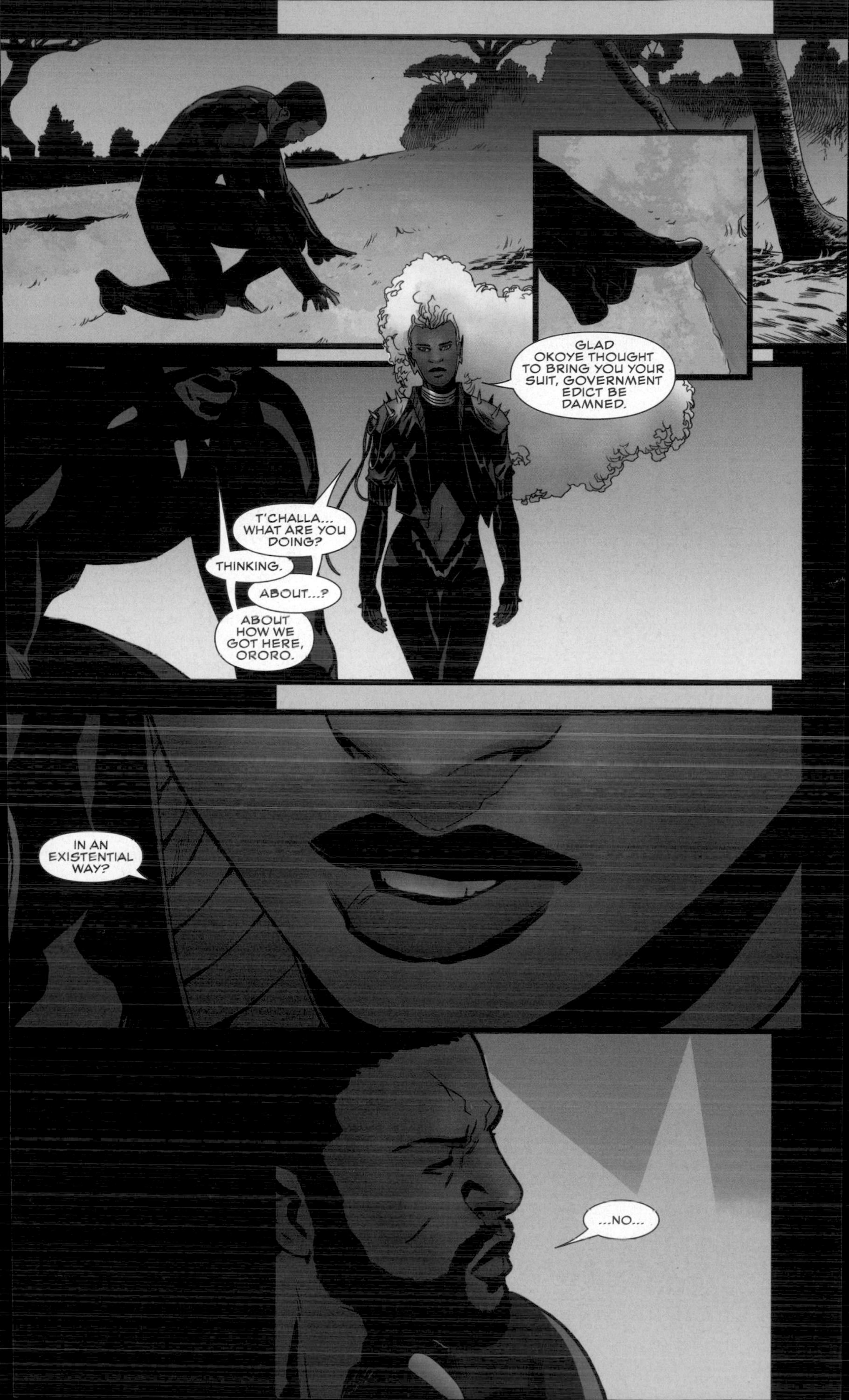
GLAD OKOYE THOUGHT TO BRING YOU YOUR SUIT, GOVERNMENT EDICT BE DAMNED.
T'CHALLA... WHAT ARE YOU DOING?
THINKING.
ABOUT...?
ABOUT HOW WE GOT HERE, ORORO.
IN AN EXISTENTIAL WAY?
...NO...

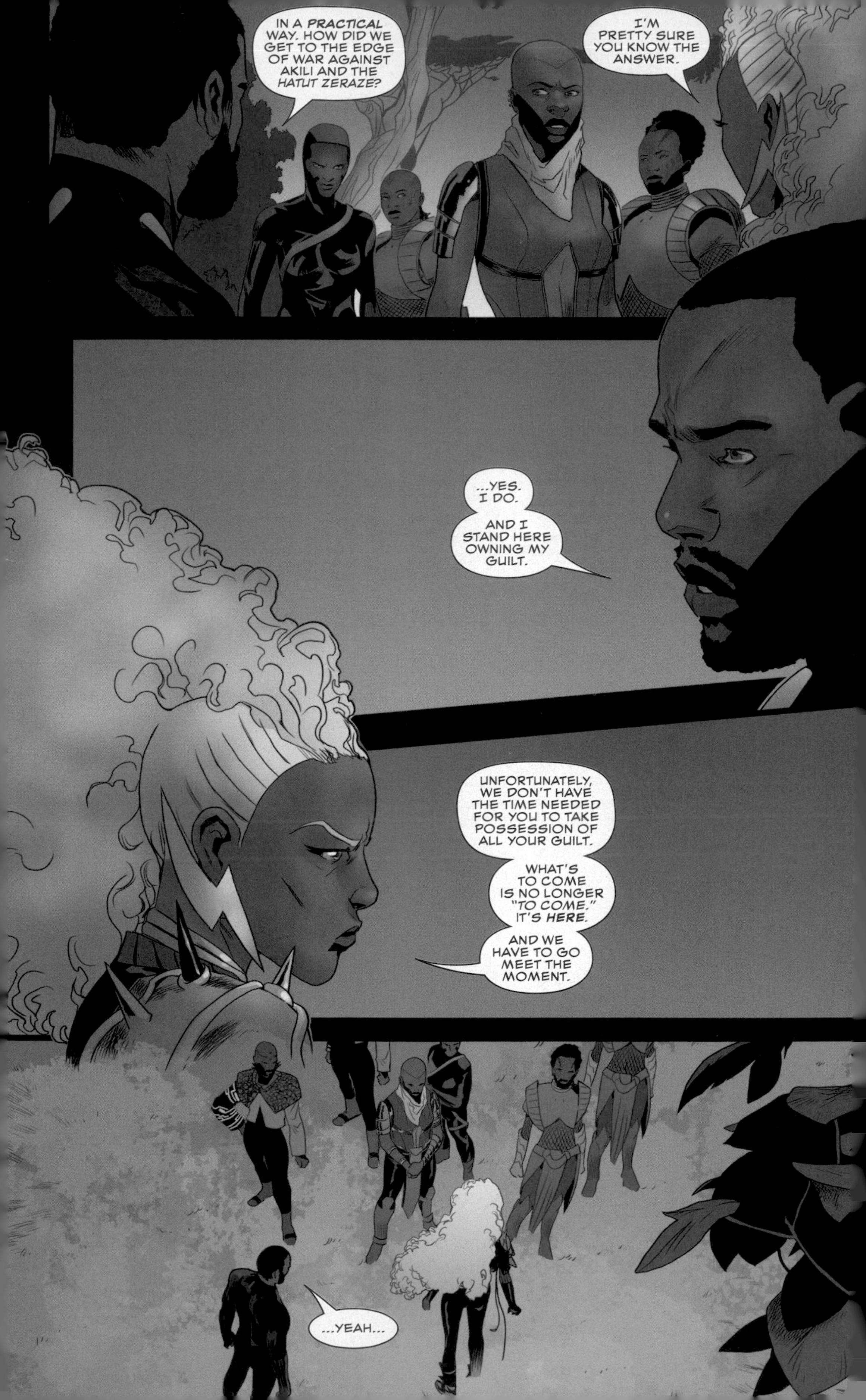
IN A PRACTICAL WAY. HOW DID WE GET TO THE EDGE OF WAR AGAINST AKILI AND THE HATUT ZERAZE?
I'M PRETTY SURE YOU KNOW THE ANSWER.
...YES. I DO.
AND I STAND HERE OWNING MY GUILT.
UNFORTUNATELY, WE DON'T HAVE THE TIME NEEDED FOR YOU TO TAKE POSSESSION OF ALL YOUR GUILT.
WHAT'S TO COME IS NO LONGER "TO COME." IT'S HERE.
AND WE HAVE TO GO MEET THE MOMENT.
...YEAH...

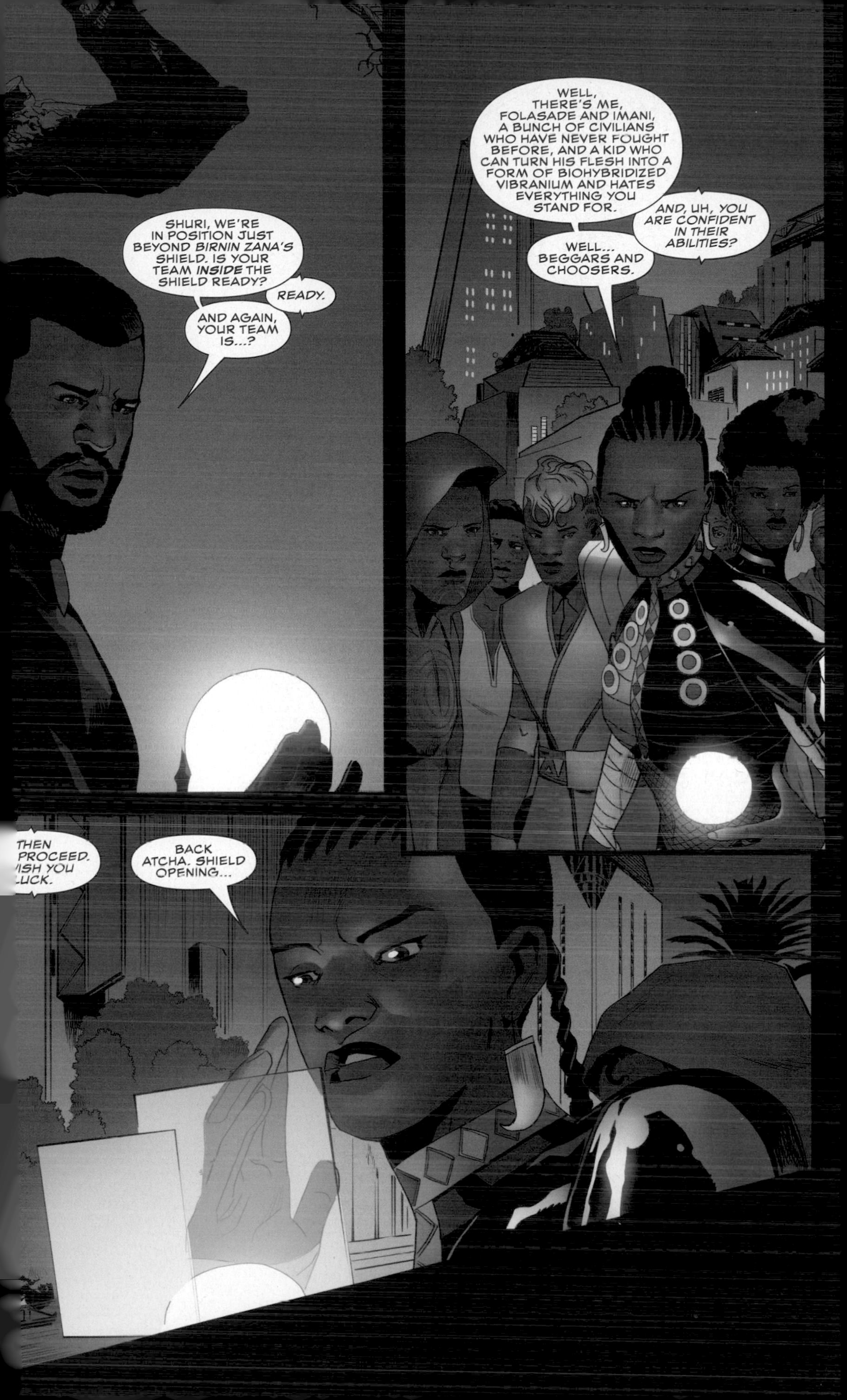
SHURI, WE'RE IN POSITION JUST BEYOND BIRNIN ZANA'S SHIELD. IS YOUR TEAM INSIDE THE SHIELD READY?
READY.
AND AGAIN, YOUR TEAM IS...?
WELL, THERE'S ME, FOLASADE AND IMANI, A BUNCH OF CIVILIANS WHO HAVE NEVER FOUGHT BEFORE, AND A KID WHO CAN TURN HIS FLESH INTO A FORM OF BIOHYBRIDIZED VIBRANIUM AND HATES EVERYTHING YOU STAND FOR.
AND, UH, YOU ARE CONFIDENT IN THEIR ABILITIES?
WELL... BEGGARS AND CHOOSERS.
THEN PROCEED. WISH YOU LUCK.
BACK ATCHA. SHIELD OPENING...

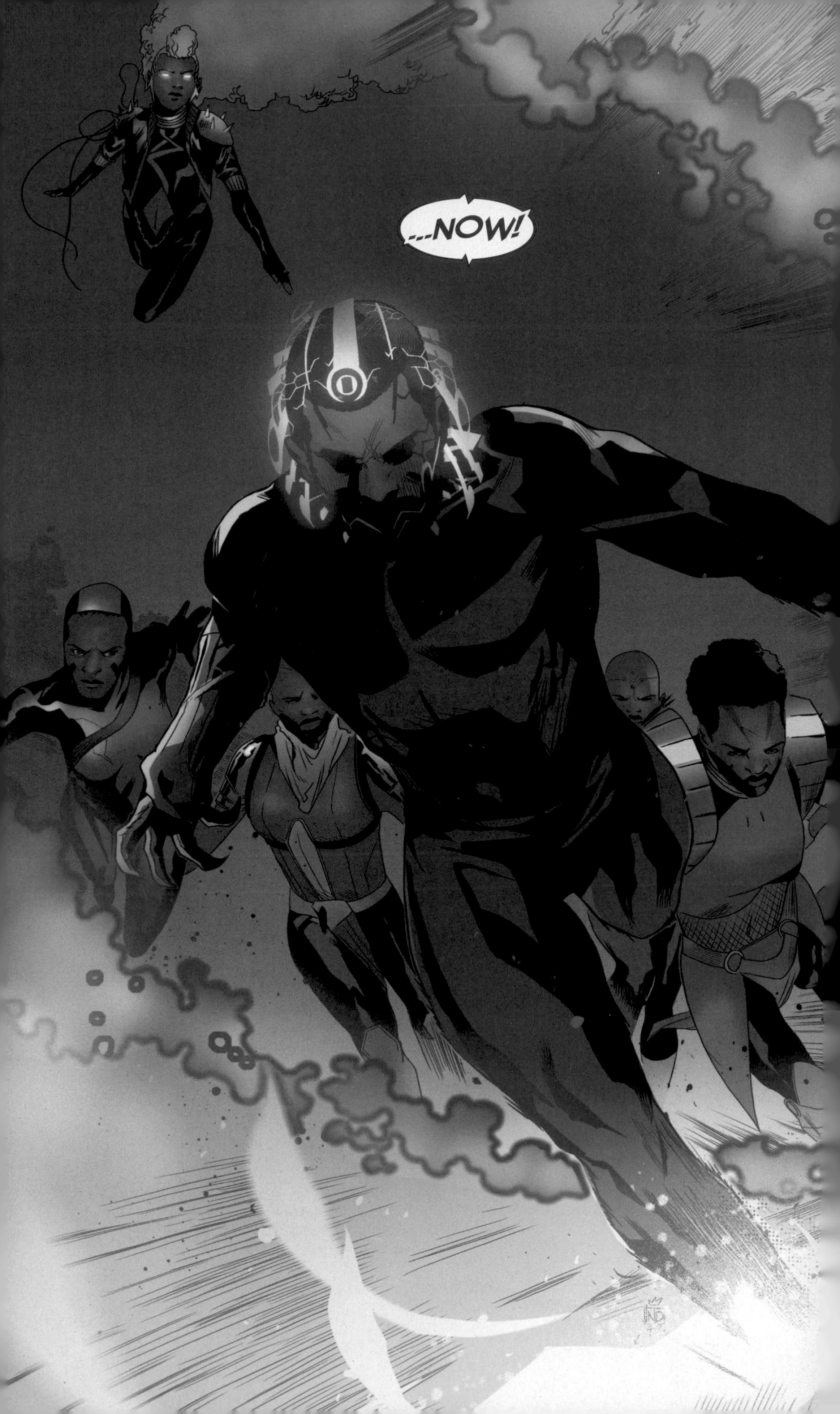
--NOW!

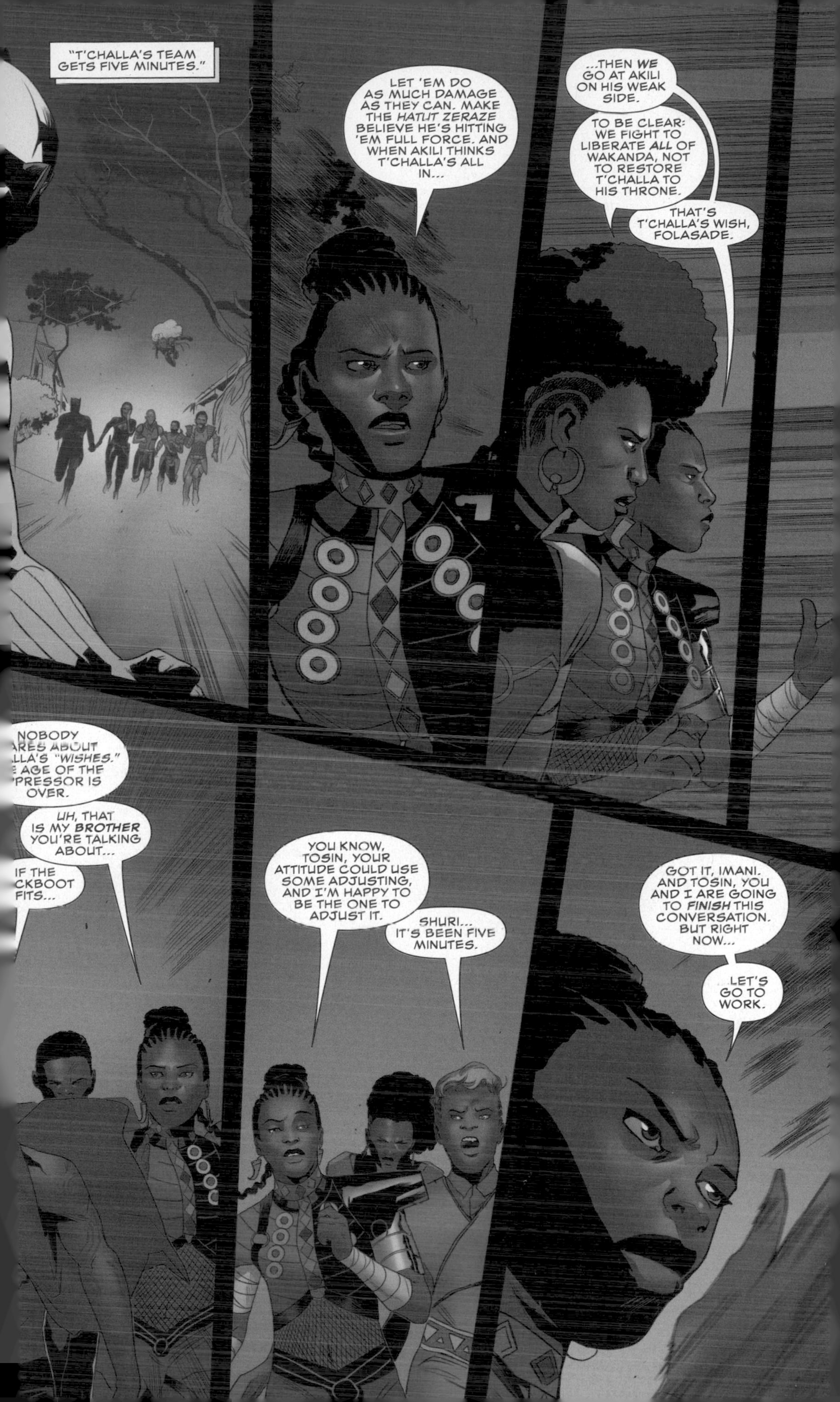
"T'CHALLA'S TEAM GETS FIVE MINUTES."
LET 'EM DO AS MUCH DAMAGE AS THEY CAN. MAKE THE HATUT ZERAZE BELIEVE HE'S HITTING 'EM FULL FORCE. AND WHEN AKILI THINKS T'CHALLA'S ALL IN...
...THEN WE GO AT AKILI ON HIS WEAK SIDE.
TO BE CLEAR: WE FIGHT TO LIBERATE ALL OF WAKANDA, NOT TO RESTORE T'CHALLA TO HIS THRONE.
THAT'S T'CHALLA'S WISH, FOLASADE.
NOBODY ARES ABOUT LLA'S "WISHES." E AGE OF THE PPRESSOR IS OVER.
UH, THAT IS MY BROTHER YOU'RE TALKING ABOUT...
IF THE CKBOOT FITS...
YOU KNOW, TOSIN, YOUR ATTITUDE COULD USE SOME ADJUSTING, AND I'M HAPPY TO BE THE ONE TO ADJUST IT.
SHURI... IT'S BEEN FIVE MINUTES.
GOT IT, IMANI. AND TOSIN, YOU AND I ARE GOING TO FINISH THIS CONVERSATION. BUT RIGHT NOW...
...LET'S GO TO WORK.

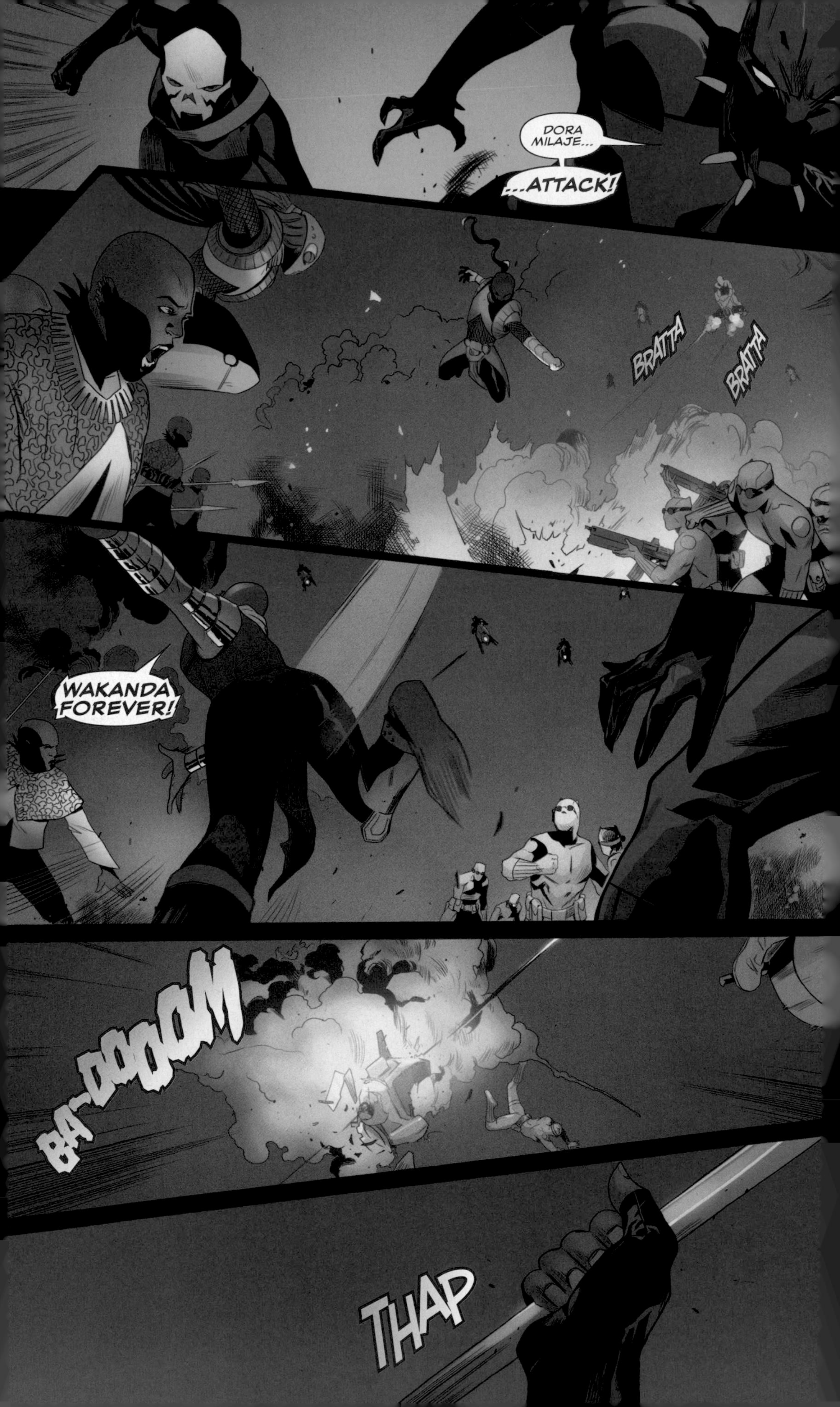
DORA MILAJE...
...ATTACK!
BRATTA
BRATTA
WAKANDA FOREVER!
BA-DOOOOM
THAP

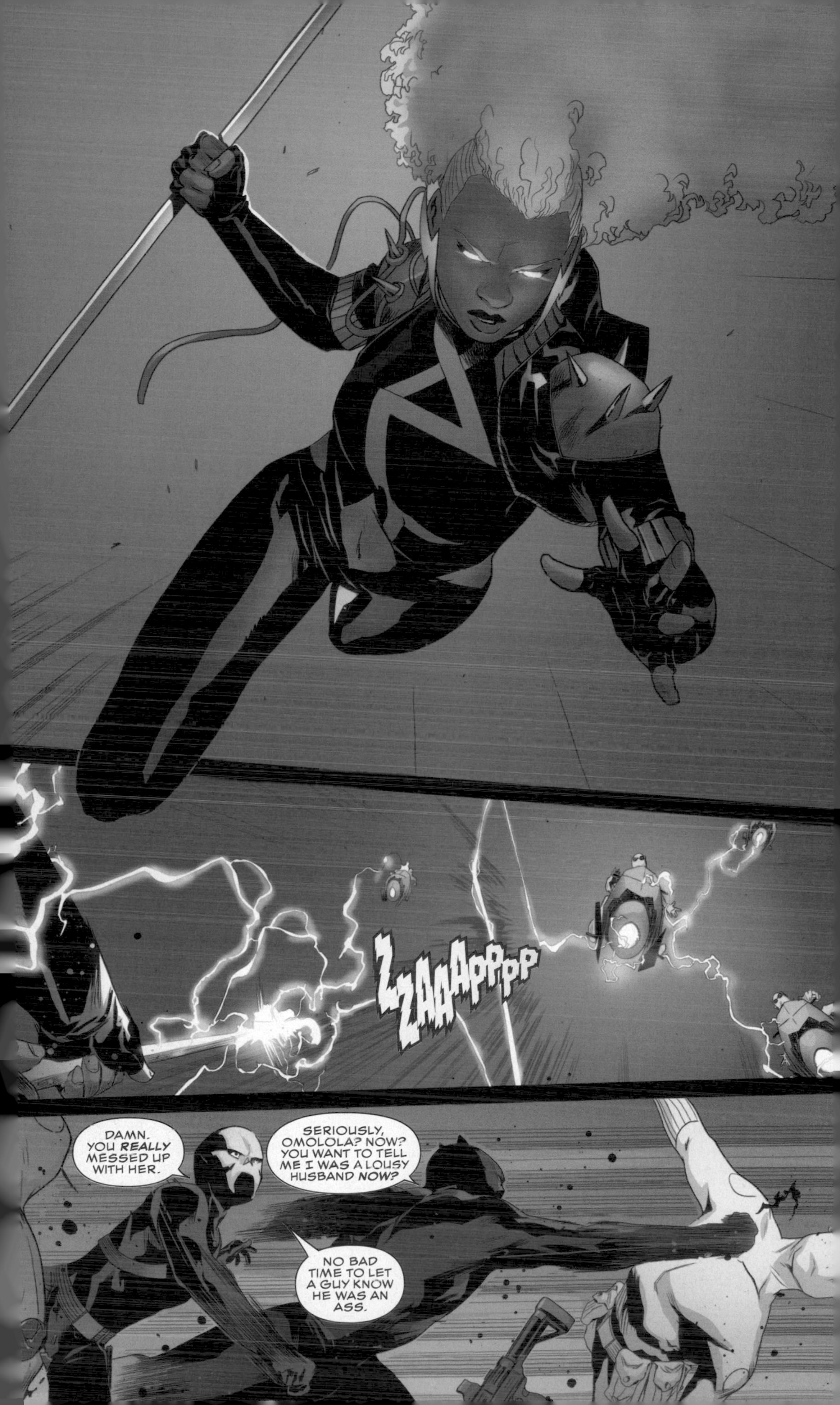
ZZAAAPPPP
DAMN. YOU REALLY MESSED UP WITH HER.
SERIOUSLY, OMOLOLA? NOW? YOU WANT TO TELL ME I WAS A LOUSY HUSBAND NOW?
NO BAD TIME TO LET A GUY KNOW HE WAS AN ASS.

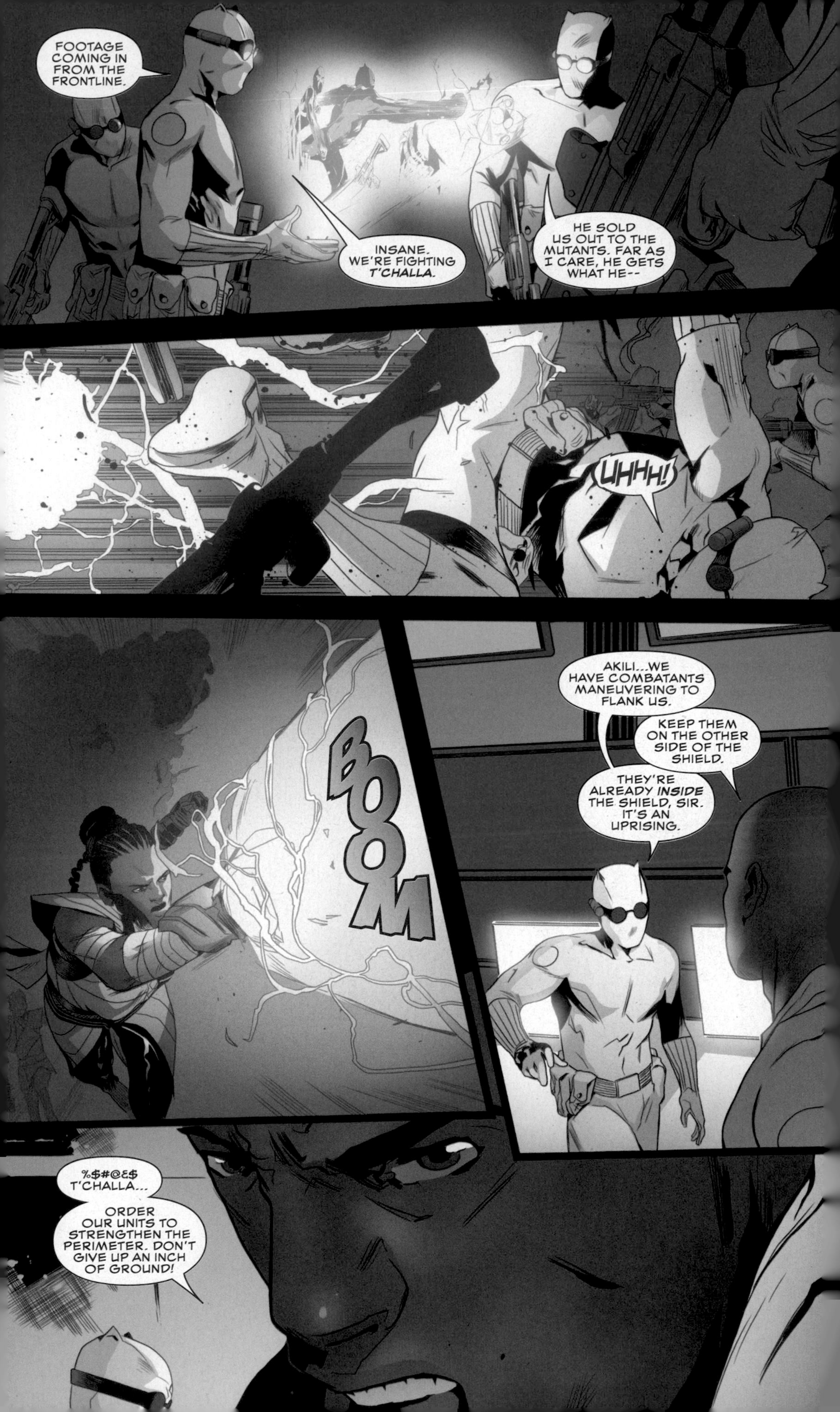
FOOTAGE COMING IN FROM THE FRONTLINE.
INSANE. WE'RE FIGHTING T'CHALLA.
HE SOLD US OUT TO THE MUTANTS. FAR AS I CARE, HE GETS WHAT HE--
UHHH!
BOOM
AKILI...WE HAVE COMBATANTS MANEUVERING TO FLANK US.
KEEP THEM ON THE OTHER SIDE OF THE SHIELD.
THEY'RE ALREADY INSIDE THE SHIELD, SIR. IT'S AN UPRISING.
%$#@&$ T'CHALLA...
ORDER OUR UNITS TO STRENGTHEN THE PERIMETER. DON'T GIVE UP AN INCH OF GROUND!

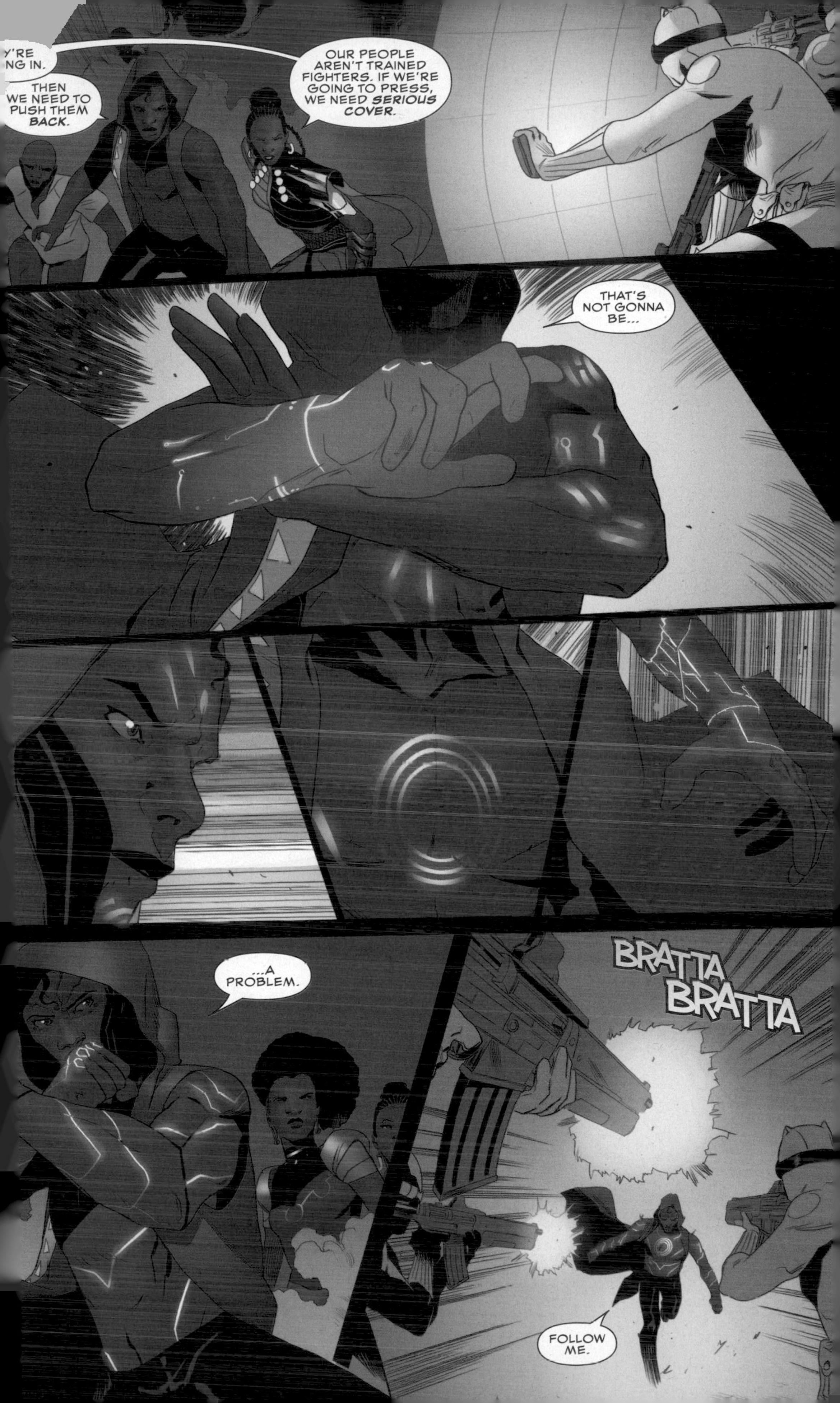
Y'RE
NG IN.
THEN WE NEED TO PUSH THEM BACK.
OUR PEOPLE AREN'T TRAINED FIGHTERS. IF WE'RE GOING TO PRESS, WE NEED SERIOUS COVER.
THAT'S NOT GONNA BE...
...A PROBLEM.
BRATTA BRATTA
FOLLOW ME.

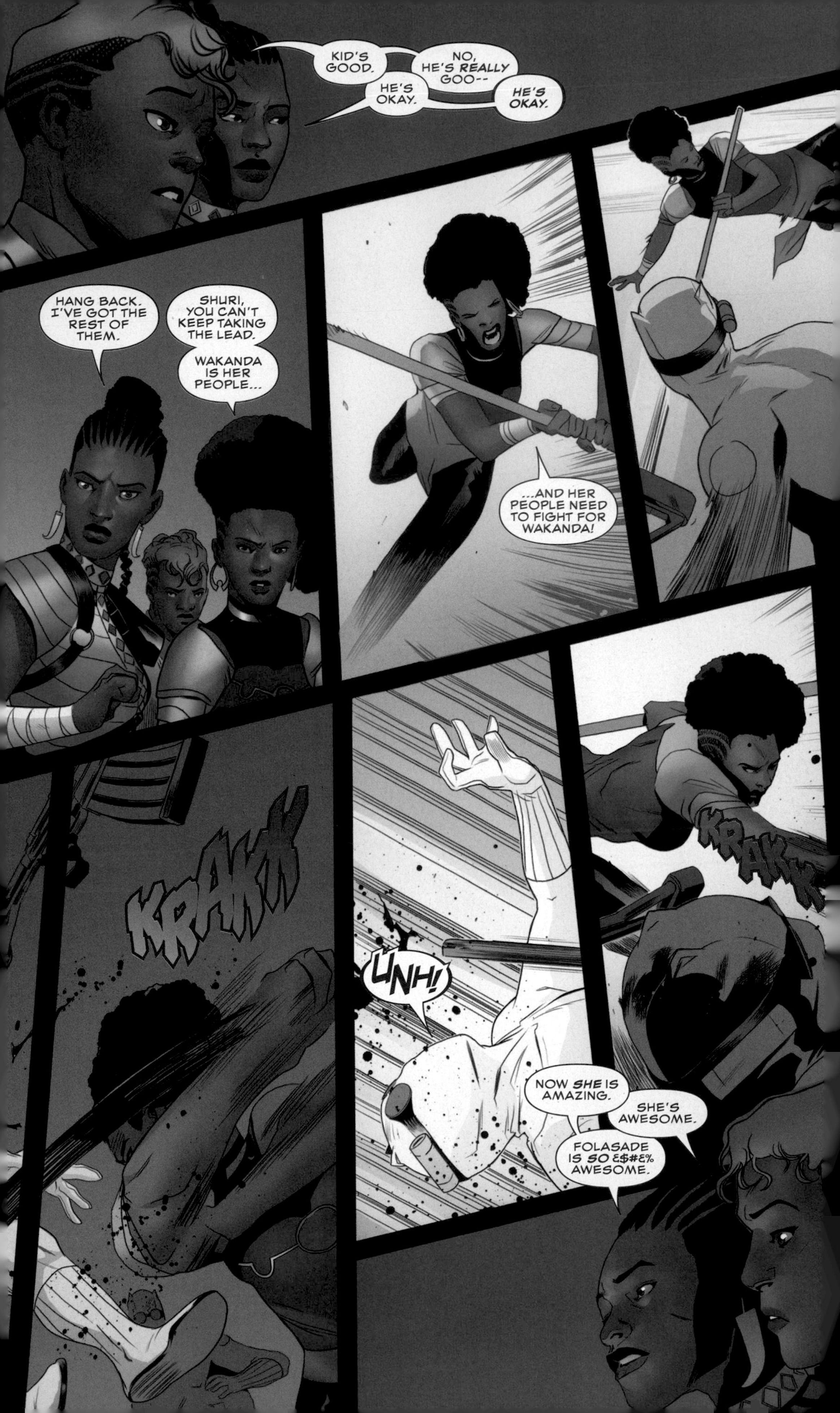
KID'S GOOD.
HE'S OKAY.
NO, HE'S REALLY GOO--
HE'S OKAY.
HANG BACK. I'VE GOT THE REST OF THEM.
SHURI, YOU CAN'T KEEP TAKING THE LEAD.
WAKANDA IS HER PEOPLE...
...AND HER PEOPLE NEED TO FIGHT FOR WAKANDA!
KRAKK
KRAKK
UNH!
NOW SHE IS AMAZING.
SHE'S AWESOME.
FOLASADE IS SO &$#&% AWESOME.

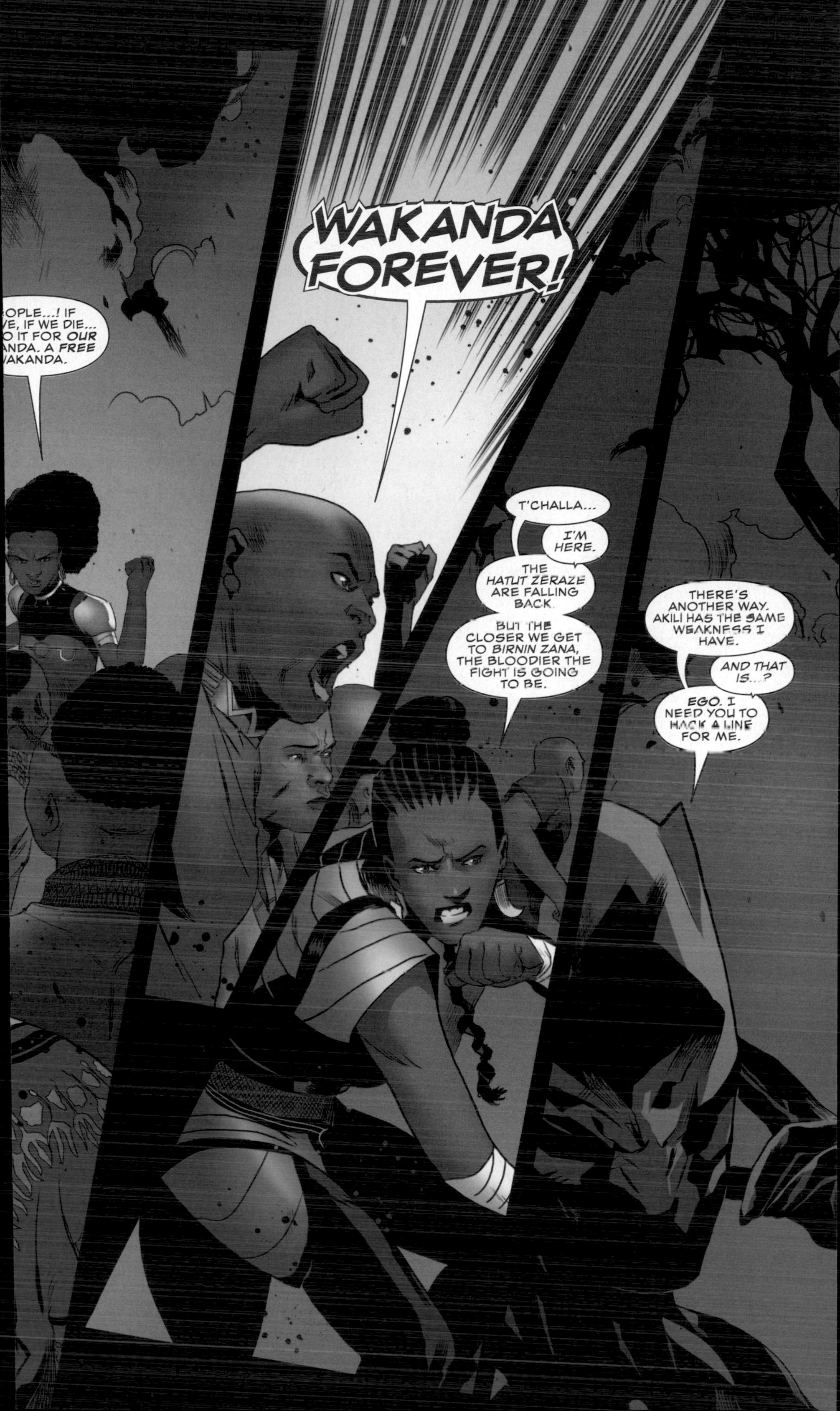

EOPLE...! IF VE, IF WE DIE... O IT FOR OUR ANDA. A FREE WAKANDA.
WAKANDA FOREVER!
T'CHALLA...
I'M HERE.
THE HATUT ZERAZE ARE FALLING BACK.
BUT THE CLOSER WE GET TO BIRNIN ZANA, THE BLOODIER THE FIGHT IS GOING TO BE.
THERE'S ANOTHER WAY. AKILI HAS THE SAME WEAKNESS I HAVE.
AND THAT IS...?
EGO. I NEED YOU TO HACK A LINE FOR ME.

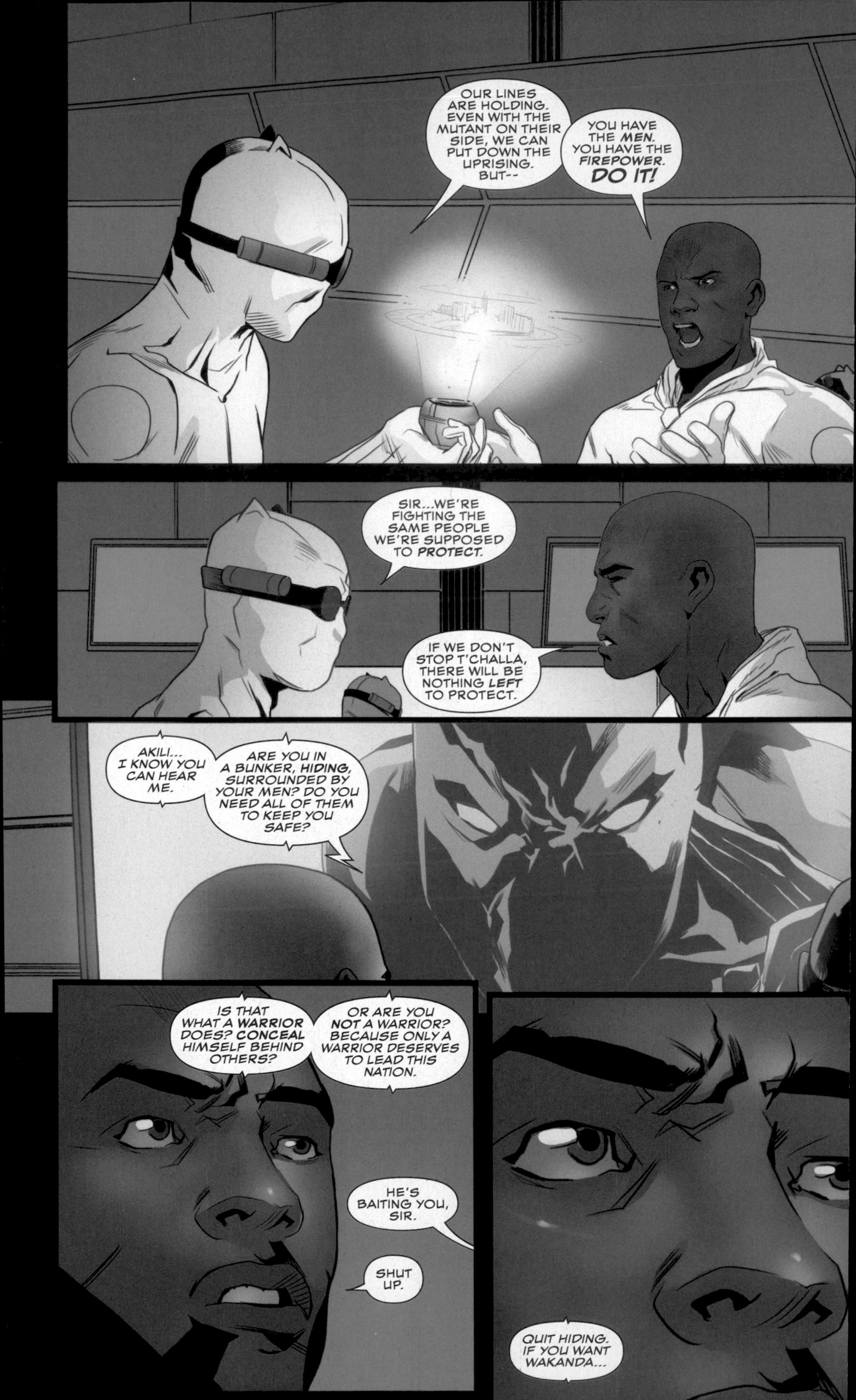

OUR LINES ARE HOLDING. EVEN WITH THE MUTANT ON THEIR SIDE, WE CAN PUT DOWN THE UPRISING. BUT--
YOU HAVE THE MEN. YOU HAVE THE FIREPOWER. DO IT!
SIR...WE'RE FIGHTING THE SAME PEOPLE WE'RE SUPPOSED TO PROTECT.
IF WE DON'T STOP T'CHALLA, THERE WILL BE NOTHING LEFT TO PROTECT.
AKILI... I KNOW YOU CAN HEAR ME.
ARE YOU IN A BUNKER, HIDING, SURROUNDED BY YOUR MEN? DO YOU NEED ALL OF THEM TO KEEP YOU SAFE?
IS THAT WHAT A WARRIOR DOES? CONCEAL HIMSELF BEHIND OTHERS?
OR ARE YOU NOT A WARRIOR? BECAUSE ONLY A WARRIOR DESERVES TO LEAD THIS NATION.
HE'S BAITING YOU, SIR.
SHUT UP.
QUIT HIDING. IF YOU WANT WAKANDA...

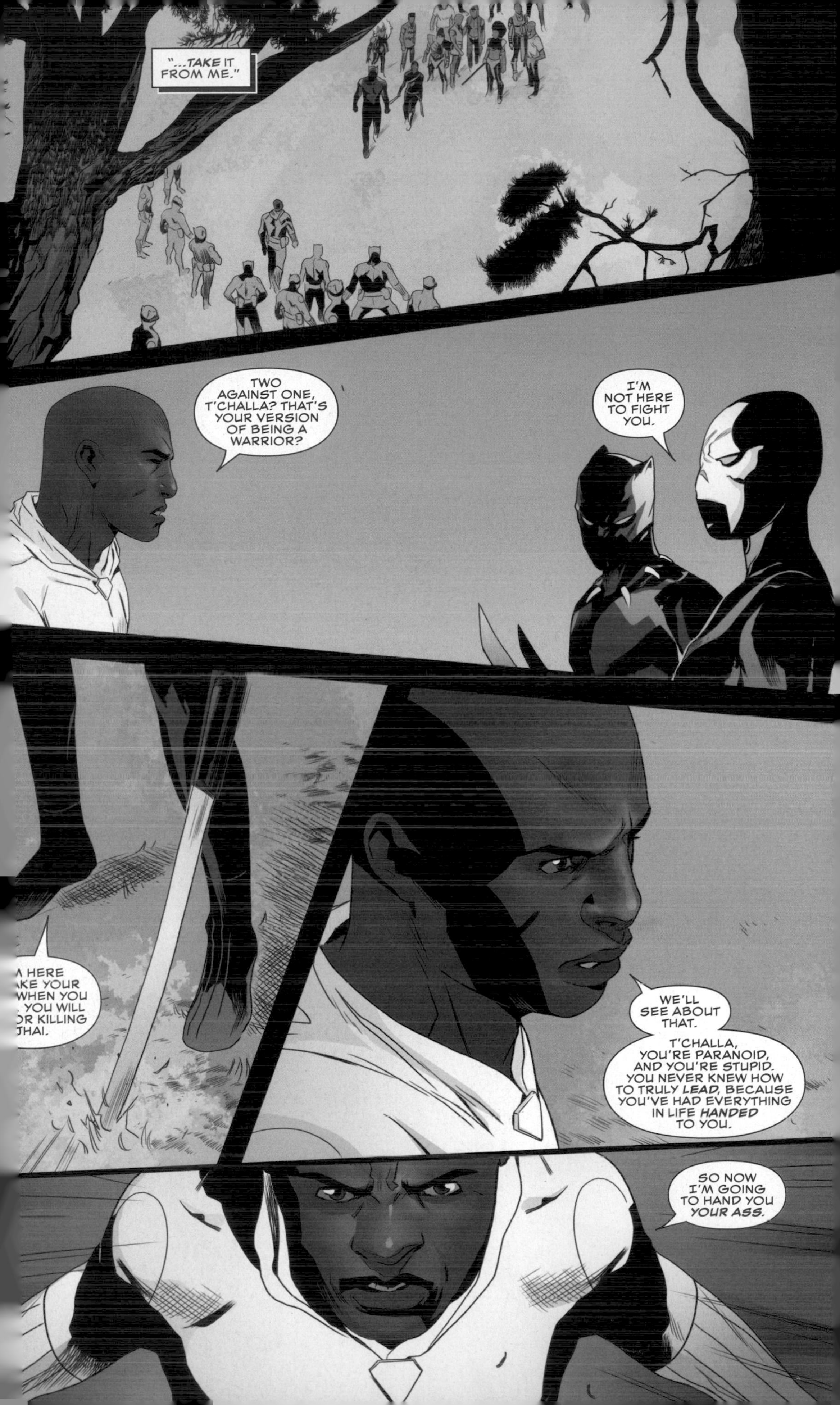

"...TAKE IT FROM ME."
TWO AGAINST ONE, T'CHALLA? THAT'S YOUR VERSION OF BEING A WARRIOR?
I'M NOT HERE TO FIGHT YOU.
M HERE AKE YOUR WHEN YOU YOU WILL OR KILLING THAI.
WE'LL SEE ABOUT THAT.
T'CHALLA, YOU'RE PARANOID, AND YOU'RE STUPID. YOU NEVER KNEW HOW TO TRULY LEAD, BECAUSE YOU'VE HAD EVERYTHING IN LIFE HANDED TO YOU.
SO NOW I'M GOING TO HAND YOU YOUR ASS.

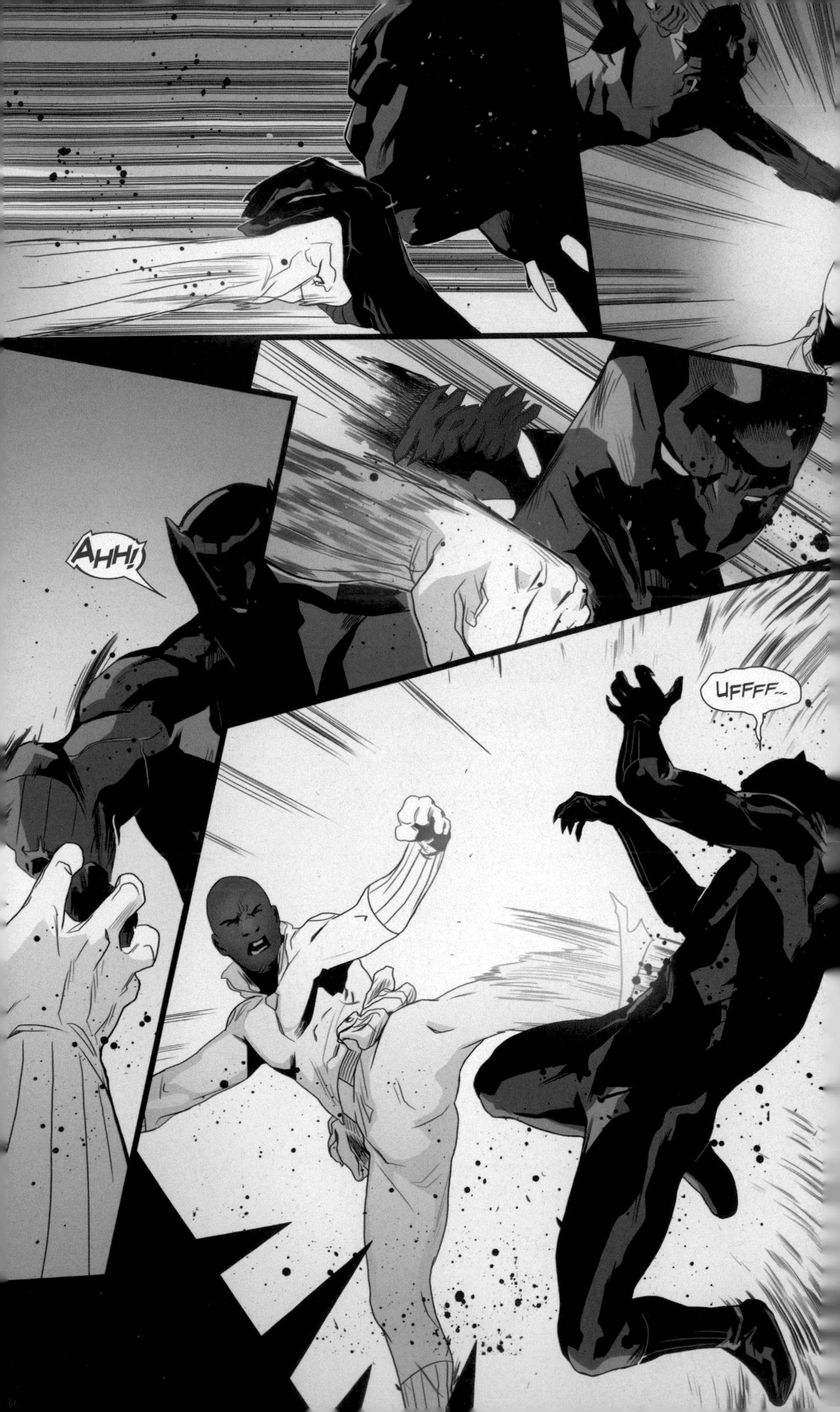
AHH!
UFFFF...

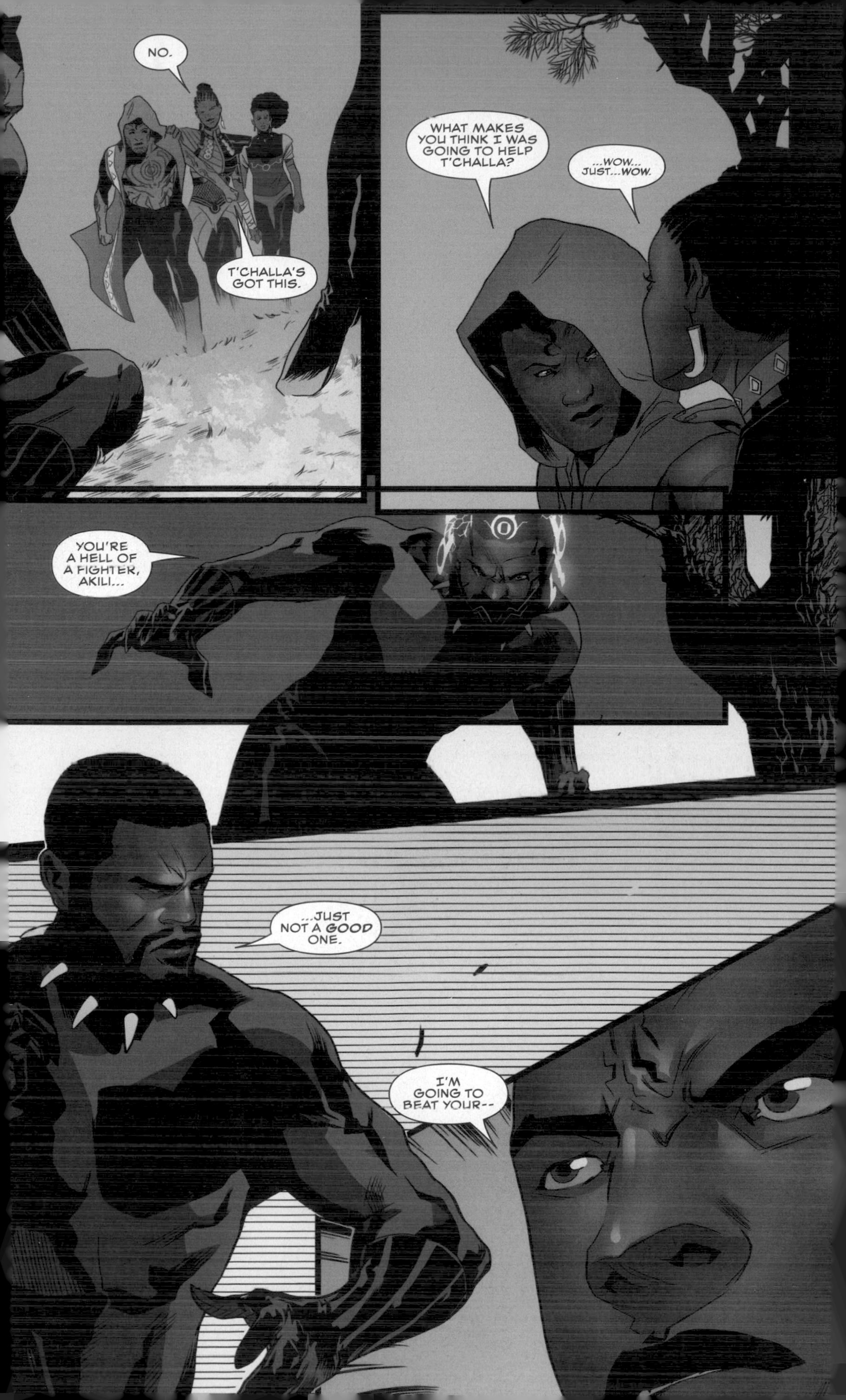
NO.
T'CHALLA'S GOT THIS.
WHAT MAKES YOU THINK I WAS GOING TO HELP T'CHALLA?
...WOW... JUST...WOW.
YOU'RE A HELL OF A FIGHTER, AKILI...
...JUST NOT A GOOD ONE.
I'M GOING TO BEAT YOUR--

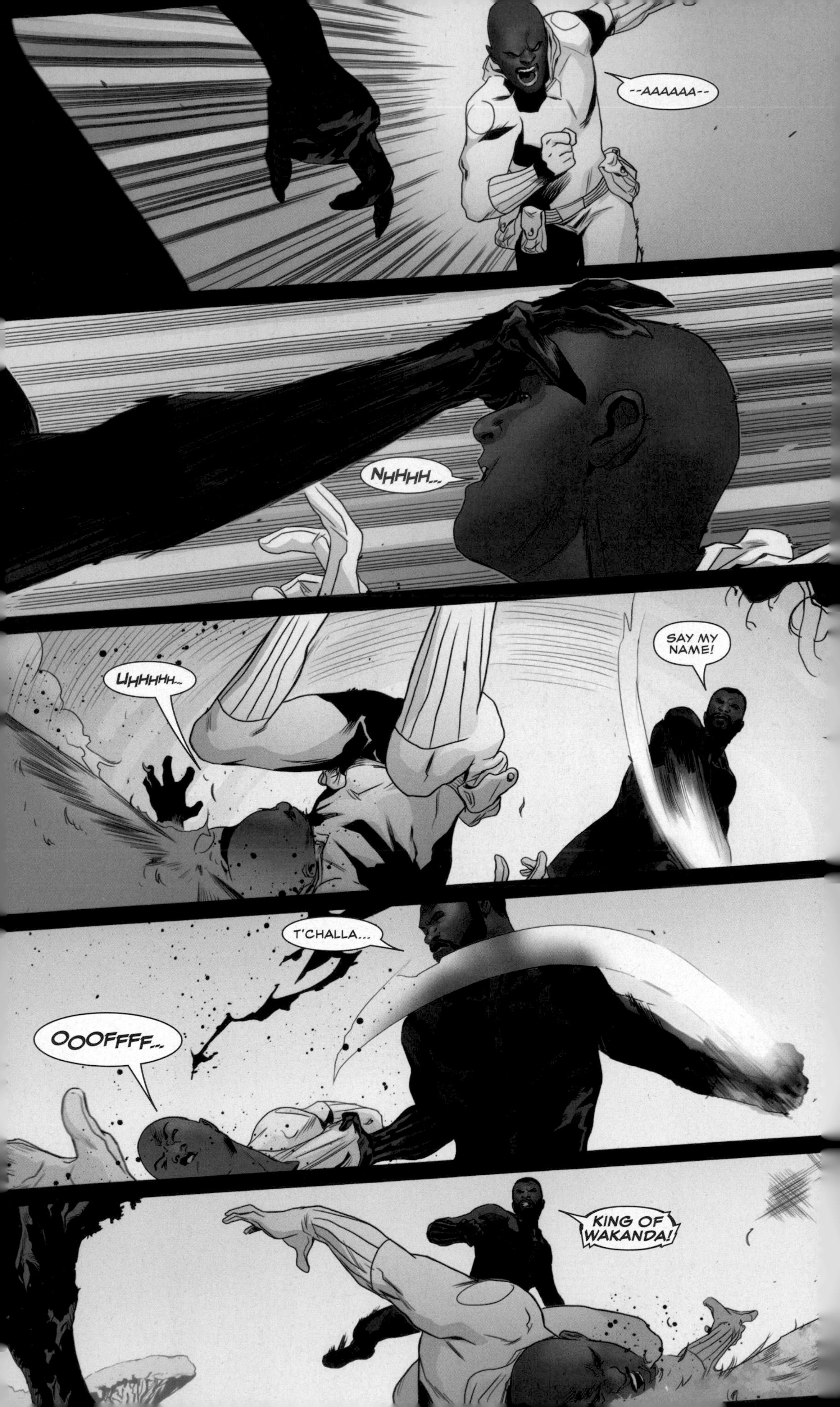
--AAAAAA--
NHHHH...
UHHHHH...
SAY MY NAME!
T'CHALLA...
OOOFFFF...
KING OF WAKANDA!

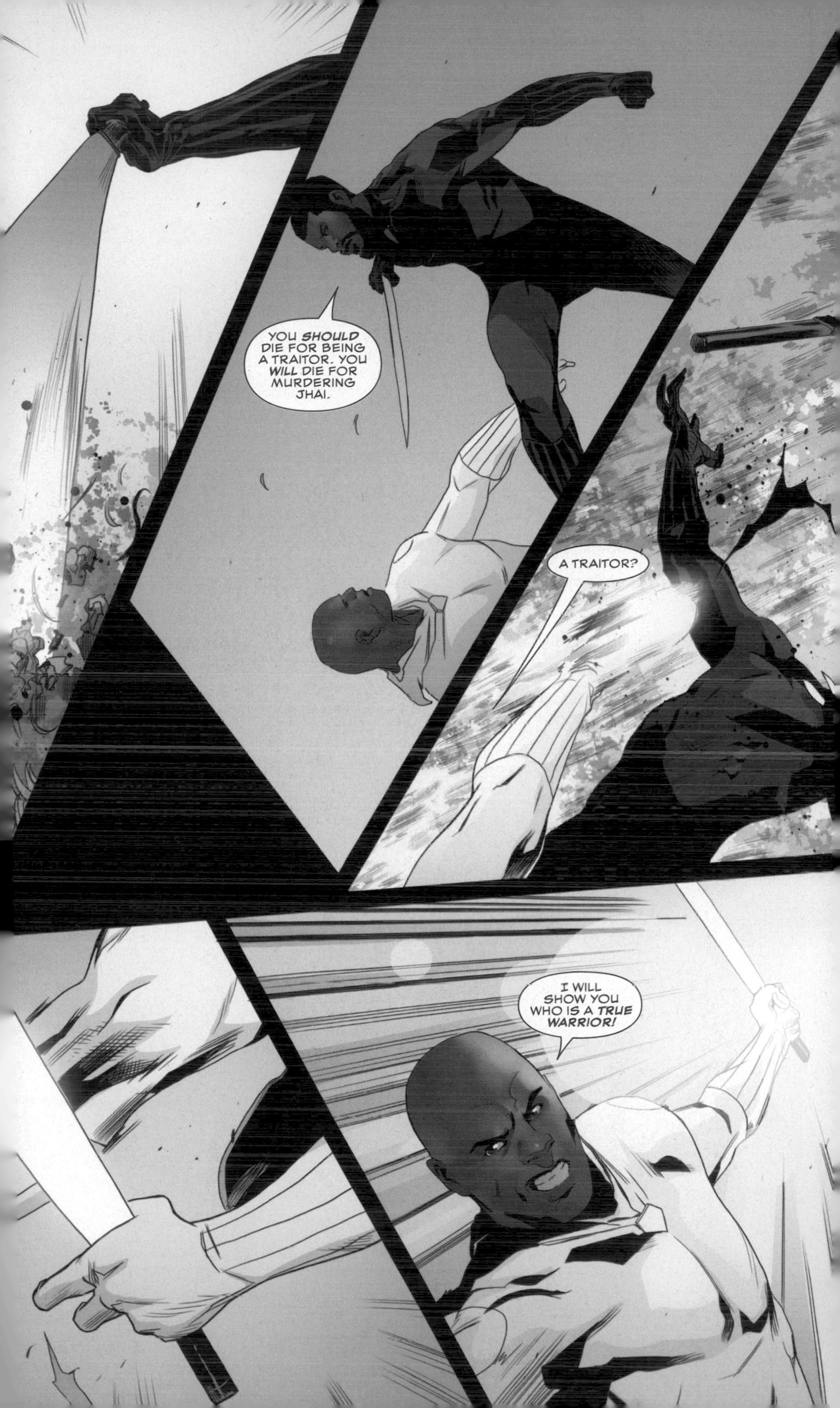
YOU SHOULD DIE FOR BEING A TRAITOR. YOU WILL DIE FOR MURDERING JHAI.
A TRAITOR?
I WILL SHOW YOU WHO IS A TRUE WARRIOR!

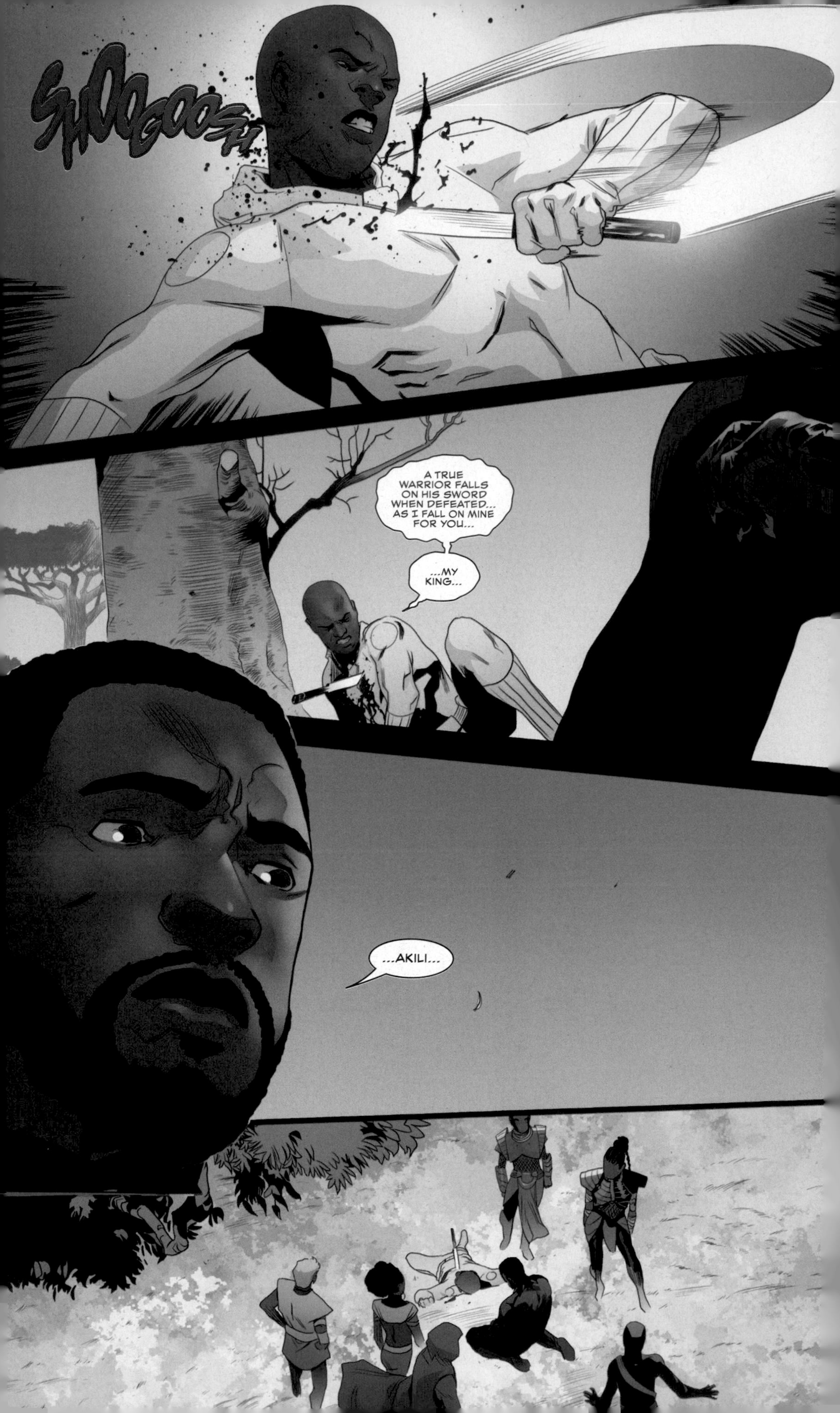
SHOOGOOSH
A TRUE WARRIOR FALLS ON HIS SWORD WHEN DEFEATED... AS I FALL ON MINE FOR YOU...
...MY KING...
...AKILI...

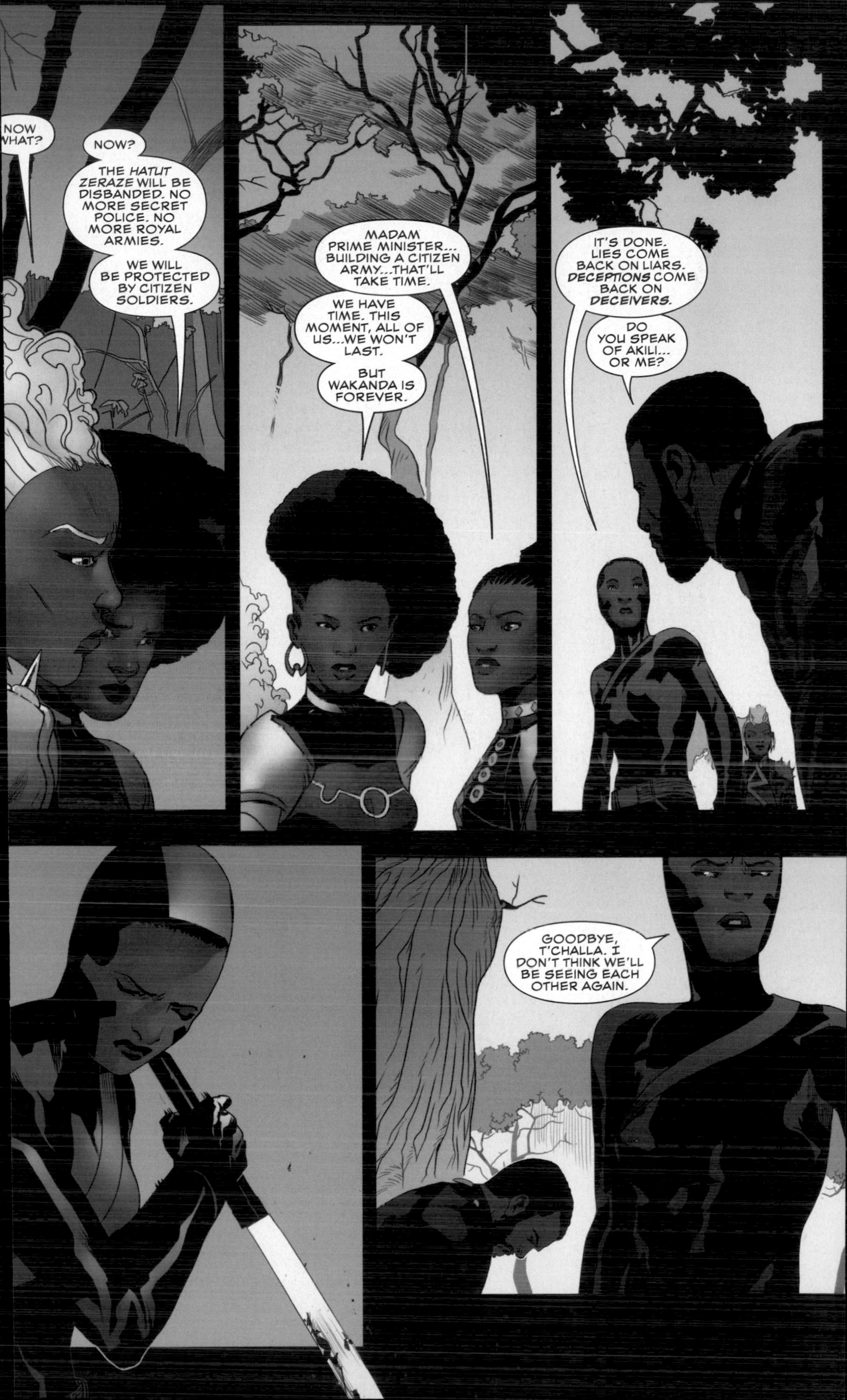
NOW WHAT?
NOW?
THE *HATUT ZERAZE* WILL BE DISBANDED. NO MORE SECRET POLICE. NO MORE ROYAL ARMIES.
WE WILL BE PROTECTED BY CITIZEN SOLDIERS.
MADAM PRIME MINISTER... BUILDING A CITIZEN ARMY...THAT'LL TAKE TIME.
WE HAVE TIME. THIS MOMENT, ALL OF US...WE WON'T LAST.
BUT WAKANDA IS FOREVER.
IT'S DONE. LIES COME BACK ON LIARS. *DECEPTIONS* COME BACK ON *DECEIVERS.*
DO YOU SPEAK OF AKILI... OR ME?
GOODBYE, T'CHALLA. I DON'T THINK WE'LL BE SEEING EACH OTHER AGAIN.

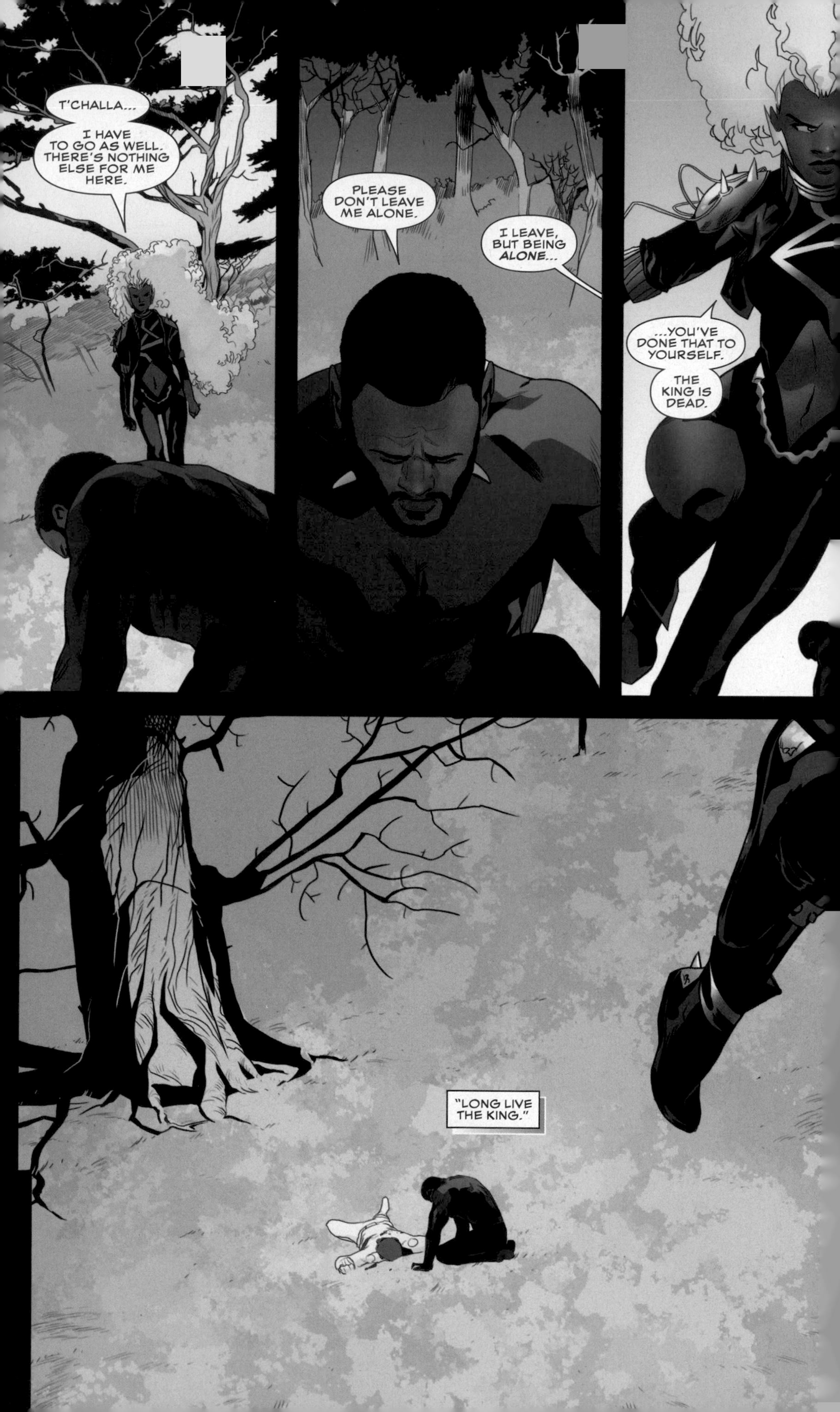
T'CHALLA...
I HAVE TO GO AS WELL. THERE'S NOTHING ELSE FOR ME HERE.
PLEASE DON'T LEAVE ME ALONE.
I LEAVE, BUT BEING ALONE...
...YOU'VE DONE THAT TO YOURSELF.
THE KING IS DEAD.
"LONG LIVE THE KING."

5 Skrull Variant |||||||||||||||||||||||||||
|||| **KHARY RANDOLPH** & **EMILIO LOPEZ**

#6 Variant |||||||||||||||||||||||||||||||||||
||**MARTIN COCCOLO** & **MATTHEW WILSON**

Stormbreakers Variant ||||||||||||||||||||||||||||||||||||||||||||||**R.B. SILVA** & **DAVID CURIEL**

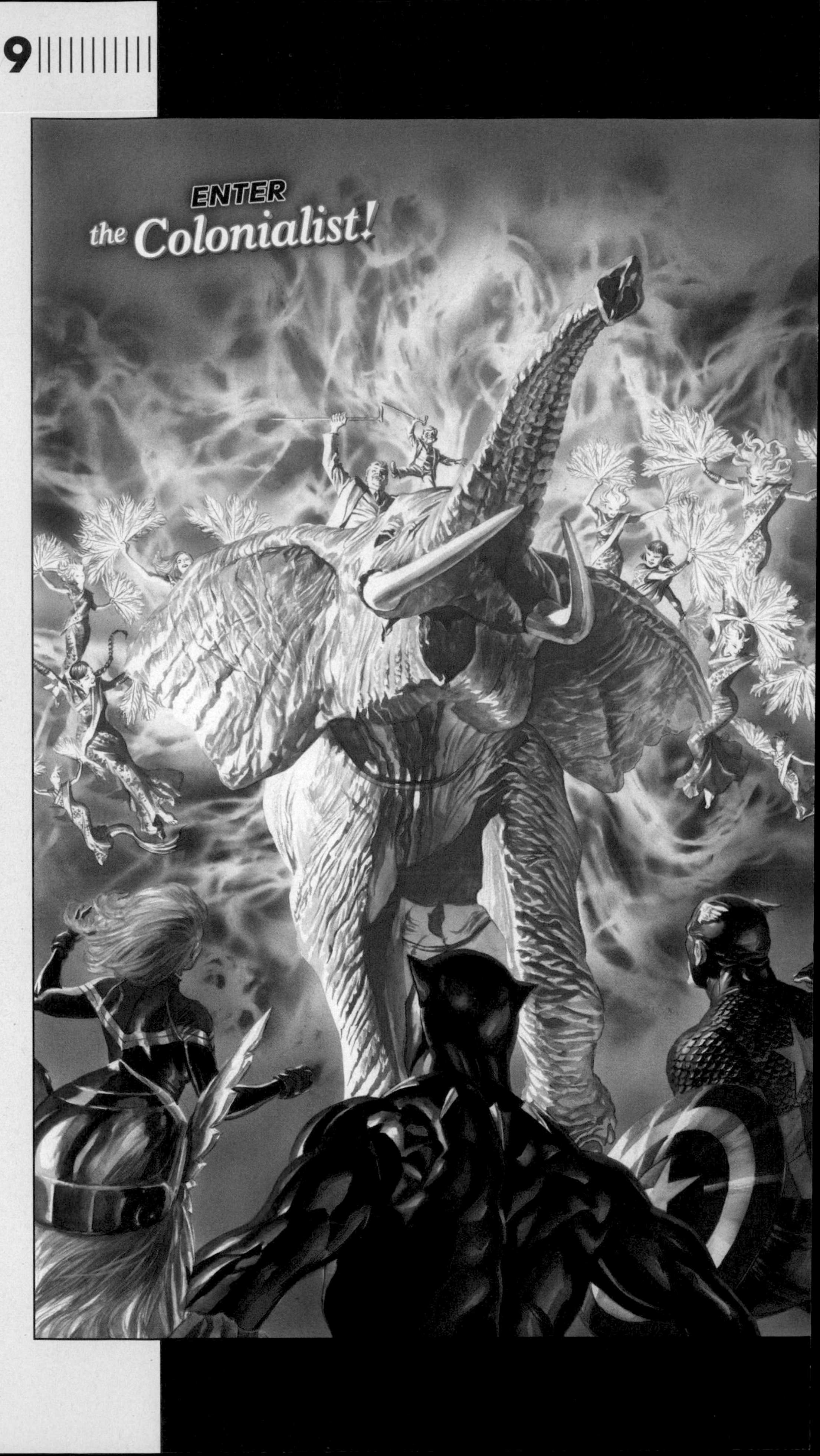
ENTER
the Colonialist!

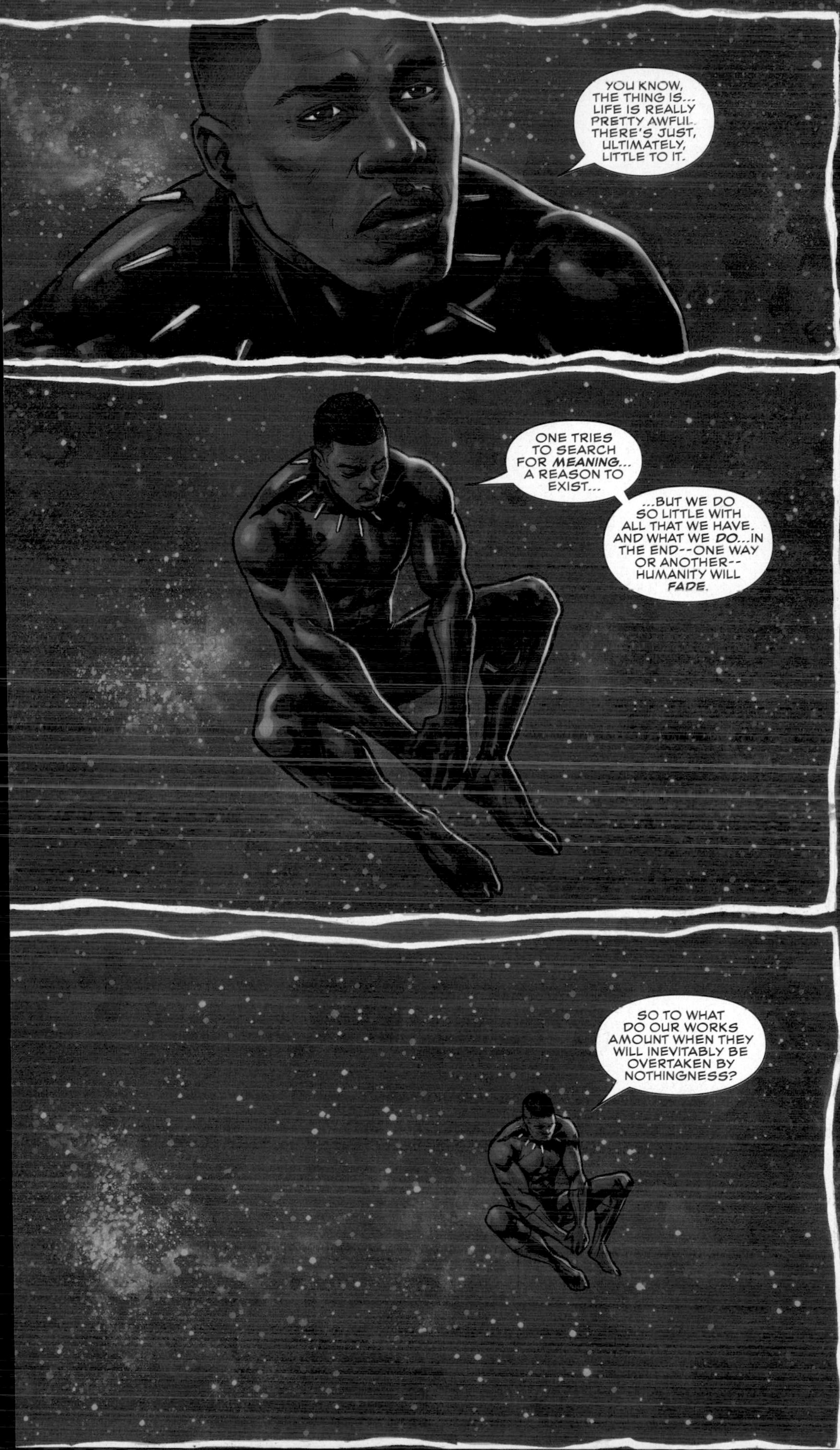
YOU KNOW, THE THING IS... LIFE IS REALLY PRETTY AWFUL. THERE'S JUST, ULTIMATELY, LITTLE TO IT.
ONE TRIES TO SEARCH FOR *MEANING*... A REASON TO EXIST...
...BUT WE DO SO LITTLE WITH ALL THAT WE HAVE. AND WHAT WE *DO*...IN THE END--ONE WAY OR ANOTHER--HUMANITY WILL *FADE*.
SO TO WHAT DO OUR WORKS AMOUNT WHEN THEY WILL INEVITABLY BE OVERTAKEN BY NOTHINGNESS?

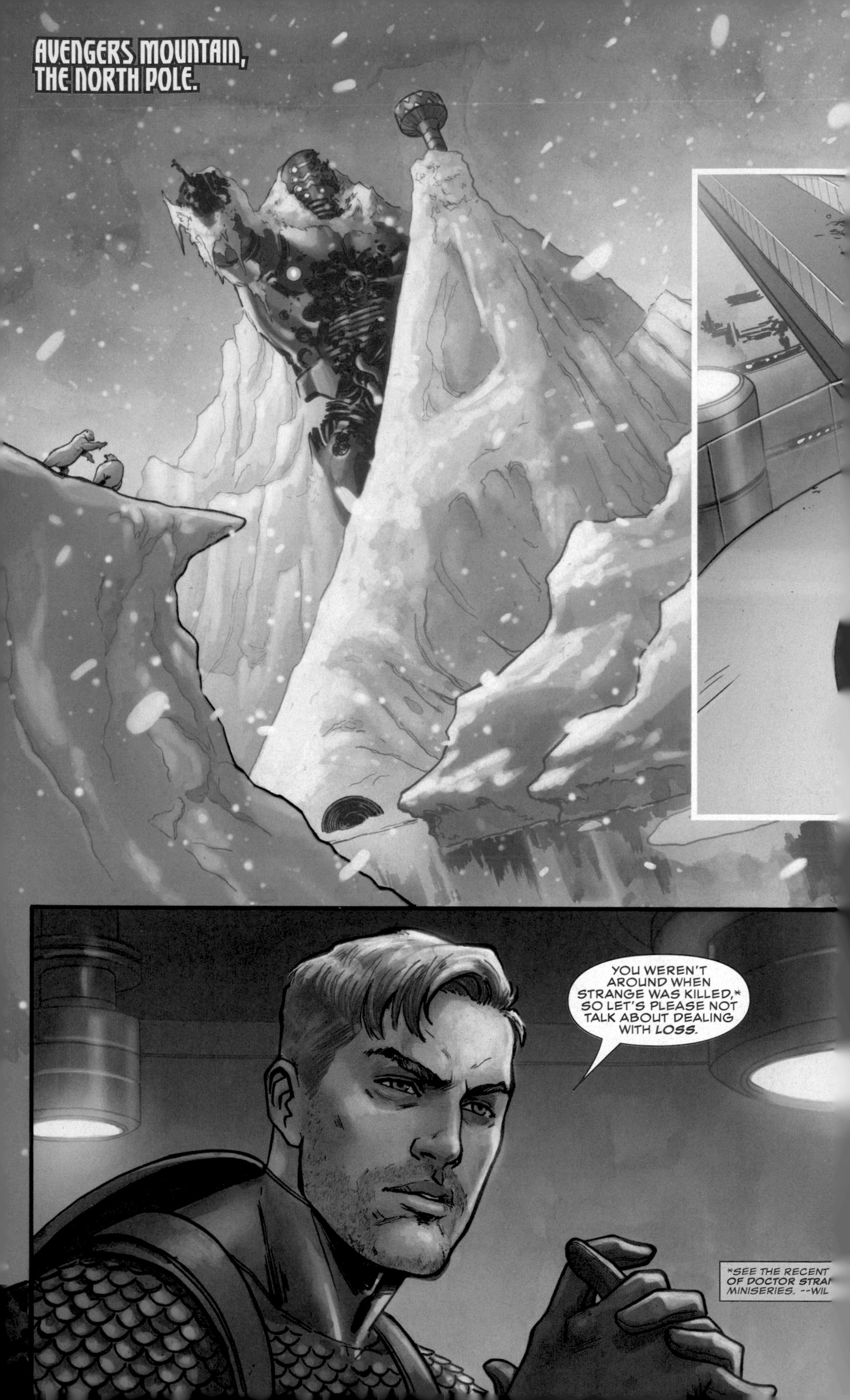
AVENGERS MOUNTAIN, THE NORTH POLE.
YOU WEREN'T AROUND WHEN STRANGE WAS KILLED,* SO LET'S PLEASE NOT TALK ABOUT DEALING WITH LOSS.
*SEE THE RECENT
OF DOCTOR STRA
MINISERIES. --WIL

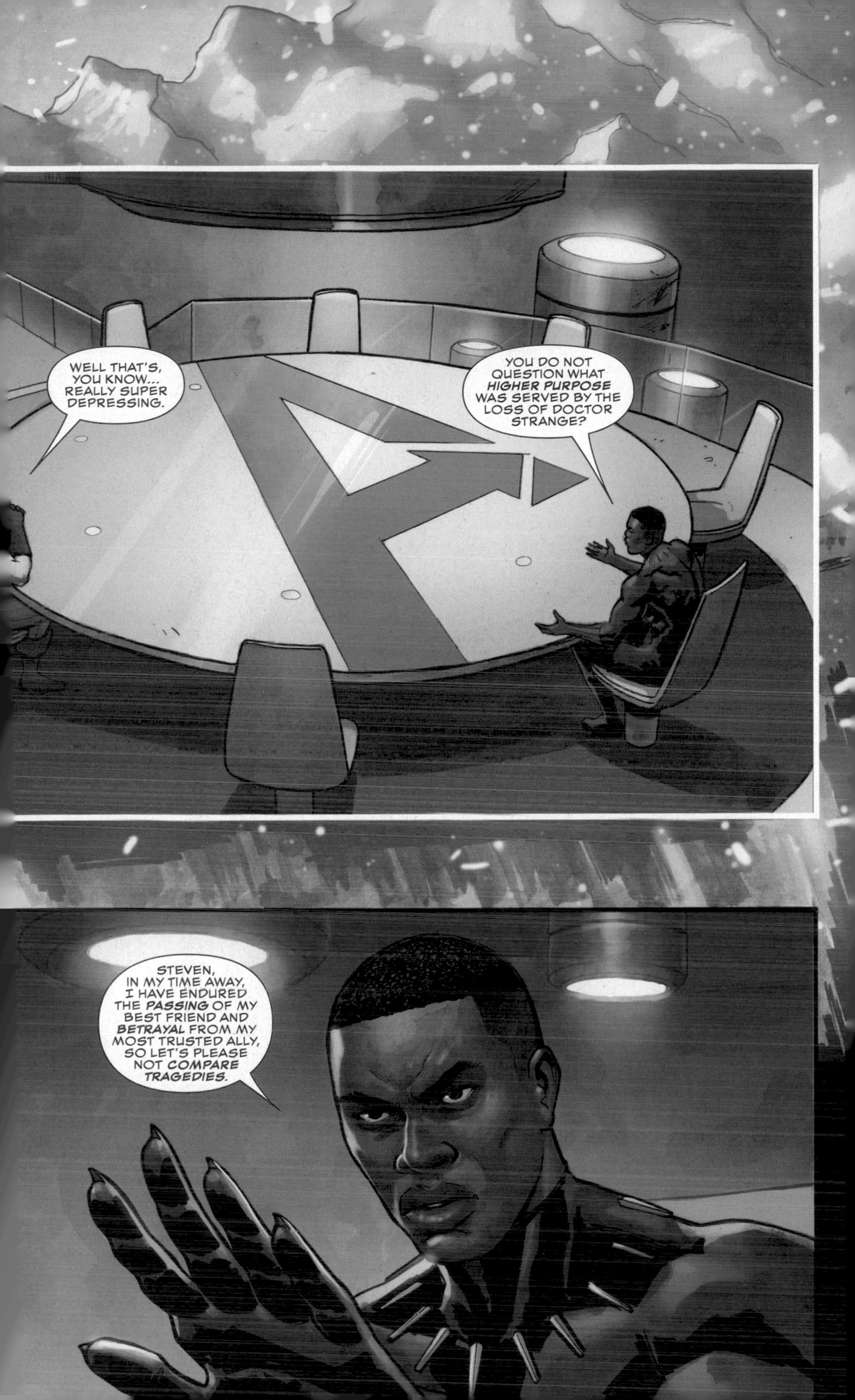
WELL THAT'S, YOU KNOW... REALLY SUPER DEPRESSING.
YOU DO NOT QUESTION WHAT HIGHER PURPOSE WAS SERVED BY THE LOSS OF DOCTOR STRANGE?
STEVEN, IN MY TIME AWAY, I HAVE ENDURED THE PASSING OF MY BEST FRIEND AND BETRAYAL FROM MY MOST TRUSTED ALLY, SO LET'S PLEASE NOT COMPARE TRAGEDIES.

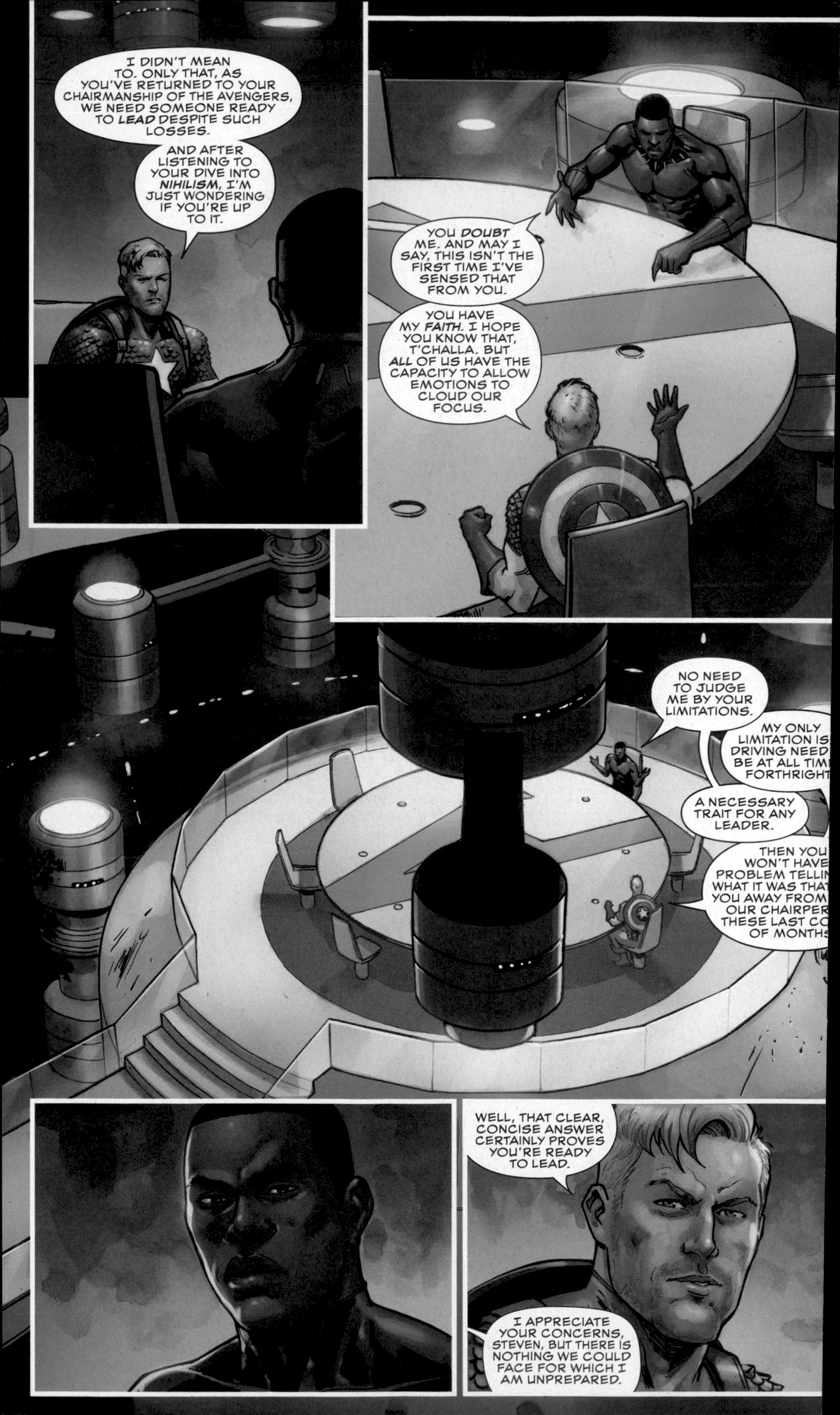
I DIDN'T MEAN TO. ONLY THAT, AS YOU'VE RETURNED TO YOUR CHAIRMANSHIP OF THE AVENGERS, WE NEED SOMEONE READY TO LEAD DESPITE SUCH LOSSES.
AND AFTER LISTENING TO YOUR DIVE INTO NIHILISM, I'M JUST WONDERING IF YOU'RE UP TO IT.
YOU DOUBT ME. AND MAY I SAY, THIS ISN'T THE FIRST TIME I'VE SENSED THAT FROM YOU.
YOU HAVE MY FAITH. I HOPE YOU KNOW THAT, T'CHALLA. BUT ALL OF US HAVE THE CAPACITY TO ALLOW EMOTIONS TO CLOUD OUR FOCUS.
NO NEED TO JUDGE ME BY YOUR LIMITATIONS.
MY ONLY LIMITATION IS DRIVING NEED BE AT ALL TIM FORTHRIGH
A NECESSARY TRAIT FOR ANY LEADER.
THEN YOU WON'T HAVE PROBLEM TELLI WHAT IT WAS THA YOU AWAY FROM OUR CHAIRPE THESE LAST C OF MONTHS
WELL, THAT CLEAR, CONCISE ANSWER CERTAINLY PROVES YOU'RE READY TO LEAD.
I APPRECIATE YOUR CONCERNS, STEVEN, BUT THERE IS NOTHING WE COULD FACE FOR WHICH I AM UNPREPARED.

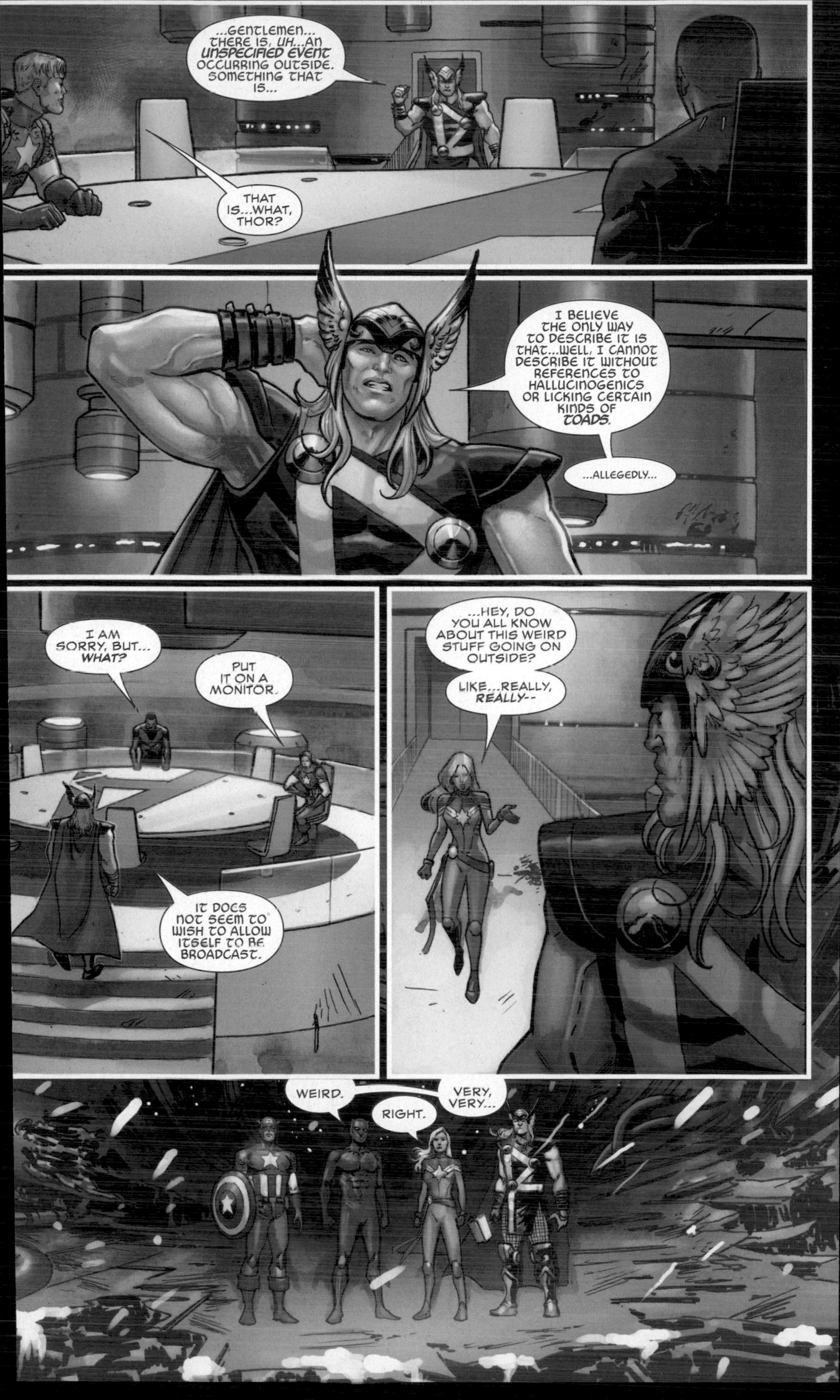
...GENTLEMEN... THERE IS, UH...AN UNSPECIFIED EVENT OCCURRING OUTSIDE. SOMETHING THAT IS...
THAT IS...WHAT, THOR?
I BELIEVE THE ONLY WAY TO DESCRIBE IT IS THAT...WELL, I CANNOT DESCRIBE IT WITHOUT REFERENCES TO HALLUCINOGENICS OR LICKING CERTAIN KINDS OF TOADS.
...ALLEGEDLY...
I AM SORRY, BUT... WHAT?
PUT IT ON A MONITOR.
IT DOES NOT SEEM TO WISH TO ALLOW ITSELF TO BE BROADCAST.
...HEY, DO YOU ALL KNOW ABOUT THIS WEIRD STUFF GOING ON OUTSIDE?
LIKE...REALLY, REALLY--
VERY, VERY...
WEIRD.
RIGHT.

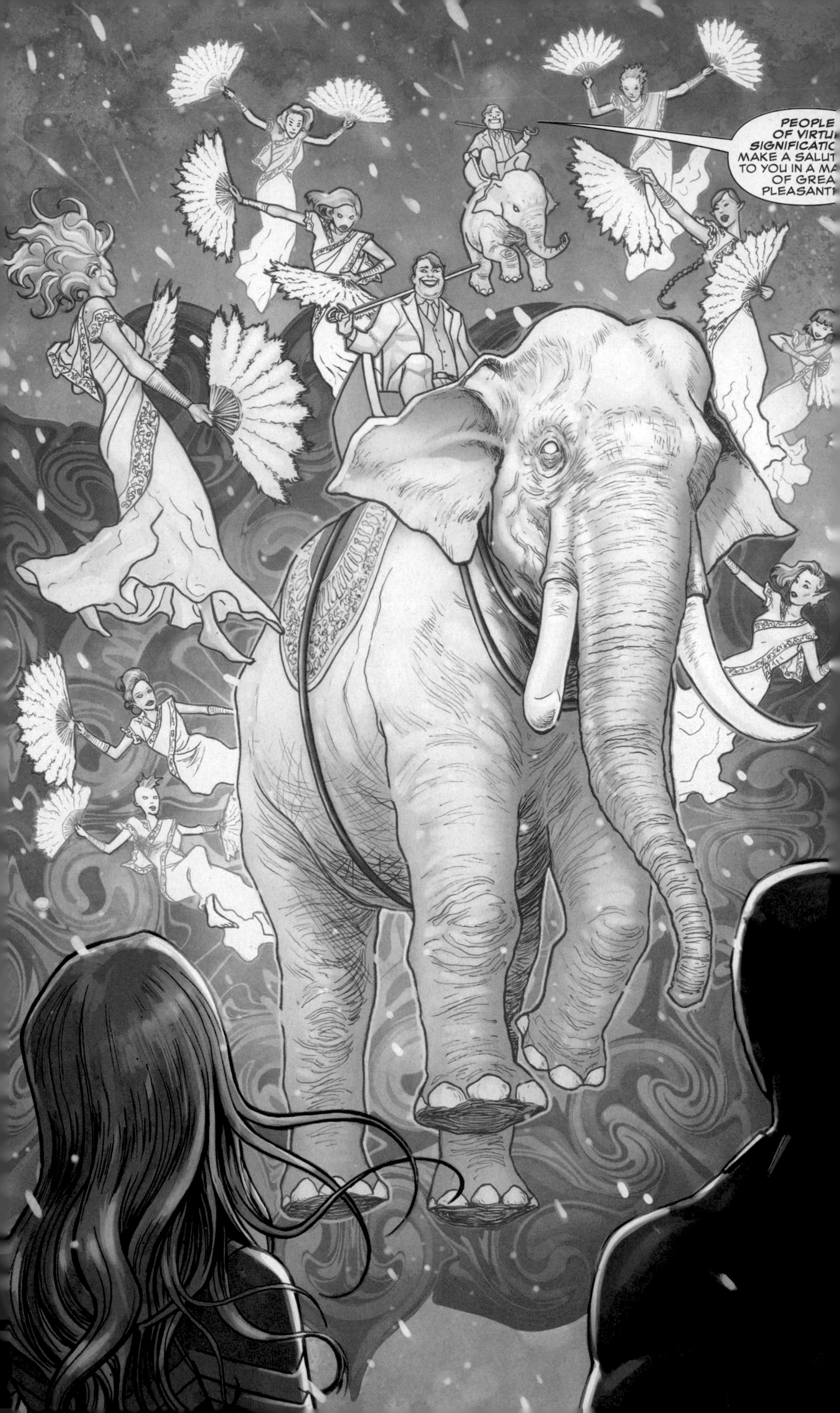
PEOPLE OF VIRTU SIGNIFICATI MAKE A SALUT TO YOU IN A MA OF GREA PLEASANT

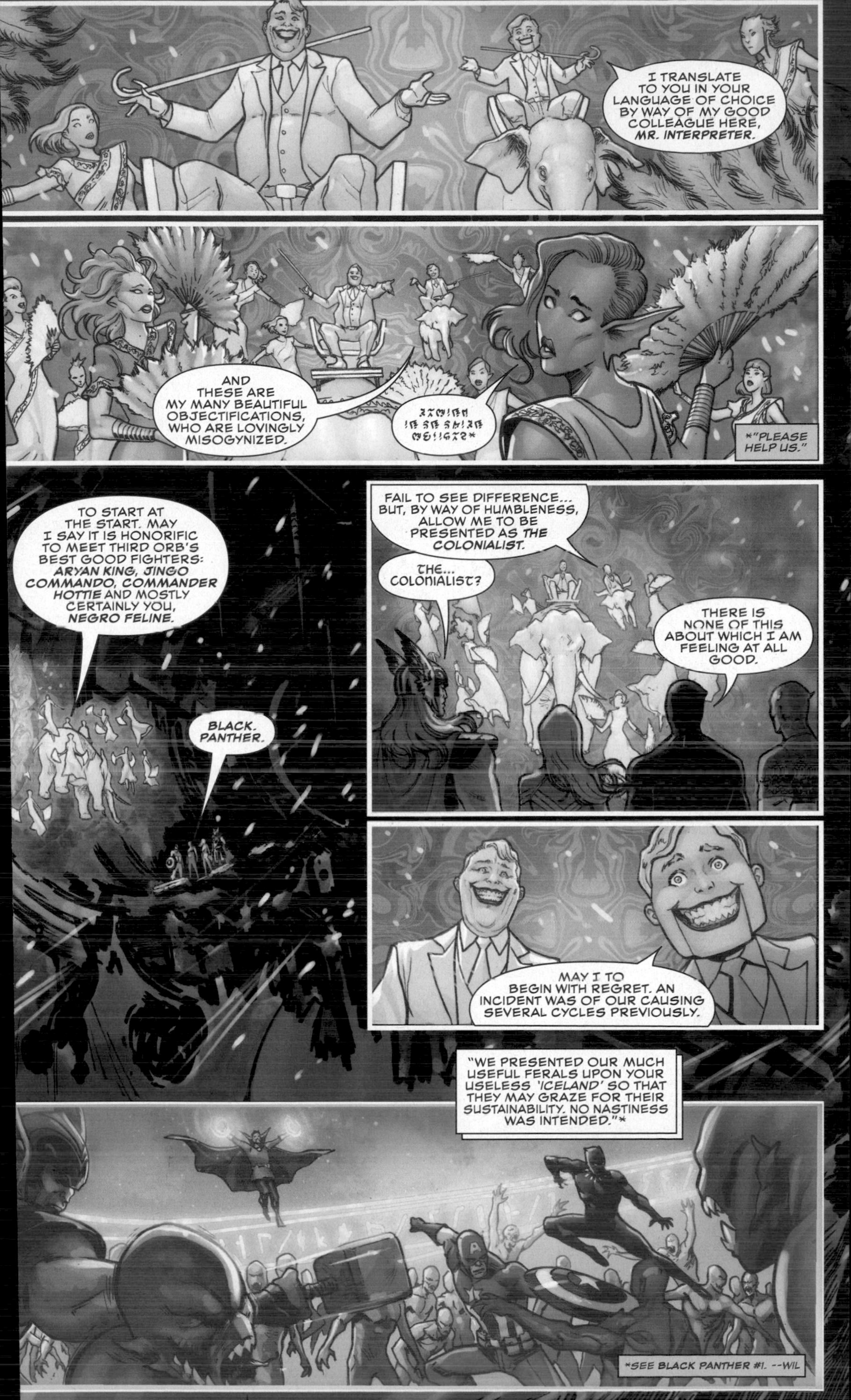
I TRANSLATE TO YOU IN YOUR LANGUAGE OF CHOICE BY WAY OF MY GOOD COLLEAGUE HERE, *MR. INTERPRETER.*
AND THESE ARE MY MANY BEAUTIFUL OBJECTIFICATIONS, WHO ARE LOVINGLY MISOGYNIZED.
*"PLEASE HELP US."
TO START AT THE START. MAY I SAY IT IS HONORIFIC TO MEET THIRD ORB'S BEST GOOD FIGHTERS: *ARYAN KING, JINGO COMMANDO, COMMANDER HOTTIE* AND MOSTLY CERTAINLY YOU, *NEGRO FELINE.*
BLACK. PANTHER.
FAIL TO SEE DIFFERENCE... BUT, BY WAY OF HUMBLENESS, ALLOW ME TO BE PRESENTED AS *THE COLONIALIST.*
THE... COLONIALIST?
THERE IS NONE OF THIS ABOUT WHICH I AM FEELING AT ALL GOOD.
MAY I TO BEGIN WITH REGRET. AN INCIDENT WAS OF OUR CAUSING SEVERAL CYCLES PREVIOUSLY.
"WE PRESENTED OUR MUCH USEFUL FERALS UPON YOUR USELESS *'ICELAND'* SO THAT THEY MAY GRAZE FOR THEIR SUSTAINABILITY. NO NASTINESS WAS INTENDED."*
*SEE *BLACK PANTHER* #1. --WIL

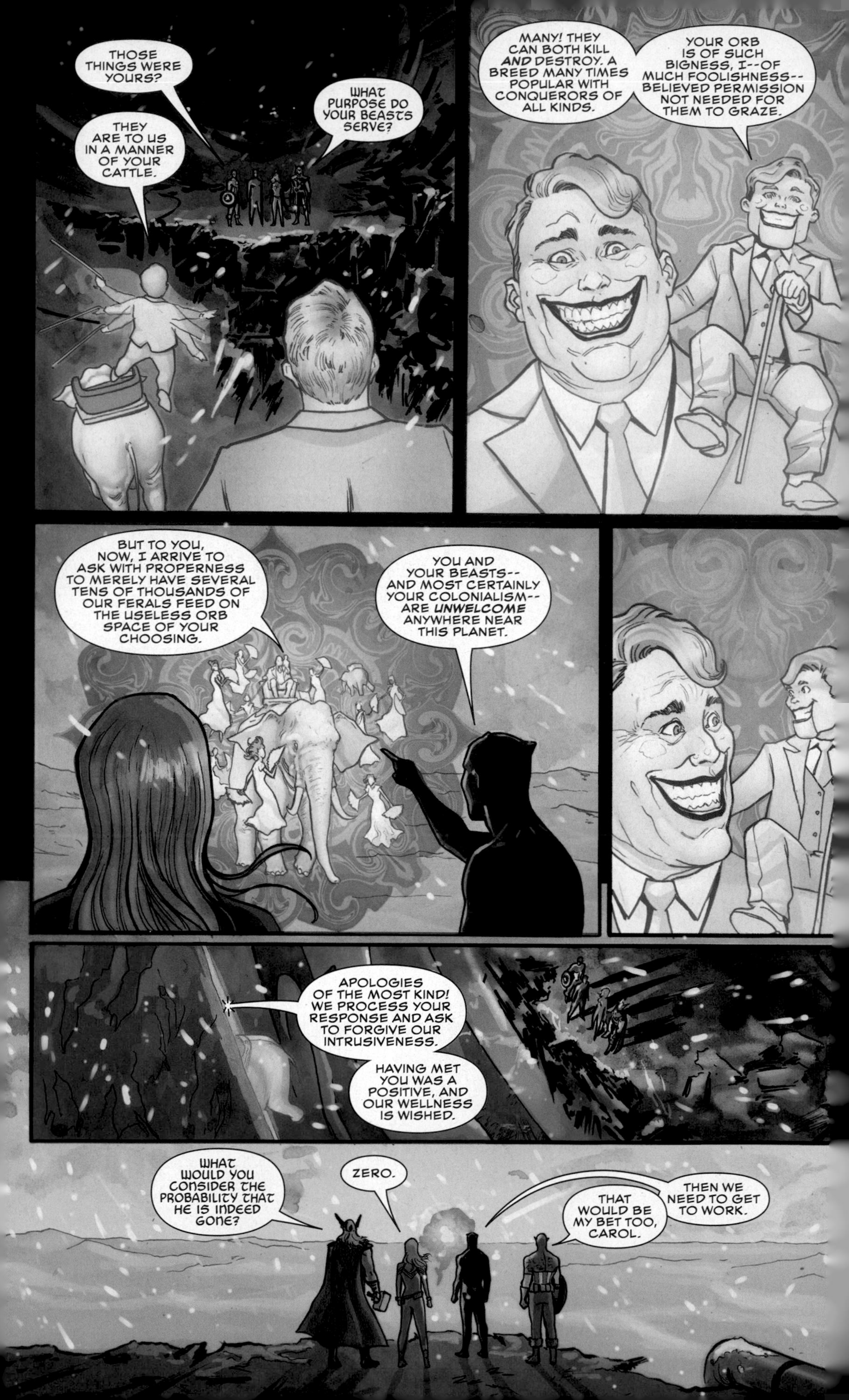
THOSE THINGS WERE YOURS?
THEY ARE TO US IN A MANNER OF YOUR CATTLE.
WHAT PURPOSE DO YOUR BEASTS SERVE?
MANY! THEY CAN BOTH KILL AND DESTROY. A BREED MANY TIMES POPULAR WITH CONQUERORS OF ALL KINDS.
YOUR ORB IS OF SUCH BIGNESS, I--OF MUCH FOOLISHNESS--BELIEVED PERMISSION NOT NEEDED FOR THEM TO GRAZE.
BUT TO YOU, NOW, I ARRIVE TO ASK WITH PROPERNESS TO MERELY HAVE SEVERAL TENS OF THOUSANDS OF OUR FERALS FEED ON THE USELESS ORB SPACE OF YOUR CHOOSING.
YOU AND YOUR BEASTS--AND MOST CERTAINLY YOUR COLONIALISM--ARE UNWELCOME ANYWHERE NEAR THIS PLANET.
APOLOGIES OF THE MOST KIND! WE PROCESS YOUR RESPONSE AND ASK TO FORGIVE OUR INTRUSIVENESS.
HAVING MET YOU WAS A POSITIVE, AND OUR WELLNESS IS WISHED.
WHAT WOULD YOU CONSIDER THE PROBABILITY THAT HE IS INDEED GONE?
ZERO.
THAT WOULD BE MY BET TOO, CAROL.
THEN WE NEED TO GET TO WORK.

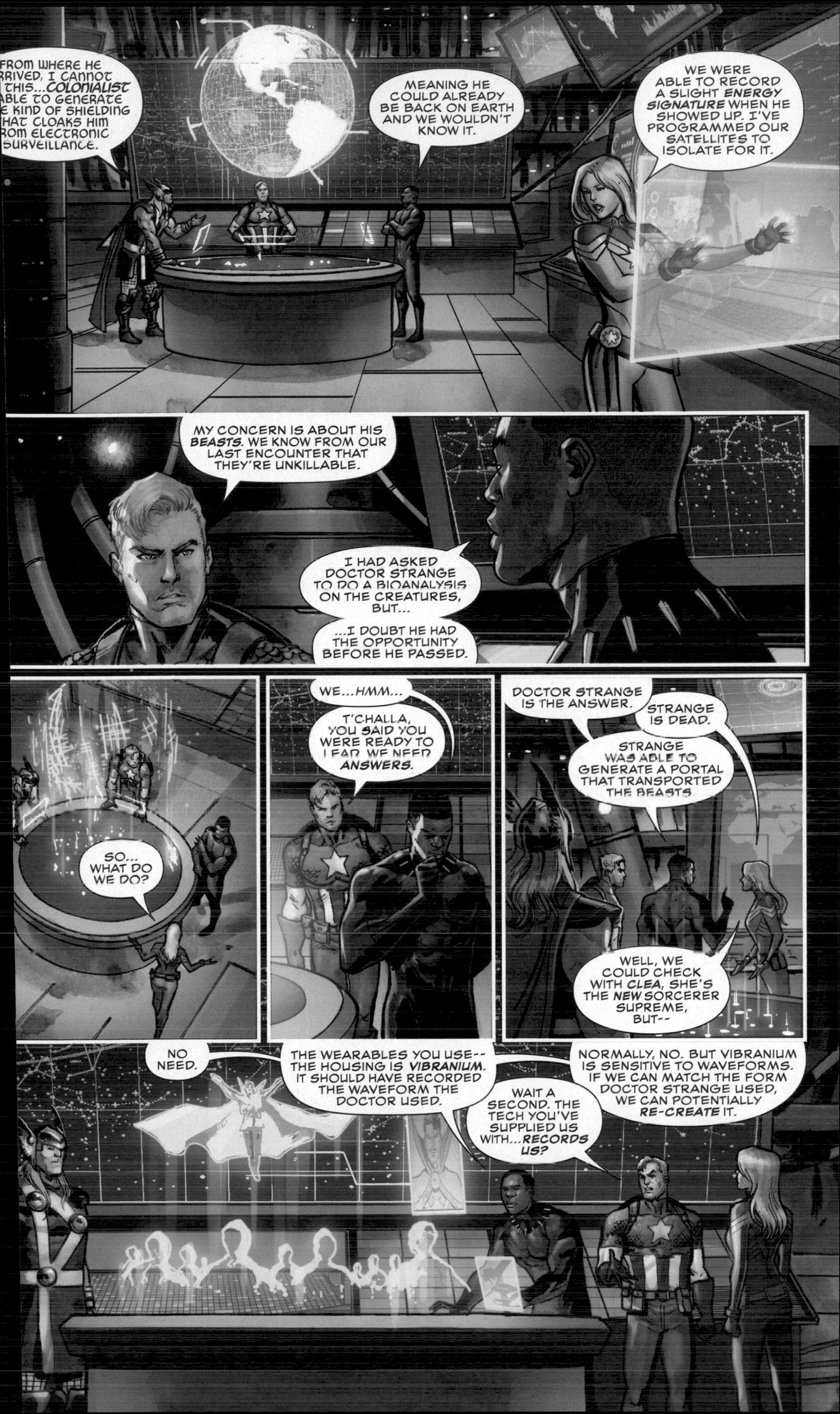
FROM WHERE HE ARRIVED, I CANNOT ... THIS...COLONIALIST ... ABLE TO GENERATE ... KIND OF SHIELDING THAT CLOAKS HIM FROM ELECTRONIC SURVEILLANCE.
MEANING HE COULD ALREADY BE BACK ON EARTH AND WE WOULDN'T KNOW IT.
WE WERE ABLE TO RECORD A SLIGHT ENERGY SIGNATURE WHEN HE SHOWED UP. I'VE PROGRAMMED OUR SATELLITES TO ISOLATE FOR IT.
MY CONCERN IS ABOUT HIS BEASTS. WE KNOW FROM OUR LAST ENCOUNTER THAT THEY'RE UNKILLABLE.
I HAD ASKED DOCTOR STRANGE TO DO A BIOANALYSIS ON THE CREATURES, BUT...
...I DOUBT HE HAD THE OPPORTUNITY BEFORE HE PASSED.
SO... WHAT DO WE DO?
WE...HMM...
T'CHALLA, YOU SAID YOU WERE READY TO LEAD. WE NEED ANSWERS.
DOCTOR STRANGE IS THE ANSWER.
STRANGE IS DEAD.
STRANGE WAS ABLE TO GENERATE A PORTAL THAT TRANSPORTED THE BEASTS.
WELL, WE COULD CHECK WITH CLEA, SHE'S THE NEW SORCERER SUPREME, BUT--
NO NEED.
THE WEARABLES YOU USE-- THE HOUSING IS VIBRANIUM. IT SHOULD HAVE RECORDED THE WAVEFORM THE DOCTOR USED.
WAIT A SECOND. THE TECH YOU'VE SUPPLIED US WITH...RECORDS US?
NORMALLY, NO. BUT VIBRANIUM IS SENSITIVE TO WAVEFORMS. IF WE CAN MATCH THE FORM DOCTOR STRANGE USED, WE CAN POTENTIALLY RE-CREATE IT.

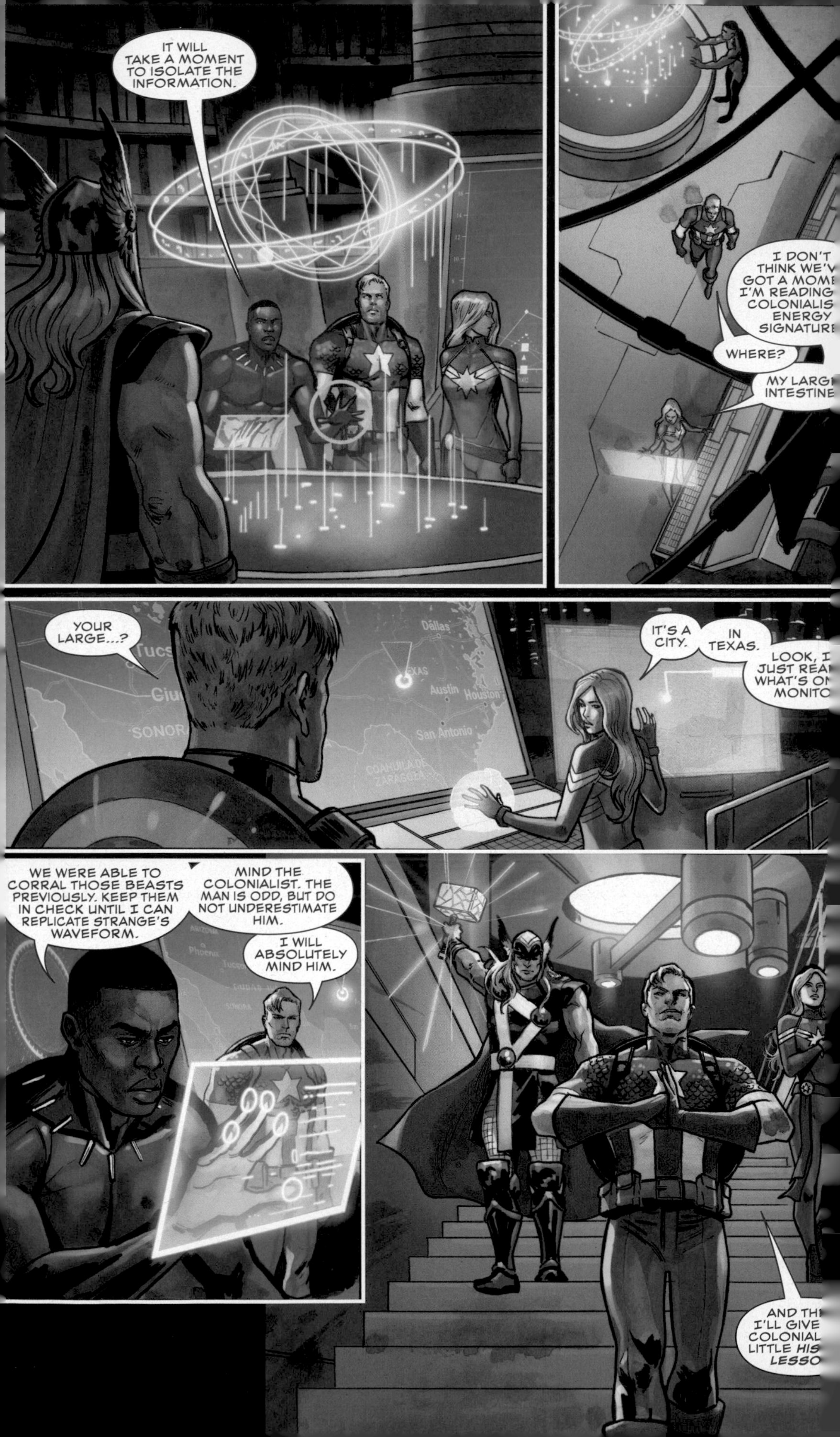
IT WILL TAKE A MOMENT TO ISOLATE THE INFORMATION.
I DON'T THINK WE'V GOT A MOME I'M READING COLONIALIS ENERGY SIGNATURE
WHERE?
MY LARG INTESTINE
YOUR LARGE...?
IT'S A CITY.
IN TEXAS.
LOOK, I JUST REA WHAT'S O MONITO
WE WERE ABLE TO CORRAL THOSE BEASTS PREVIOUSLY. KEEP THEM IN CHECK UNTIL I CAN REPLICATE STRANGE'S WAVEFORM.
MIND THE COLONIALIST. THE MAN IS ODD, BUT DO NOT UNDERESTIMATE HIM.
I WILL ABSOLUTELY MIND HIM.
AND TH I'LL GIVE COLONIAL LITTLE *HIS* *LESSO*

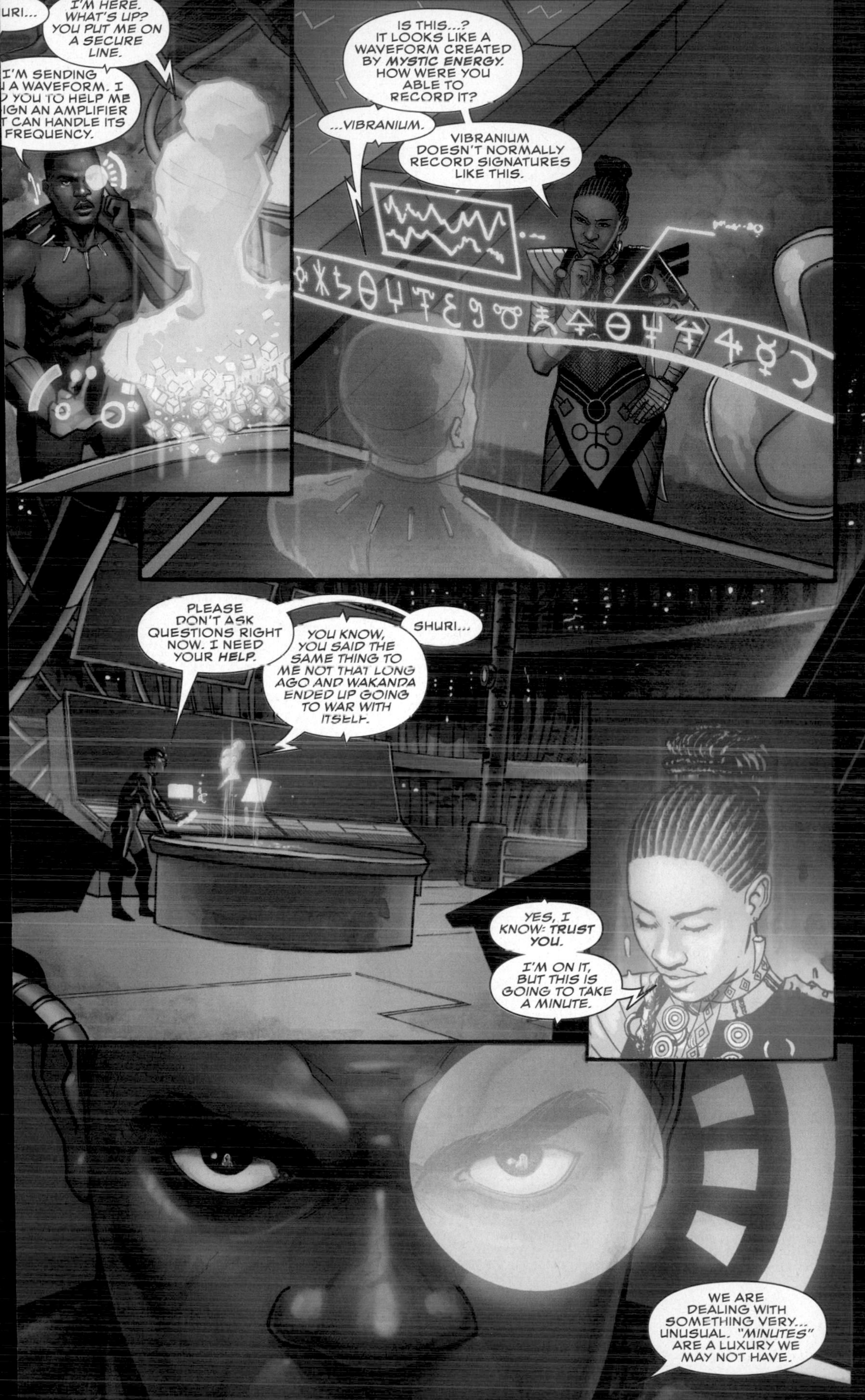
URI...
I'M HERE. WHAT'S UP? YOU PUT ME ON A SECURE LINE.
I'M SENDING A WAVEFORM. I YOU TO HELP ME IGN AN AMPLIFIER CAN HANDLE ITS FREQUENCY.
IS THIS...? IT LOOKS LIKE A WAVEFORM CREATED BY MYSTIC ENERGY. HOW WERE YOU ABLE TO RECORD IT?
...VIBRANIUM.
VIBRANIUM DOESN'T NORMALLY RECORD SIGNATURES LIKE THIS.
PLEASE DON'T ASK QUESTIONS RIGHT NOW. I NEED YOUR HELP.
SHURI...
YOU KNOW, YOU SAID THE SAME THING TO ME NOT THAT LONG AGO AND WAKANDA ENDED UP GOING TO WAR WITH ITSELF.
YES, I KNOW: TRUST YOU.
I'M ON IT, BUT THIS IS GOING TO TAKE A MINUTE.
WE ARE DEALING WITH SOMETHING VERY... UNUSUAL. "MINUTES" ARE A LUXURY WE MAY NOT HAVE.

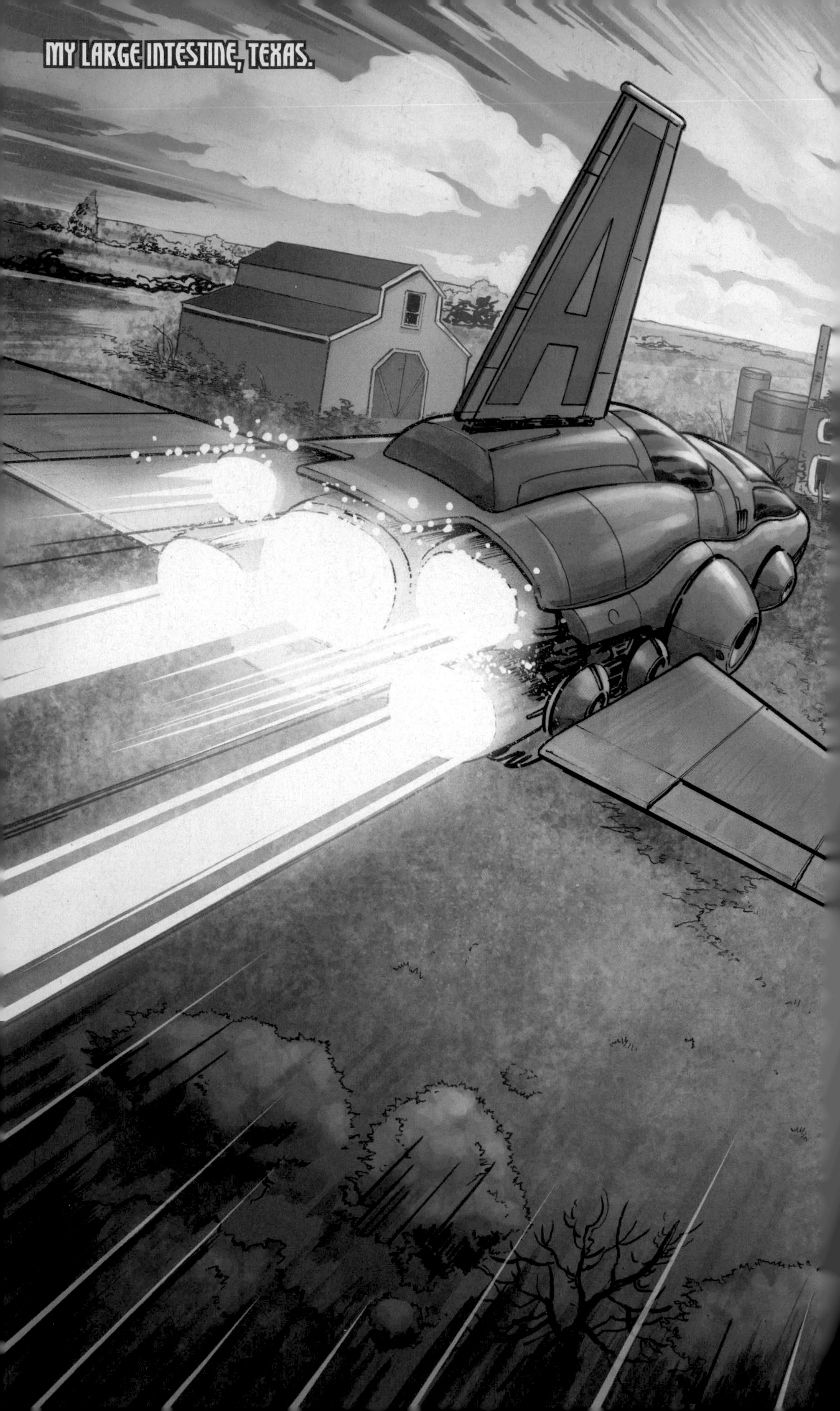
MY LARGE INTESTINE, TEXAS.

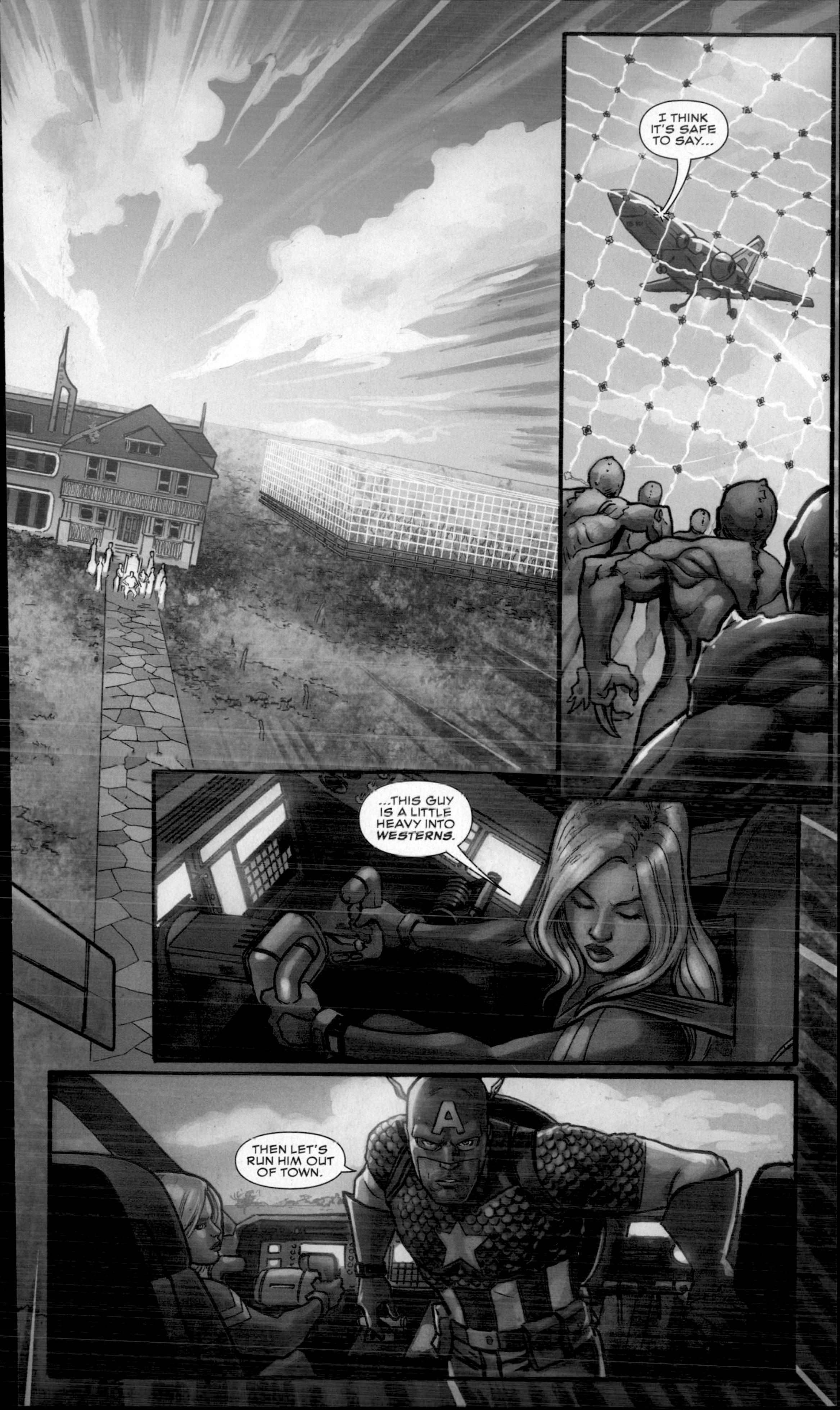
I THINK IT'S SAFE TO SAY...
...THIS GUY IS A LITTLE HEAVY INTO WESTERNS.
THEN LET'S RUN HIM OUT OF TOWN.

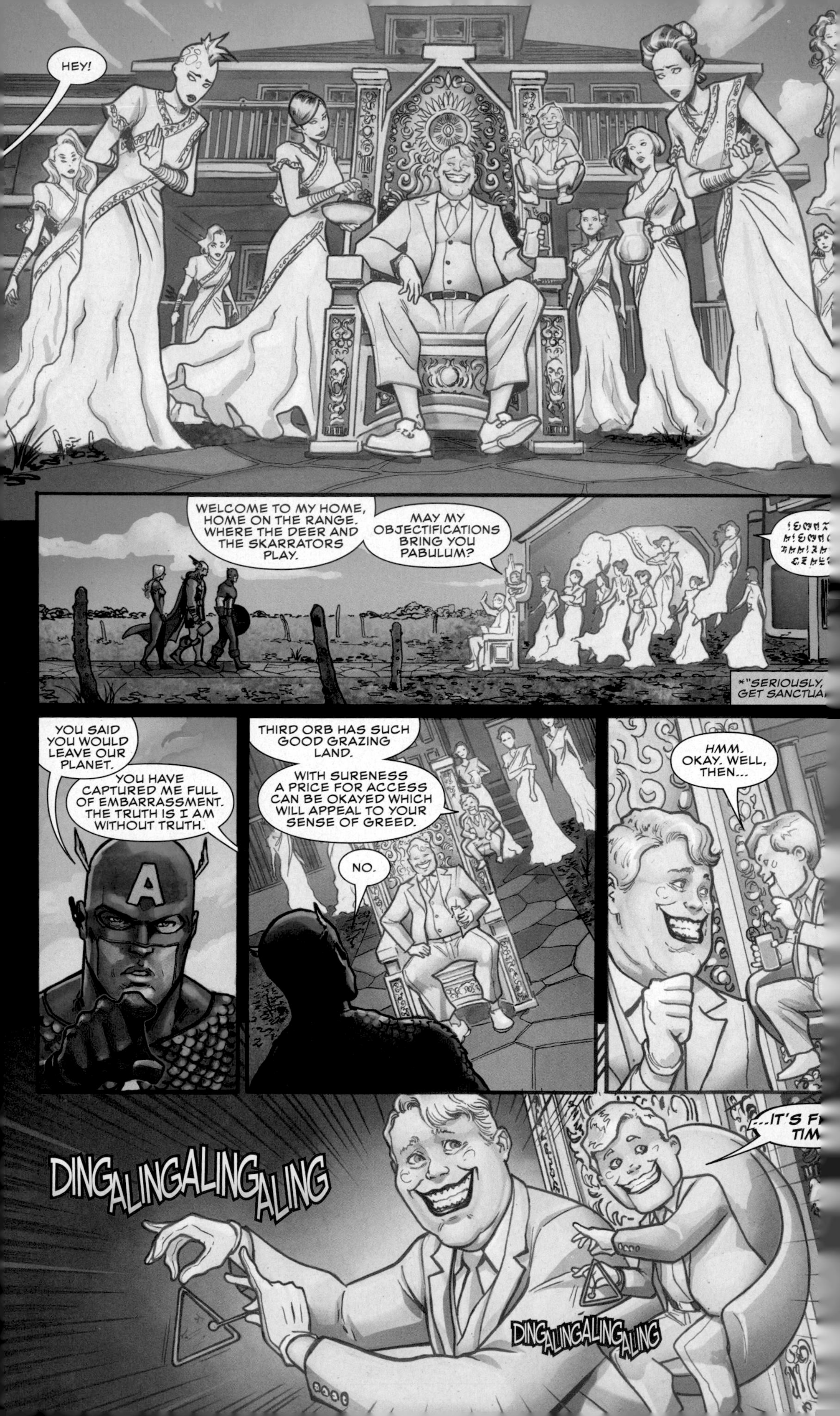
HEY!
WELCOME TO MY HOME, HOME ON THE RANGE. WHERE THE DEER AND THE SKARRATORS PLAY.
MAY MY OBJECTIFICATIONS BRING YOU PABULUM?
*"SERIOUSLY, GET SANCTUA
YOU SAID YOU WOULD LEAVE OUR PLANET.
YOU HAVE CAPTURED ME FULL OF EMBARRASSMENT. THE TRUTH IS I AM WITHOUT TRUTH.
THIRD ORB HAS SUCH GOOD GRAZING LAND.
WITH SURENESS A PRICE FOR ACCESS CAN BE OKAYED WHICH WILL APPEAL TO YOUR SENSE OF GREED.
NO.
HMM. OKAY. WELL, THEN...
DINGALINGALINGALING
...IT'S F TIM
DINGALINGALINGALING

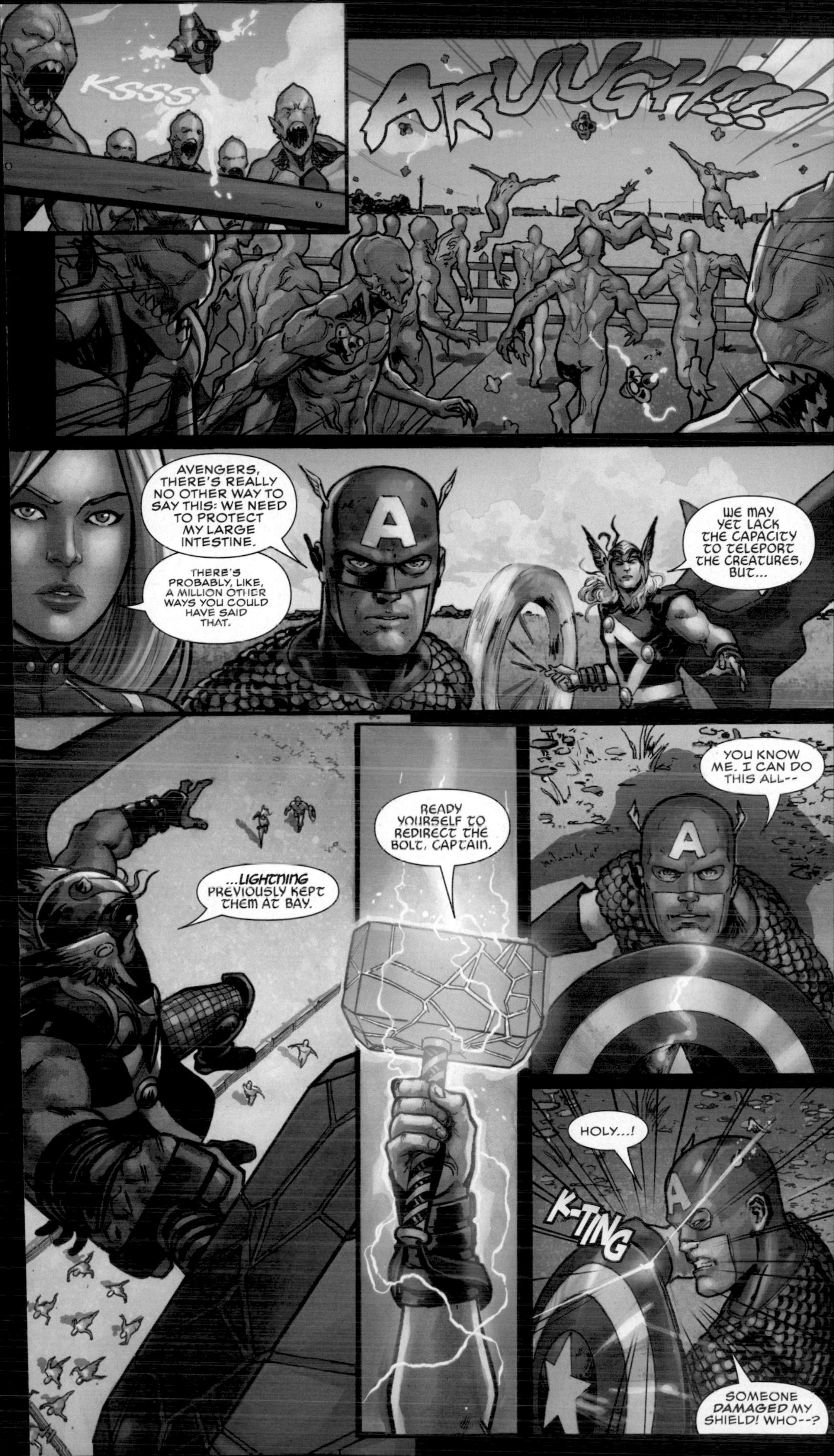
KSSS
ARUUGH!!!
AVENGERS, THERE'S REALLY NO OTHER WAY TO SAY THIS: WE NEED TO PROTECT MY LARGE INTESTINE.
THERE'S PROBABLY, LIKE, A MILLION OTHER WAYS YOU COULD HAVE SAID THAT.
WE MAY YET LACK THE CAPACITY TO TELEPORT THE CREATURES, BUT...
...LIGHTNING PREVIOUSLY KEPT THEM AT BAY.
READY YOURSELF TO REDIRECT THE BOLT, CAPTAIN.
YOU KNOW ME. I CAN DO THIS ALL--
HOLY...!
K-TING
SOMEONE DAMAGED MY SHIELD! WHO--?

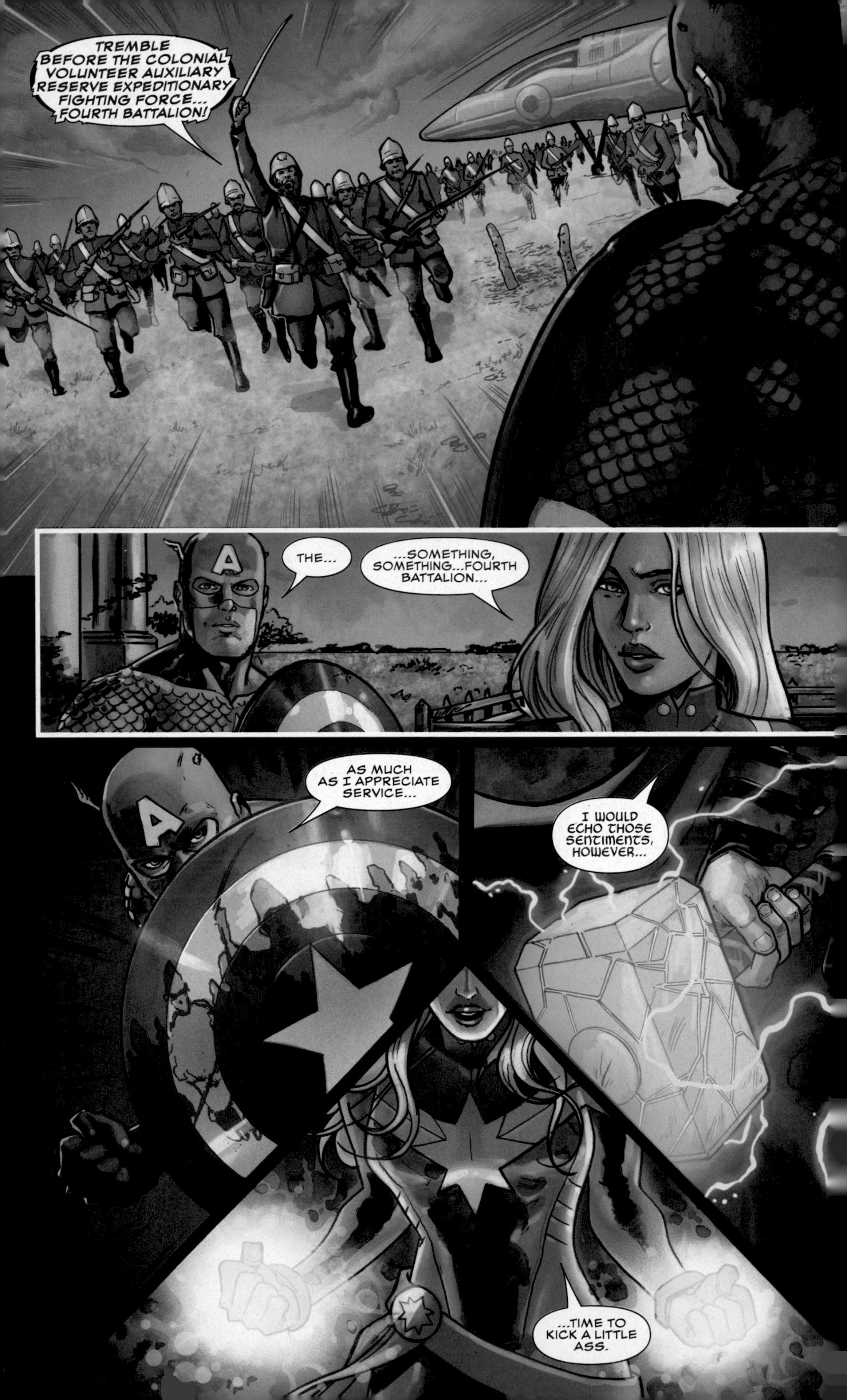
TREMBLE BEFORE THE COLONIAL VOLUNTEER AUXILIARY RESERVE EXPEDITIONARY FIGHTING FORCE... FOURTH BATTALION!
THE...
...SOMETHING, SOMETHING...FOURTH BATTALION...
AS MUCH AS I APPRECIATE SERVICE...
I WOULD ECHO THOSE SENTIMENTS, HOWEVER...
...TIME TO KICK A LITTLE ASS.

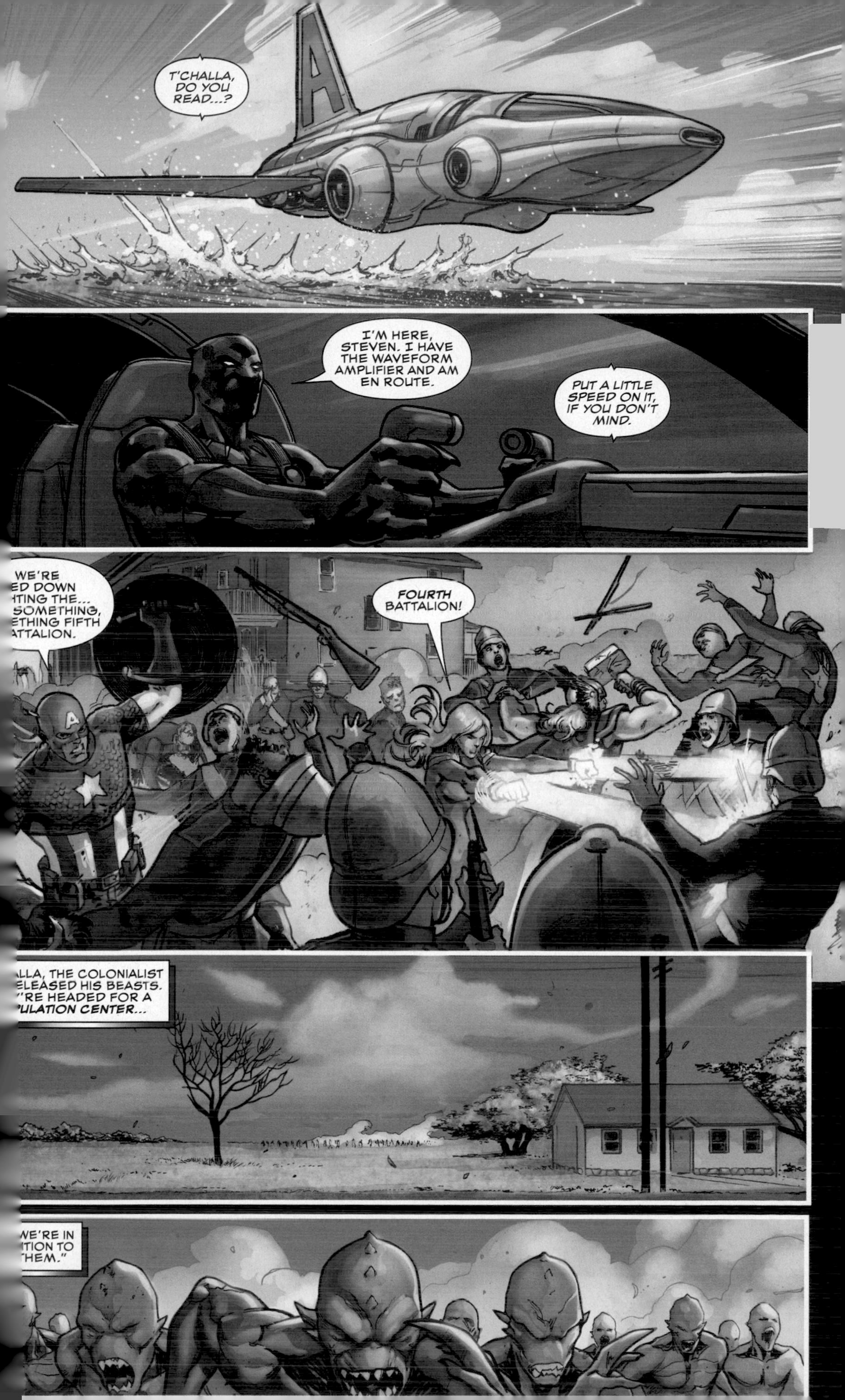
T'CHALLA, DO YOU READ...?
I'M HERE, STEVEN. I HAVE THE WAVEFORM AMPLIFIER AND AM EN ROUTE.
PUT A LITTLE SPEED ON IT, IF YOU DON'T MIND.
WE'RE ED DOWN HTING THE... SOMETHING, ETHING FIFTH ATTALION.
FOURTH BATTALION!
ALLA, THE COLONIALIST ELEASED HIS BEASTS. 'RE HEADED FOR A PULATION CENTER...
WE'RE IN TION TO THEM."

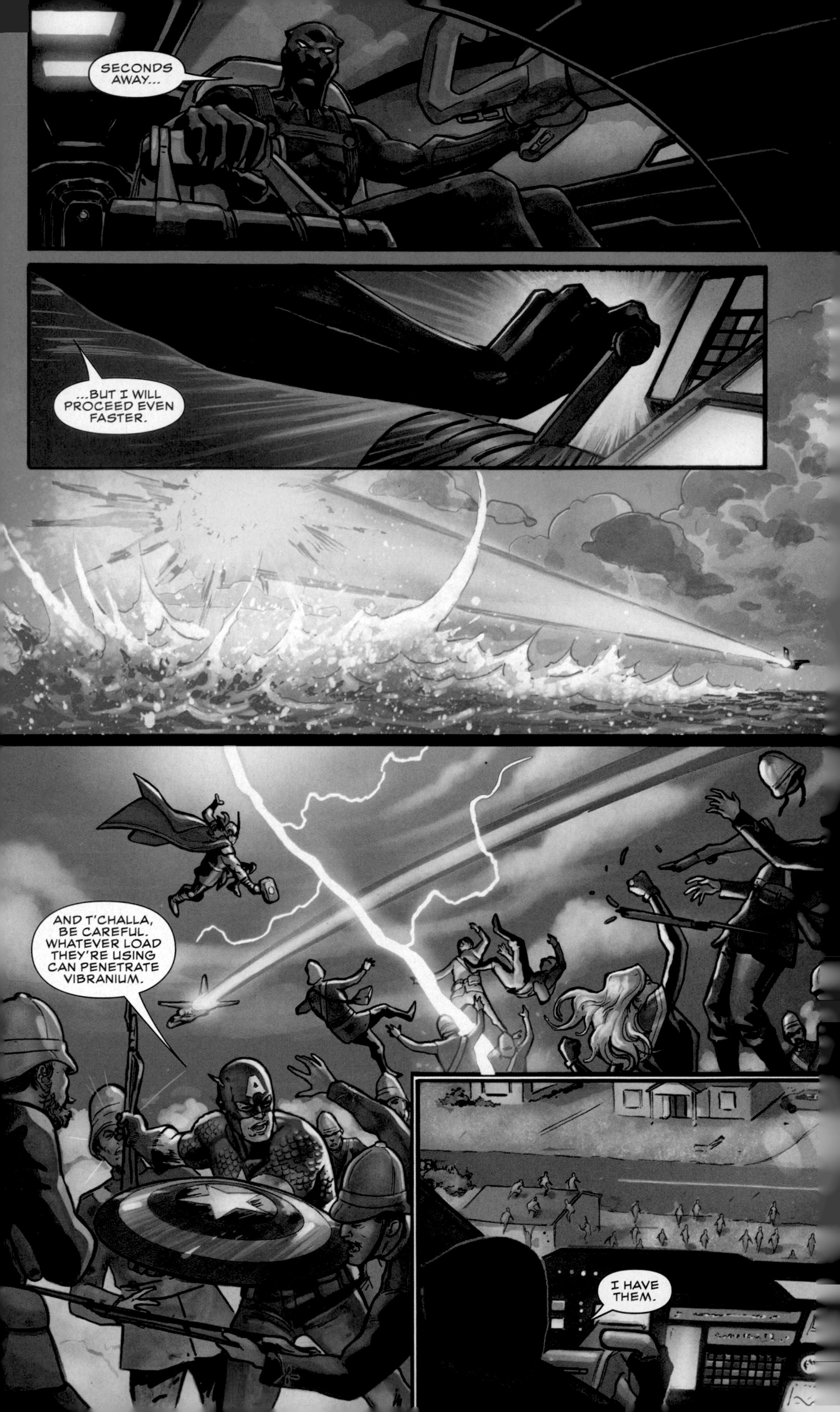
SECONDS AWAY...
...BUT I WILL PROCEED EVEN FASTER.
AND T'CHALLA, BE CAREFUL. WHATEVER LOAD THEY'RE USING CAN PENETRATE VIBRANIUM.
I HAVE THEM.

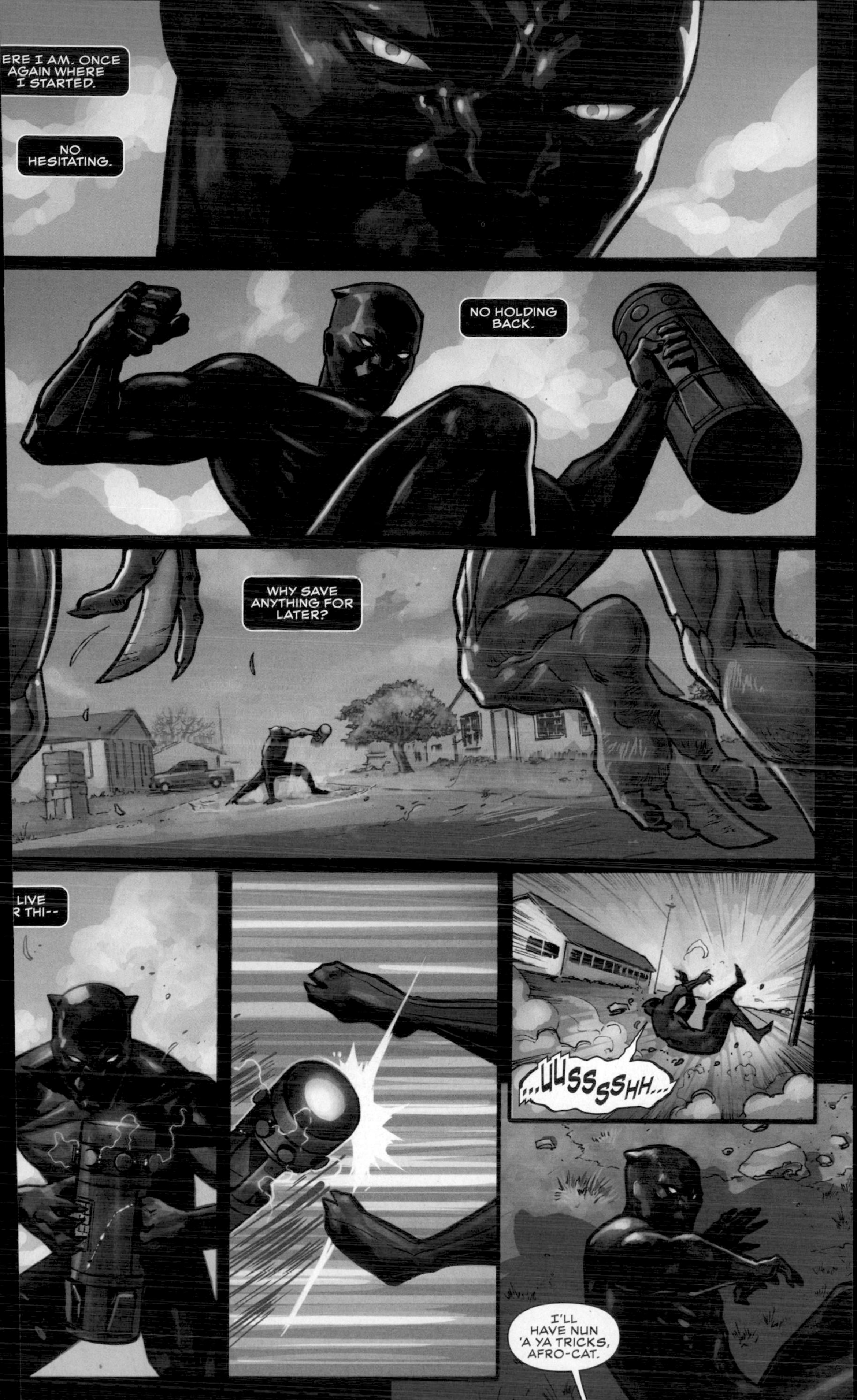
ERE I AM. ONCE AGAIN WHERE I STARTED.
NO HESITATING.
NO HOLDING BACK.
WHY SAVE ANYTHING FOR LATER?
LIVE R THI--
...UUSSSSHH...
I'LL HAVE NUN 'A YA TRICKS, AFRO-CAT.

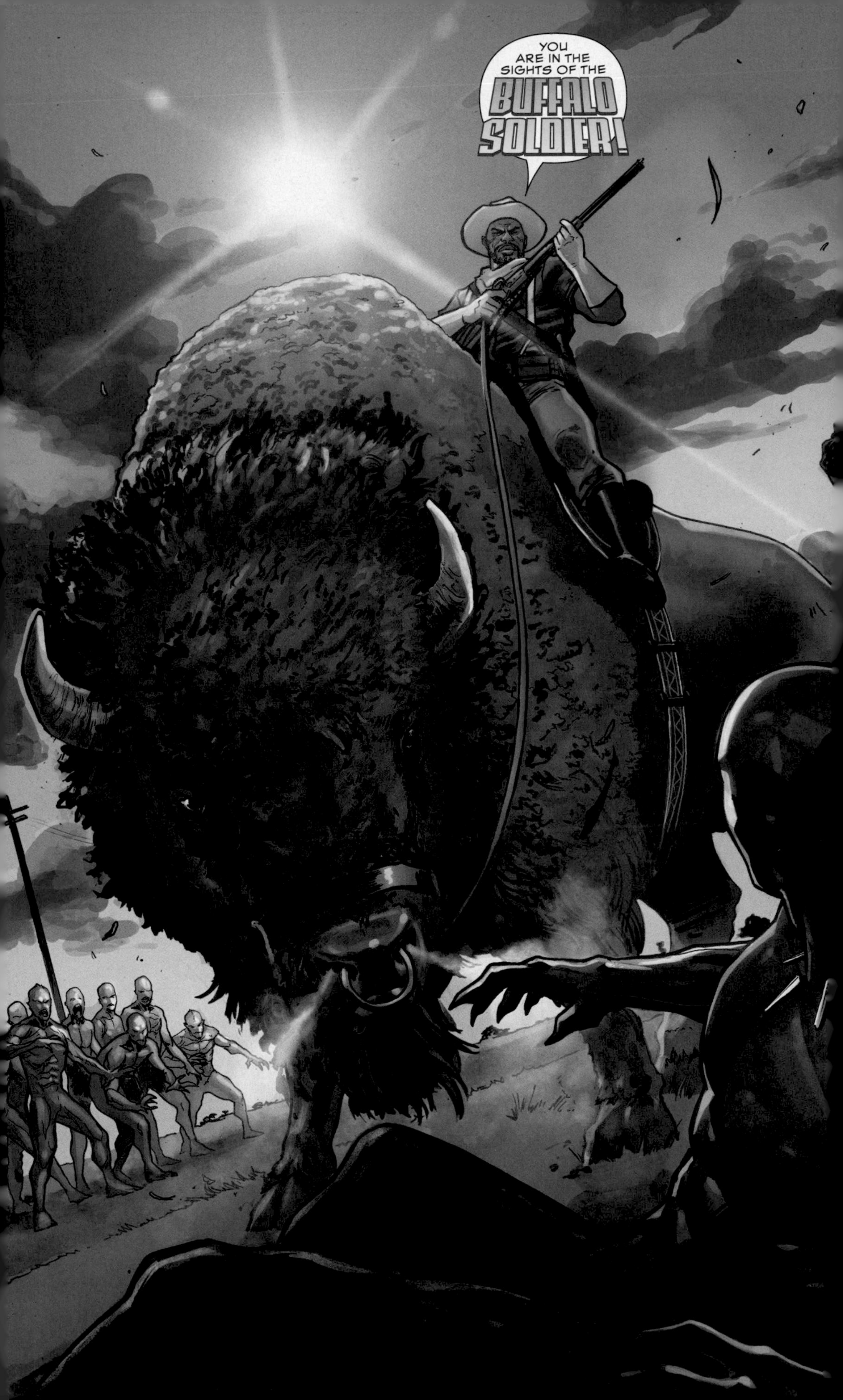
YOU ARE IN THE SIGHTS OF THE BUFFALO SOLDIER!

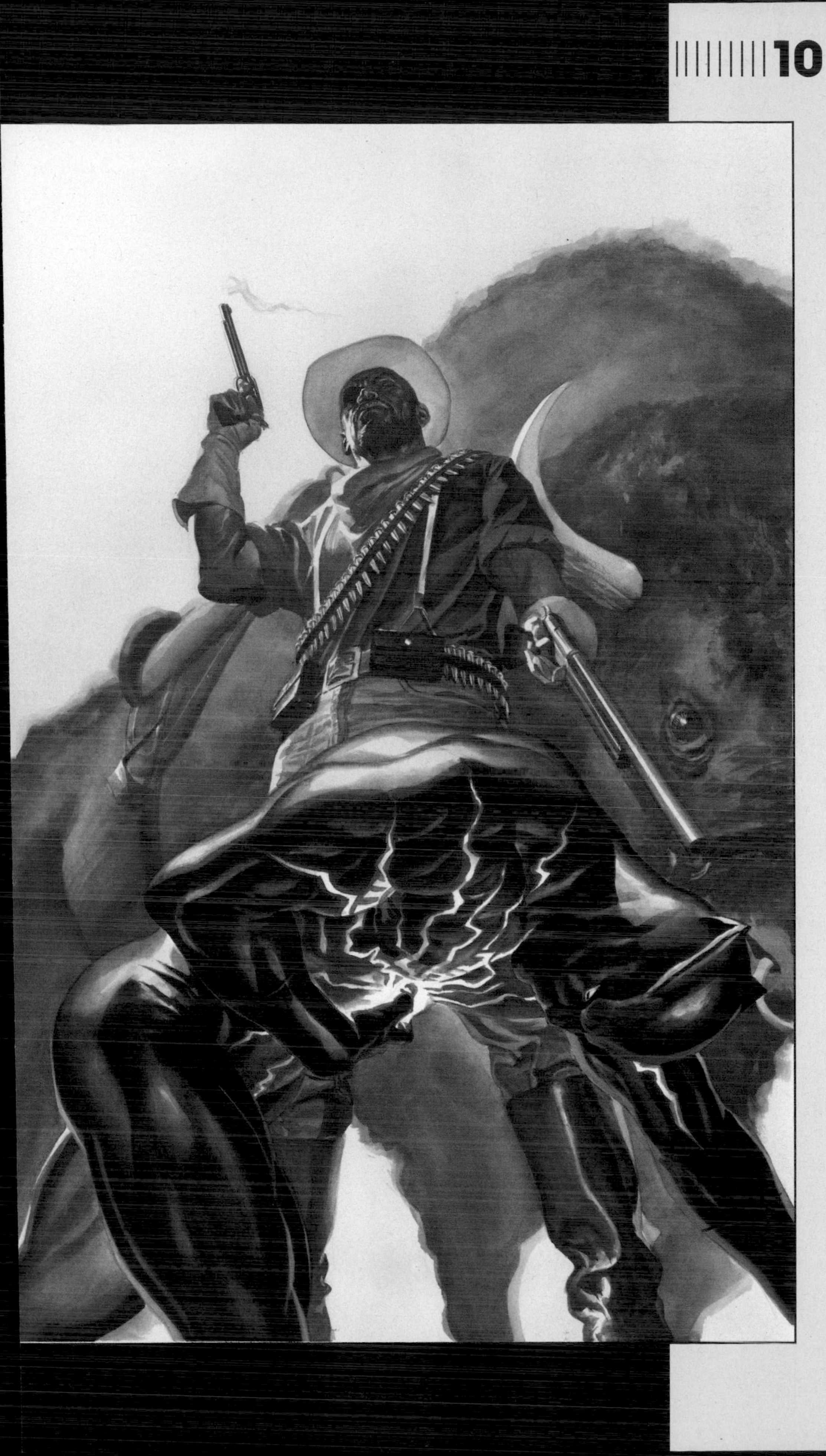

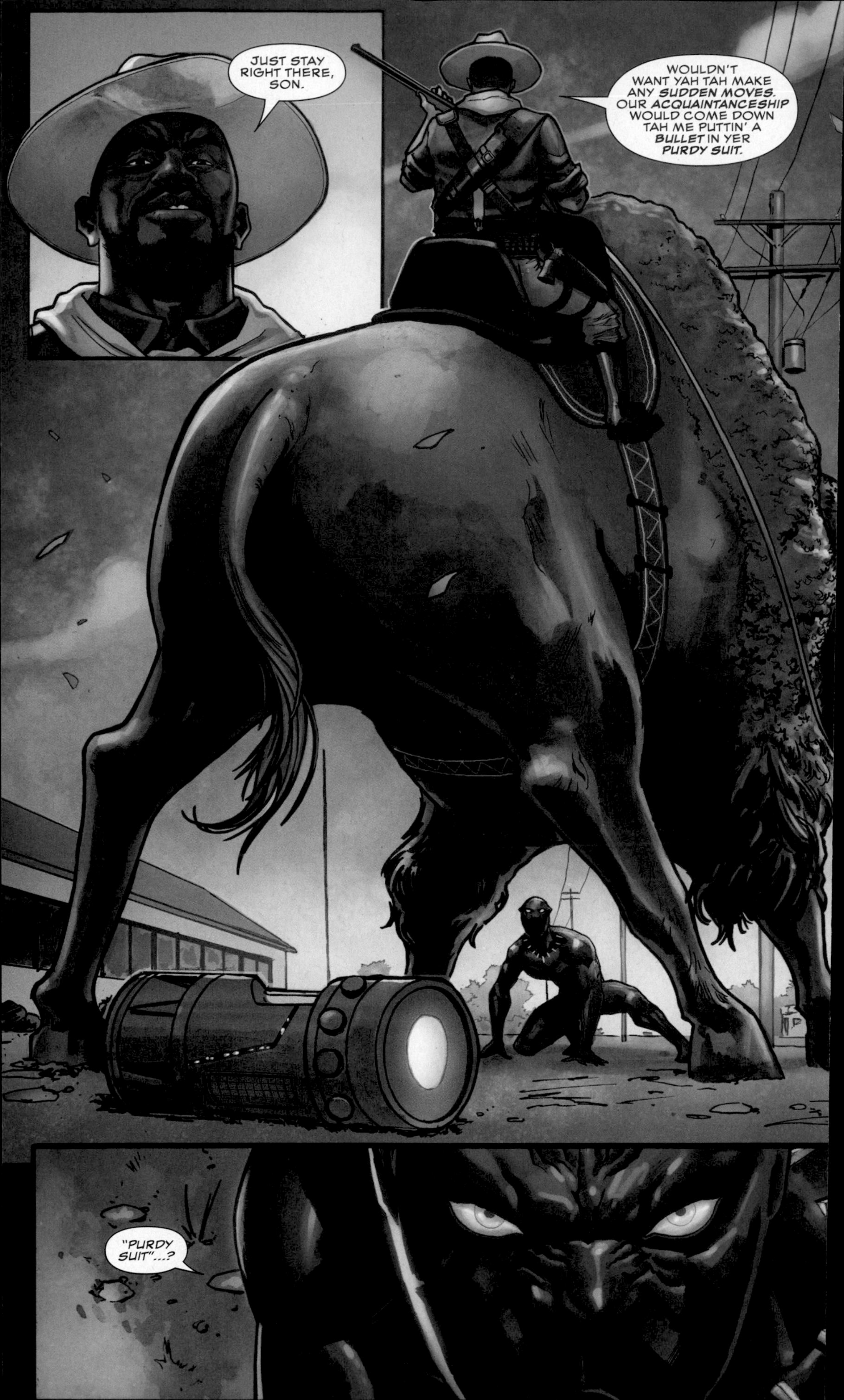
JUST STAY RIGHT THERE, SON.
WOULDN'T WANT YAH TAH MAKE ANY SUDDEN MOVES. OUR ACQUAINTANCESHIP WOULD COME DOWN TAH ME PUTTIN' A BULLET IN YER PURDY SUIT.
"PURDY SUIT"...?

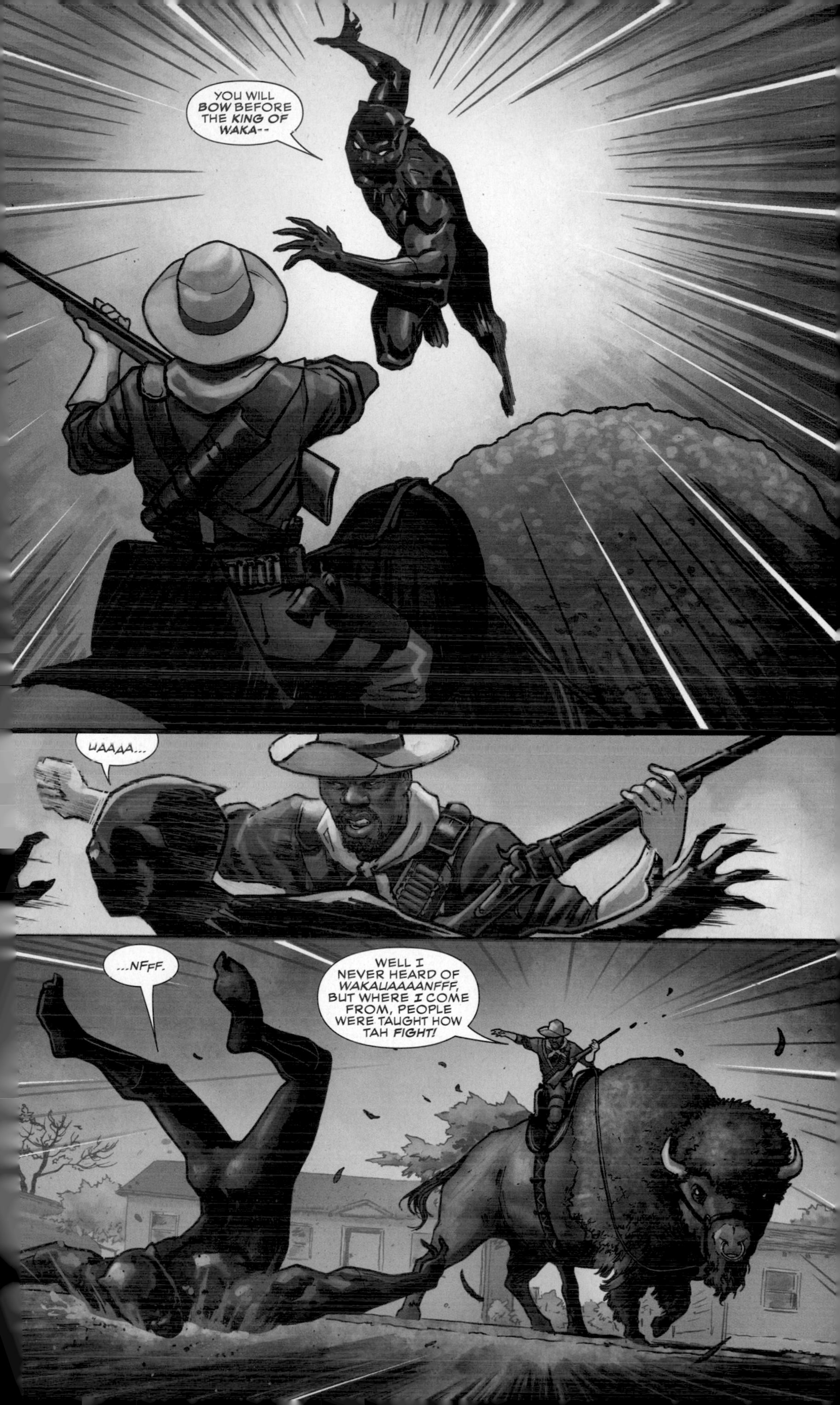

YOU WILL BOW BEFORE THE KING OF WAKA--
UAAAA...
...NFFF.
WELL I NEVER HEARD OF WAKAUAAAANFFF, BUT WHERE I COME FROM, PEOPLE WERE TAUGHT HOW TAH FIGHT!

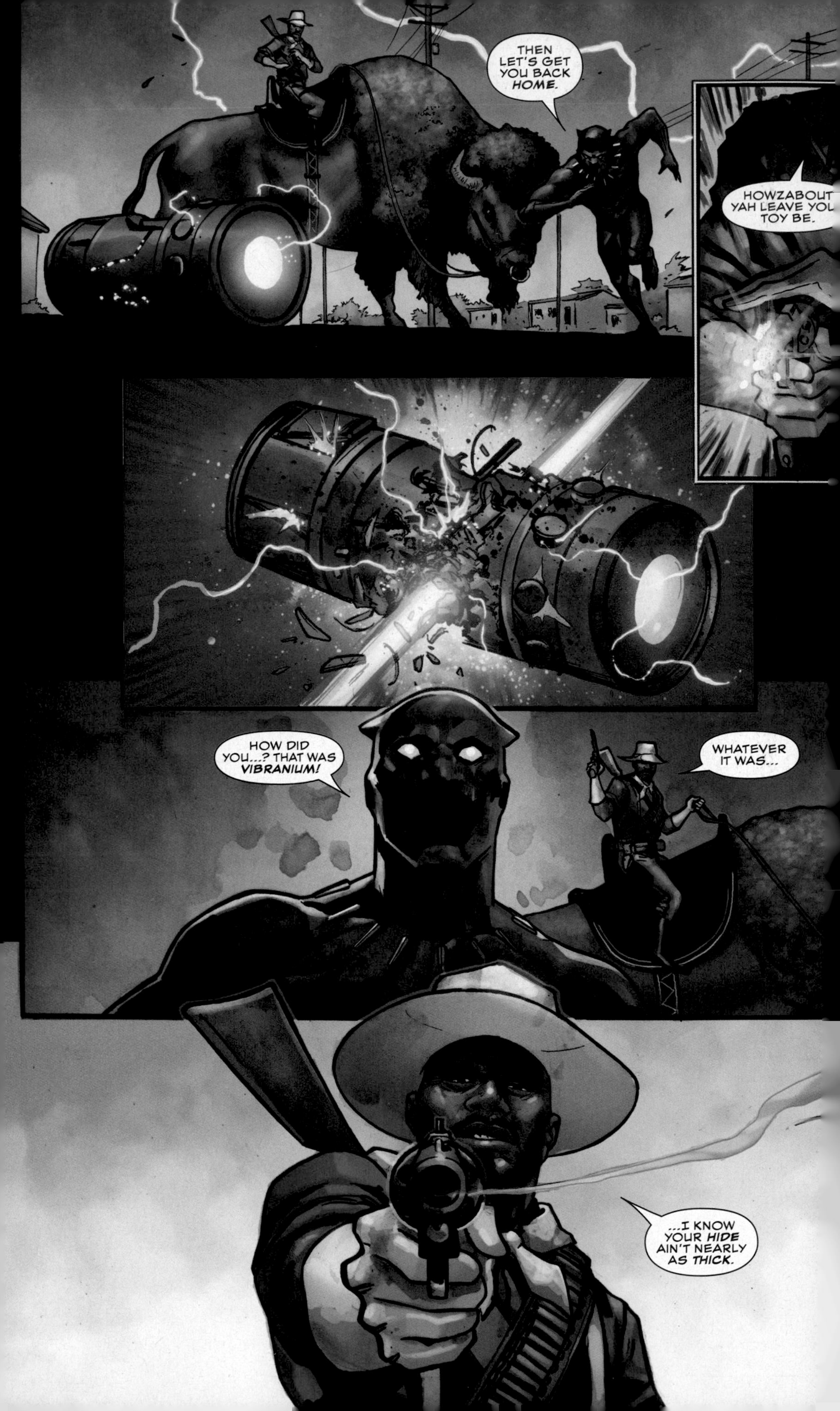
THEN LET'S GET YOU BACK HOME.
HOWZABOUT YAH LEAVE YOU TOY BE.
HOW DID YOU...? THAT WAS VIBRANIUM!
WHATEVER IT WAS...
...I KNOW YOUR HIDE AIN'T NEARLY AS THICK.

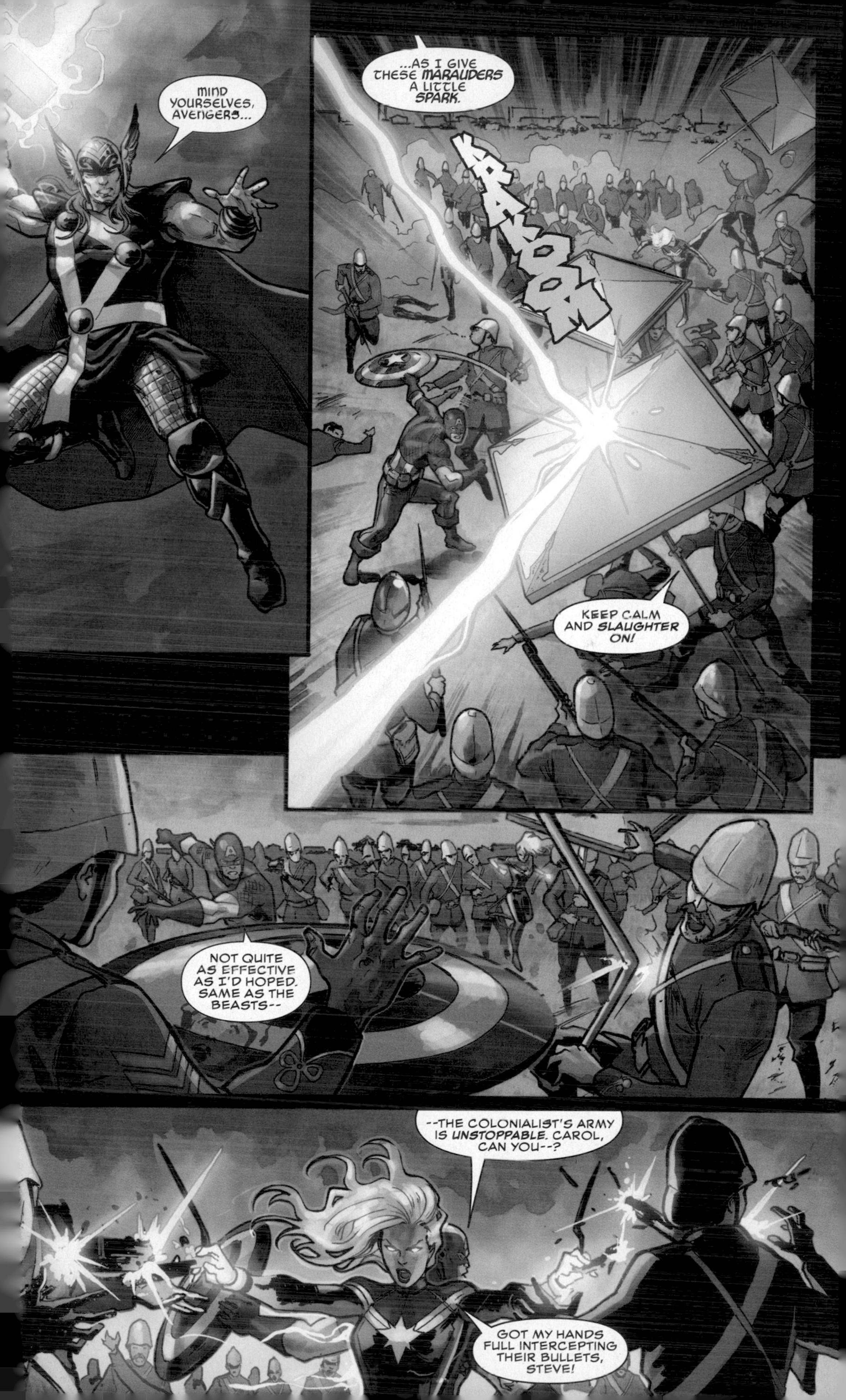
MIND YOURSELVES, AVENGERS...
...AS I GIVE THESE MARAUDERS A LITTLE SPARK.
KRAKOOM
KEEP CALM AND SLAUGHTER ON!
NOT QUITE AS EFFECTIVE AS I'D HOPED. SAME AS THE BEASTS--
--THE COLONIALIST'S ARMY IS UNSTOPPABLE. CAROL, CAN YOU--?
GOT MY HANDS FULL INTERCEPTING THEIR BULLETS, STEVE!

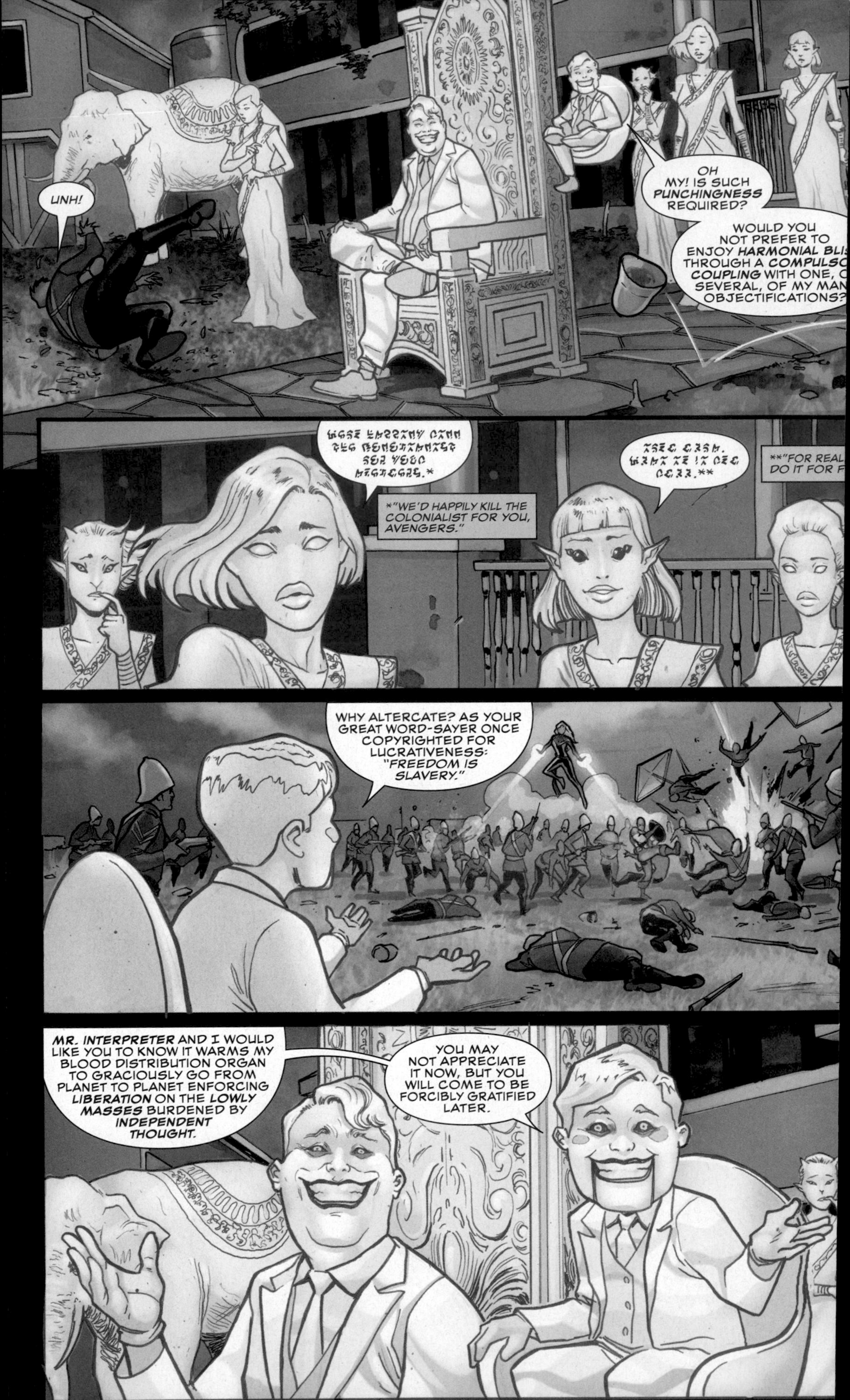
UNH!
OH MY! IS SUCH PUNCHINGNESS REQUIRED?
WOULD YOU NOT PREFER TO ENJOY HARMONIAL BLIS THROUGH A COMPULSO COUPLING WITH ONE, O SEVERAL, OF MY MAN OBJECTIFICATIONS?
*"WE'D HAPPILY KILL THE COLONIALIST FOR YOU, AVENGERS."
**"FOR REAL DO IT FOR F
WHY ALTERCATE? AS YOUR GREAT WORD-SAYER ONCE COPYRIGHTED FOR LUCRATIVENESS: "FREEDOM IS SLAVERY."
MR. INTERPRETER AND I WOULD LIKE YOU TO KNOW IT WARMS MY BLOOD DISTRIBUTION ORGAN TO GRACIOUSLY GO FROM PLANET TO PLANET ENFORCING LIBERATION ON THE LOWLY MASSES BURDENED BY INDEPENDENT THOUGHT.
YOU MAY NOT APPRECIATE IT NOW, BUT YOU WILL COME TO BE FORCIBLY GRATIFIED LATER.

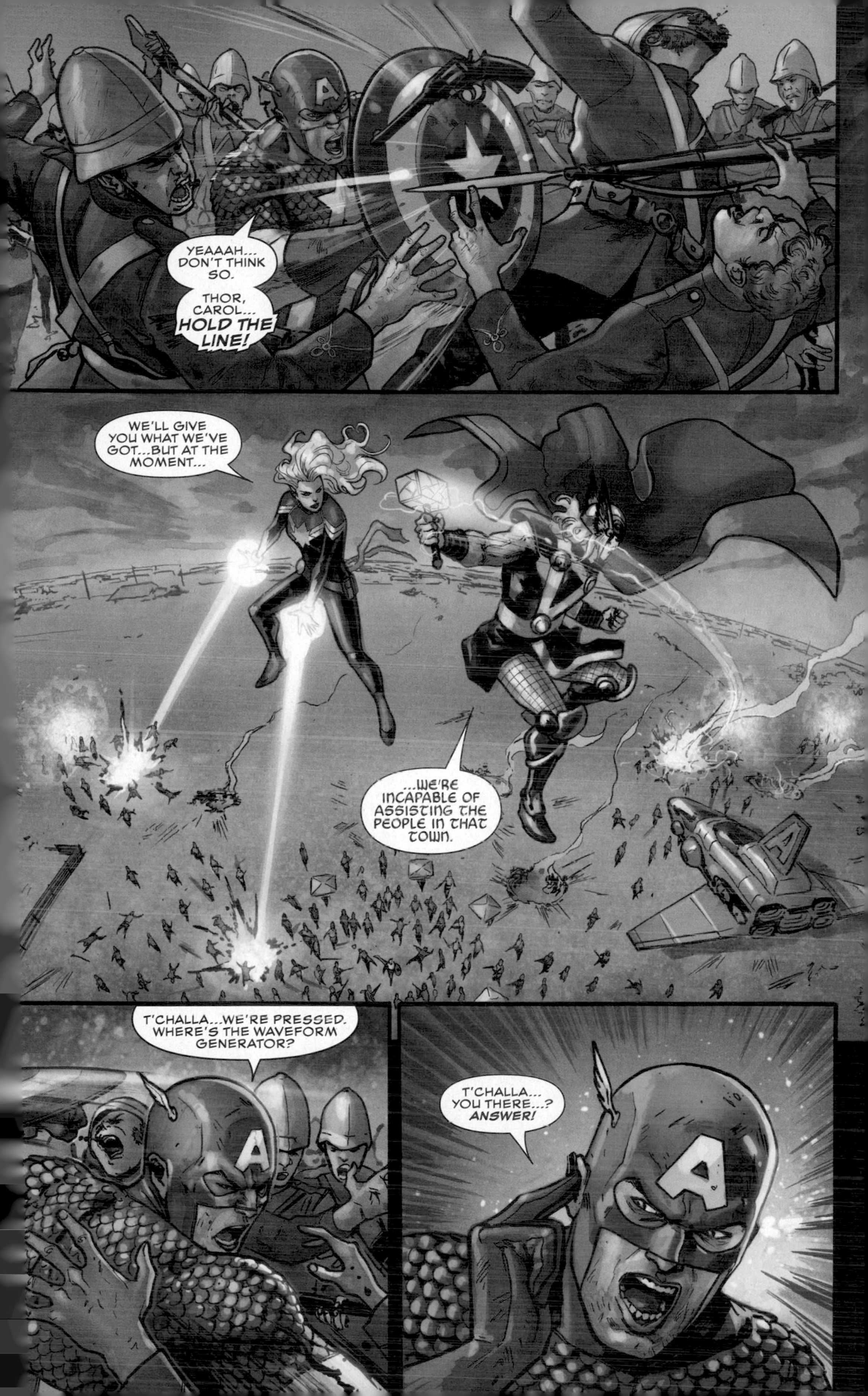
YEAAAH... DON'T THINK SO.
THOR, CAROL... HOLD THE LINE!
WE'LL GIVE YOU WHAT WE'VE GOT...BUT AT THE MOMENT...
...WE'RE INCAPABLE OF ASSISTING THE PEOPLE IN THAT TOWN.
T'CHALLA...WE'RE PRESSED. WHERE'S THE WAVEFORM GENERATOR?
T'CHALLA... YOU THERE...? ANSWER!

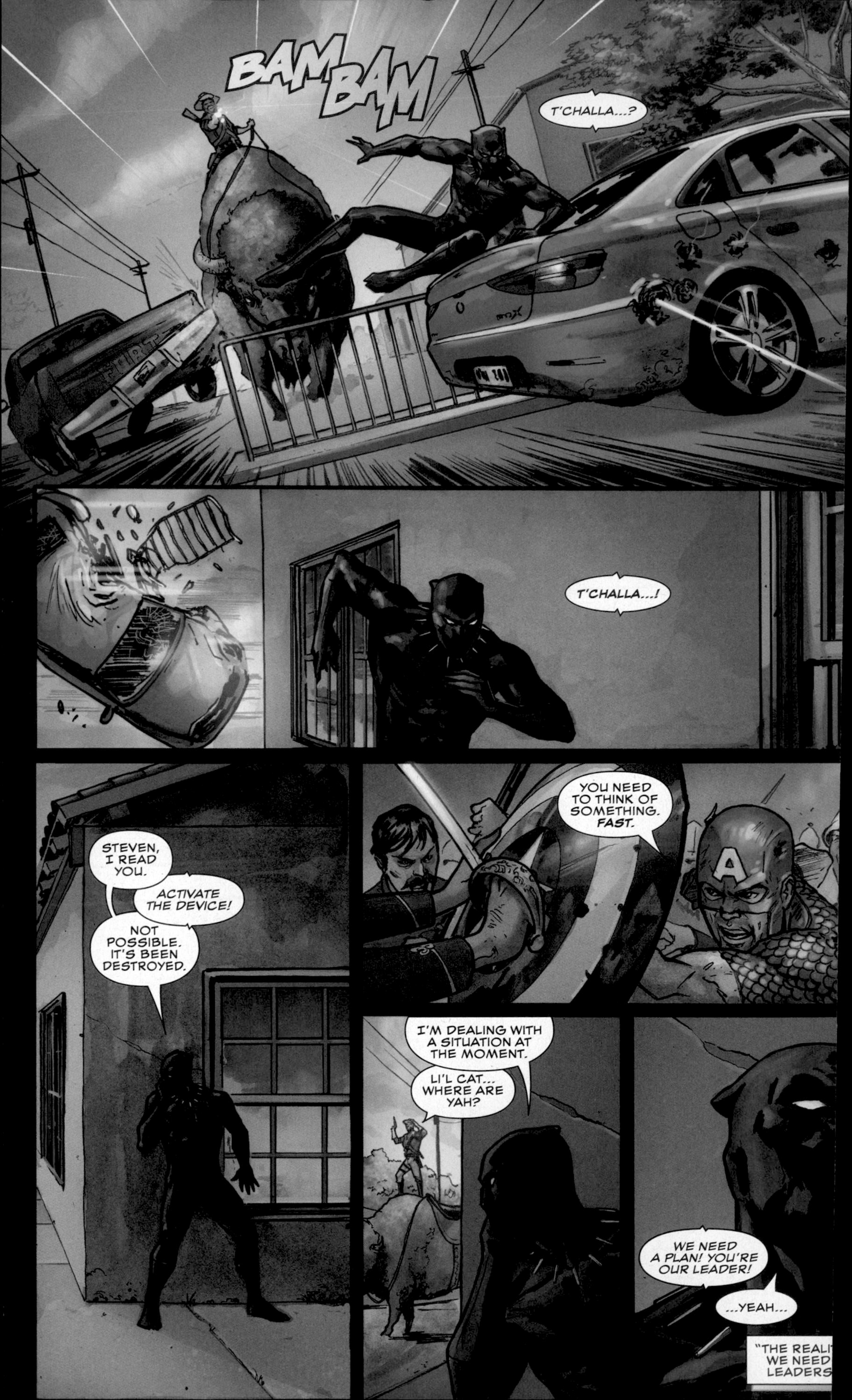
BAM BAM
T'CHALLA...?
T'CHALLA...!
STEVEN, I READ YOU.
ACTIVATE THE DEVICE!
NOT POSSIBLE. IT'S BEEN DESTROYED.
YOU NEED TO THINK OF SOMETHING. FAST.
I'M DEALING WITH A SITUATION AT THE MOMENT.
LI'L CAT... WHERE ARE YAH?
WE NEED A PLAN! YOU'RE OUR LEADER!
...YEAH...
"THE REALI
WE NEED
LEADERS

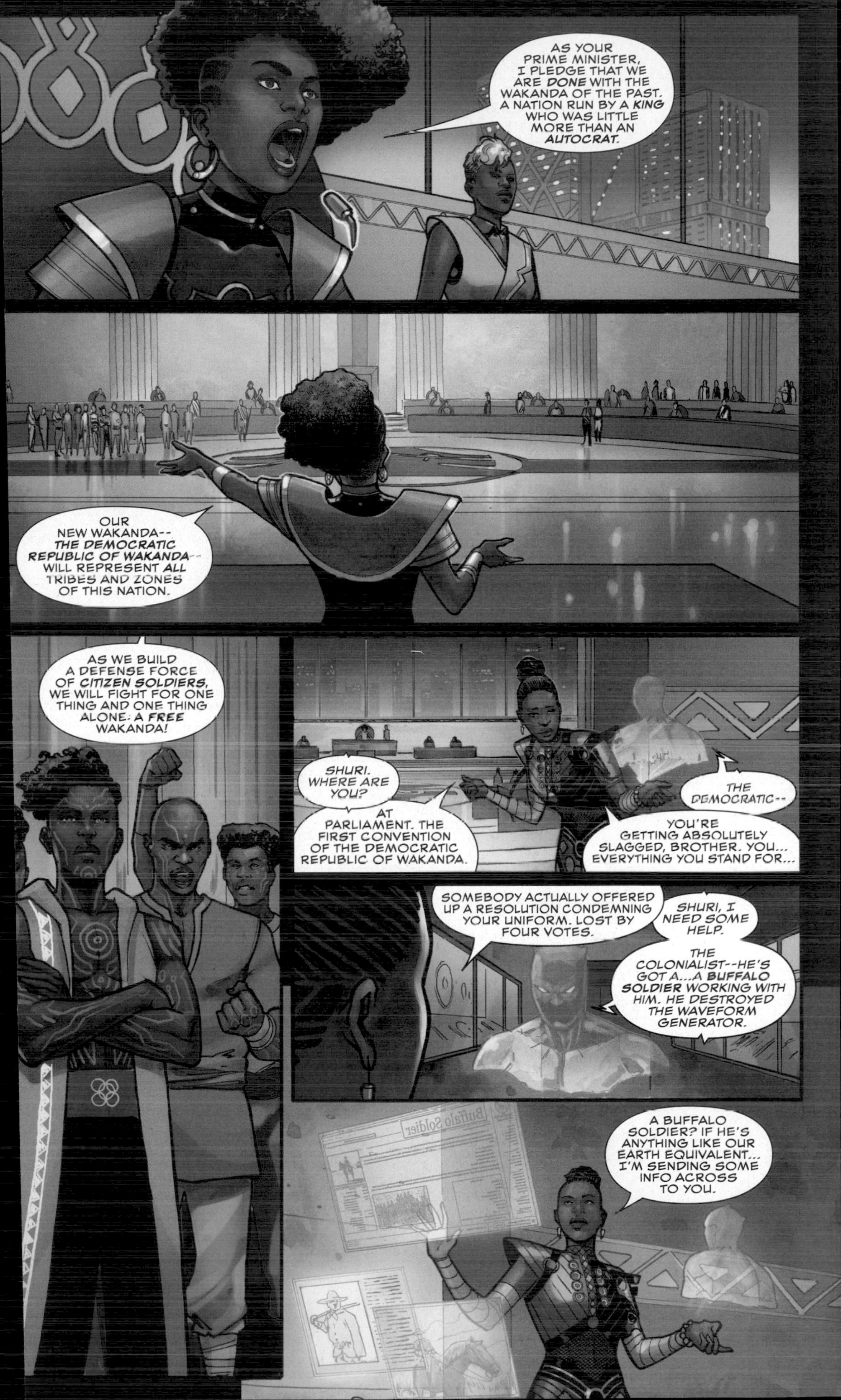
AS YOUR PRIME MINISTER, I PLEDGE THAT WE ARE DONE WITH THE WAKANDA OF THE PAST. A NATION RUN BY A KING WHO WAS LITTLE MORE THAN AN AUTOCRAT.
OUR NEW WAKANDA-- THE DEMOCRATIC REPUBLIC OF WAKANDA-- WILL REPRESENT ALL TRIBES AND ZONES OF THIS NATION.
AS WE BUILD A DEFENSE FORCE OF CITIZEN SOLDIERS, WE WILL FIGHT FOR ONE THING AND ONE THING ALONE: A FREE WAKANDA!
SHURI. WHERE ARE YOU?
AT PARLIAMENT. THE FIRST CONVENTION OF THE DEMOCRATIC REPUBLIC OF WAKANDA.
THE DEMOCRATIC--
YOU'RE GETTING ABSOLUTELY SLAGGED, BROTHER. YOU... EVERYTHING YOU STAND FOR...
SOMEBODY ACTUALLY OFFERED UP A RESOLUTION CONDEMNING YOUR UNIFORM. LOST BY FOUR VOTES.
SHURI, I NEED SOME HELP.
THE COLONIALIST--HE'S GOT A...A BUFFALO SOLDIER WORKING WITH HIM. HE DESTROYED THE WAVEFORM GENERATOR.
Buffalo Soldier
A BUFFALO SOLDIER? IF HE'S ANYTHING LIKE OUR EARTH EQUIVALENT... I'M SENDING SOME INFO ACROSS TO YOU.

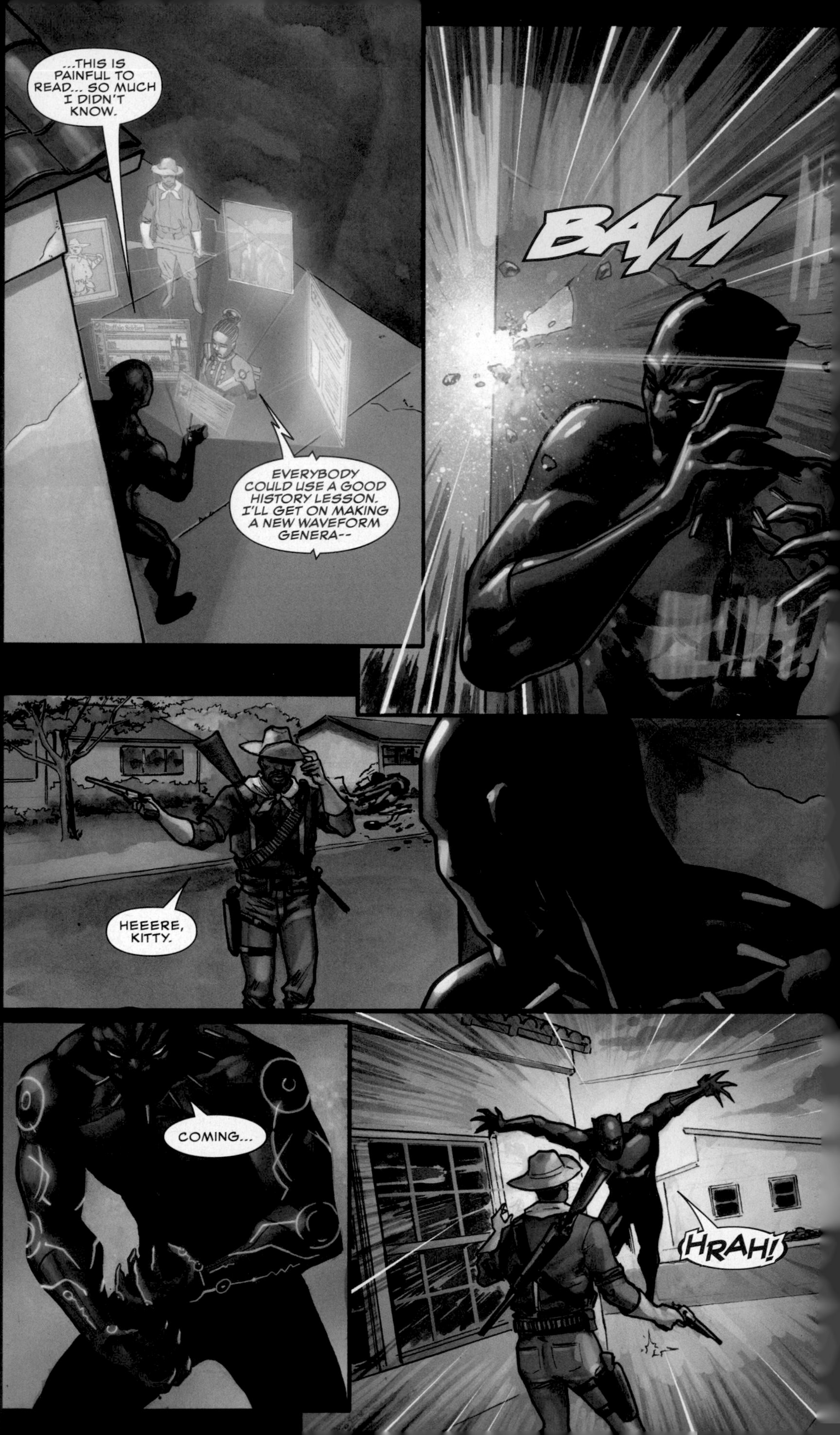
...THIS IS PAINFUL TO READ... SO MUCH I DIDN'T KNOW.
EVERYBODY COULD USE A GOOD HISTORY LESSON. I'LL GET ON MAKING A NEW WAVEFORM GENERA--
BAM
HEEERE, KITTY.
COMING...
HRAH!

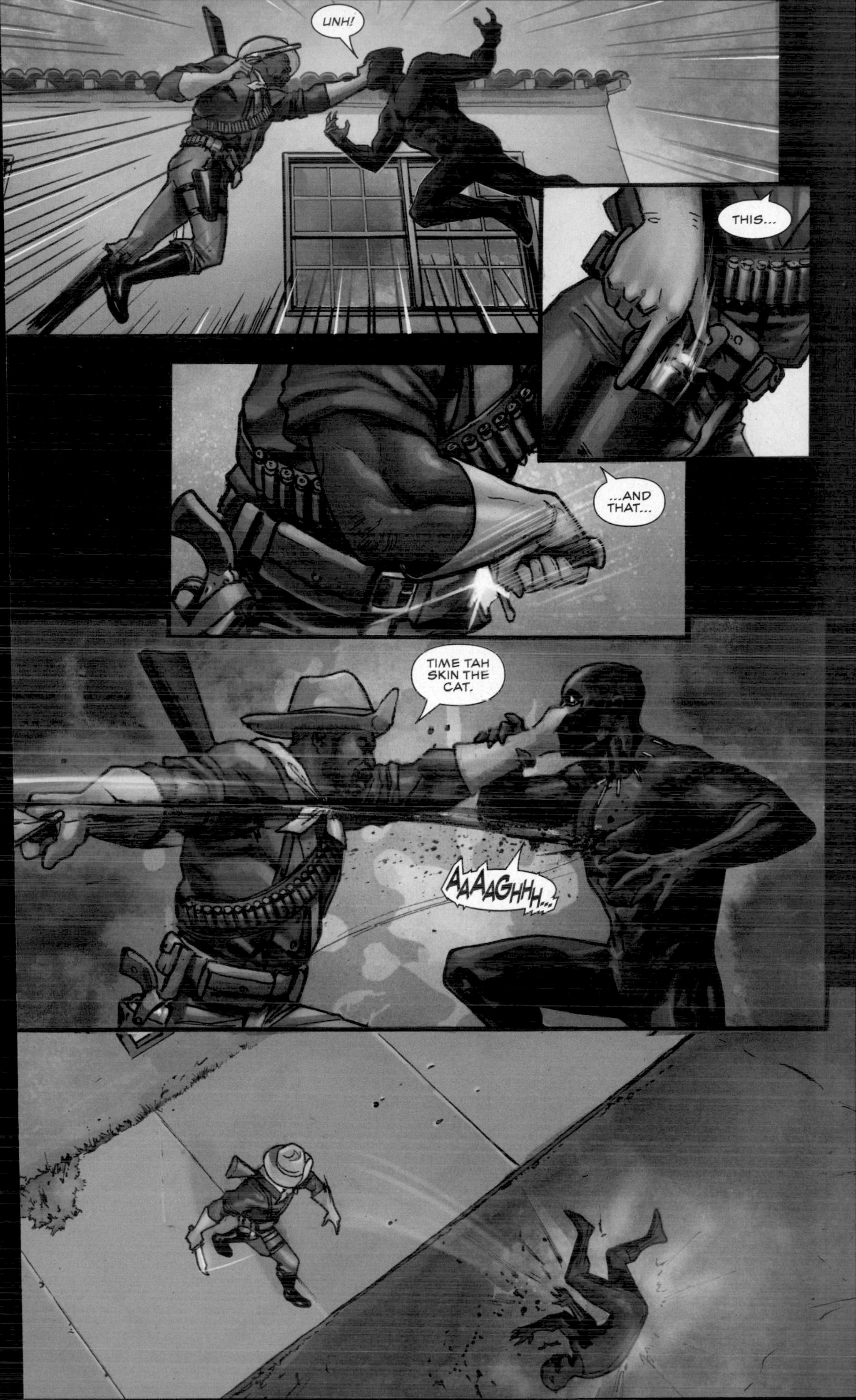
UNH!
THIS...
...AND THAT...
TIME TAH SKIN THE CAT.
AAAAGHHH...

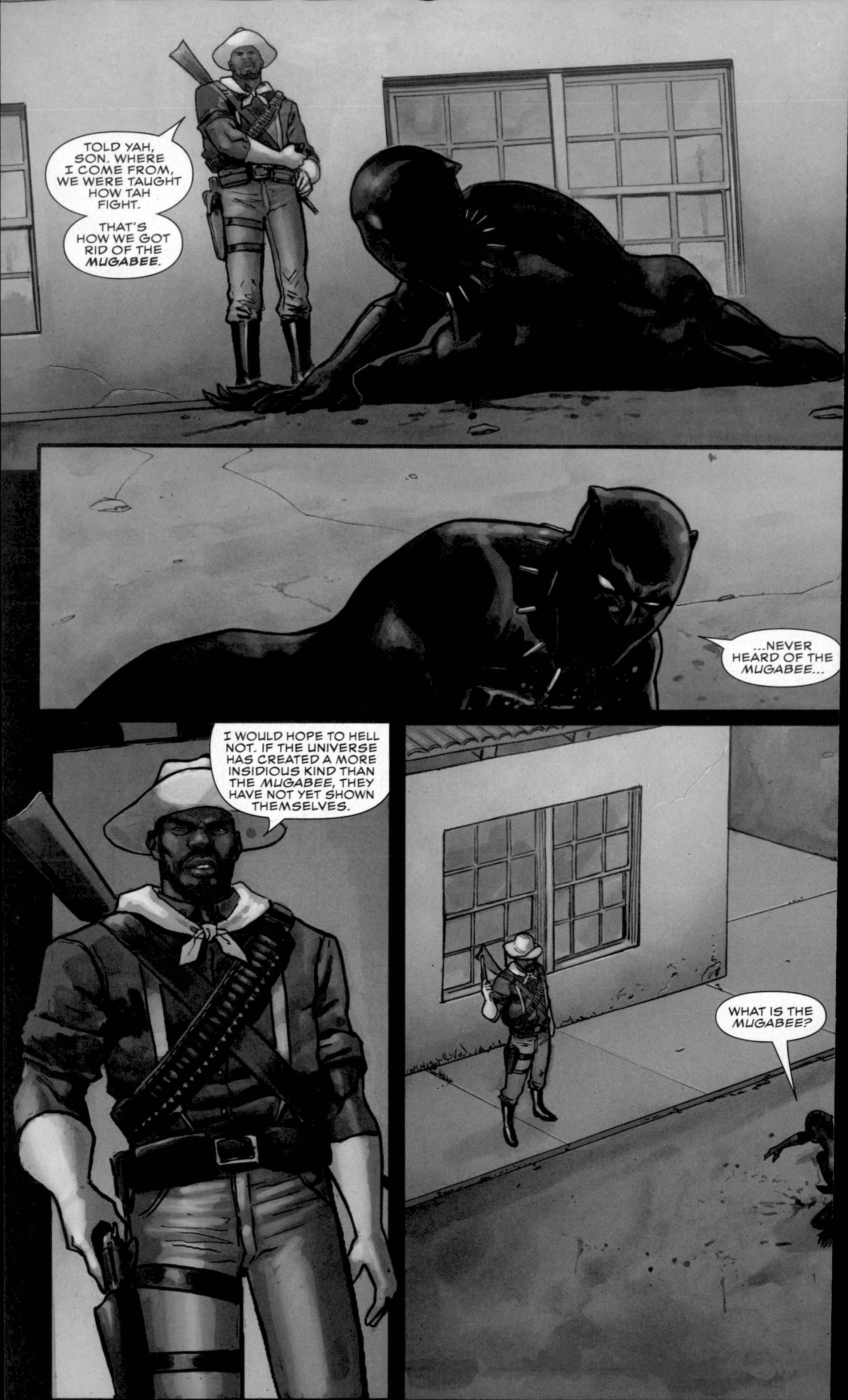
TOLD YAH, SON. WHERE I COME FROM, WE WERE TAUGHT HOW TAH FIGHT.
THAT'S HOW WE GOT RID OF THE *MUGABEE*.
...NEVER HEARD OF THE *MUGABEE*...
I WOULD HOPE TO HELL NOT. IF THE UNIVERSE HAS CREATED A MORE INSIDIOUS KIND THAN THE *MUGABEE*, THEY HAVE NOT YET SHOWN THEMSELVES.
WHAT IS THE *MUGABEE*?

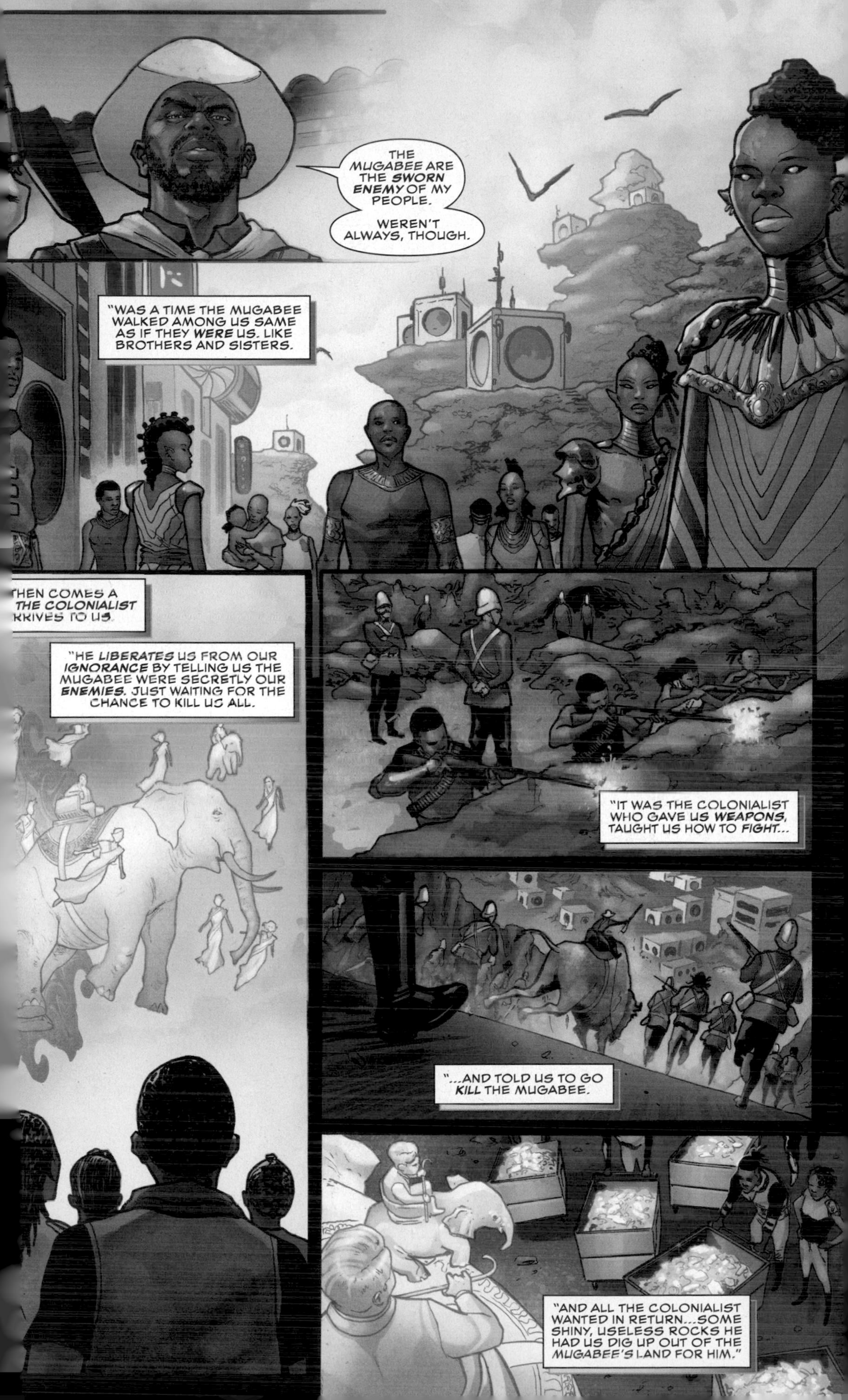
THE MUGABEE ARE THE SWORN ENEMY OF MY PEOPLE.
WEREN'T ALWAYS, THOUGH.
"WAS A TIME THE MUGABEE WALKED AMONG US SAME AS IF THEY WERE US. LIKE BROTHERS AND SISTERS.
THEN COMES A THE COLONIALIST RRIVES TO US.
"HE LIBERATES US FROM OUR IGNORANCE BY TELLING US THE MUGABEE WERE SECRETLY OUR ENEMIES. JUST WAITING FOR THE CHANCE TO KILL US ALL.
"IT WAS THE COLONIALIST WHO GAVE US WEAPONS, TAUGHT US HOW TO FIGHT...
"...AND TOLD US TO GO KILL THE MUGABEE.
"AND ALL THE COLONIALIST WANTED IN RETURN...SOME SHINY, USELESS ROCKS HE HAD US DIG UP OUT OF THE MUGABEE'S LAND FOR HIM."

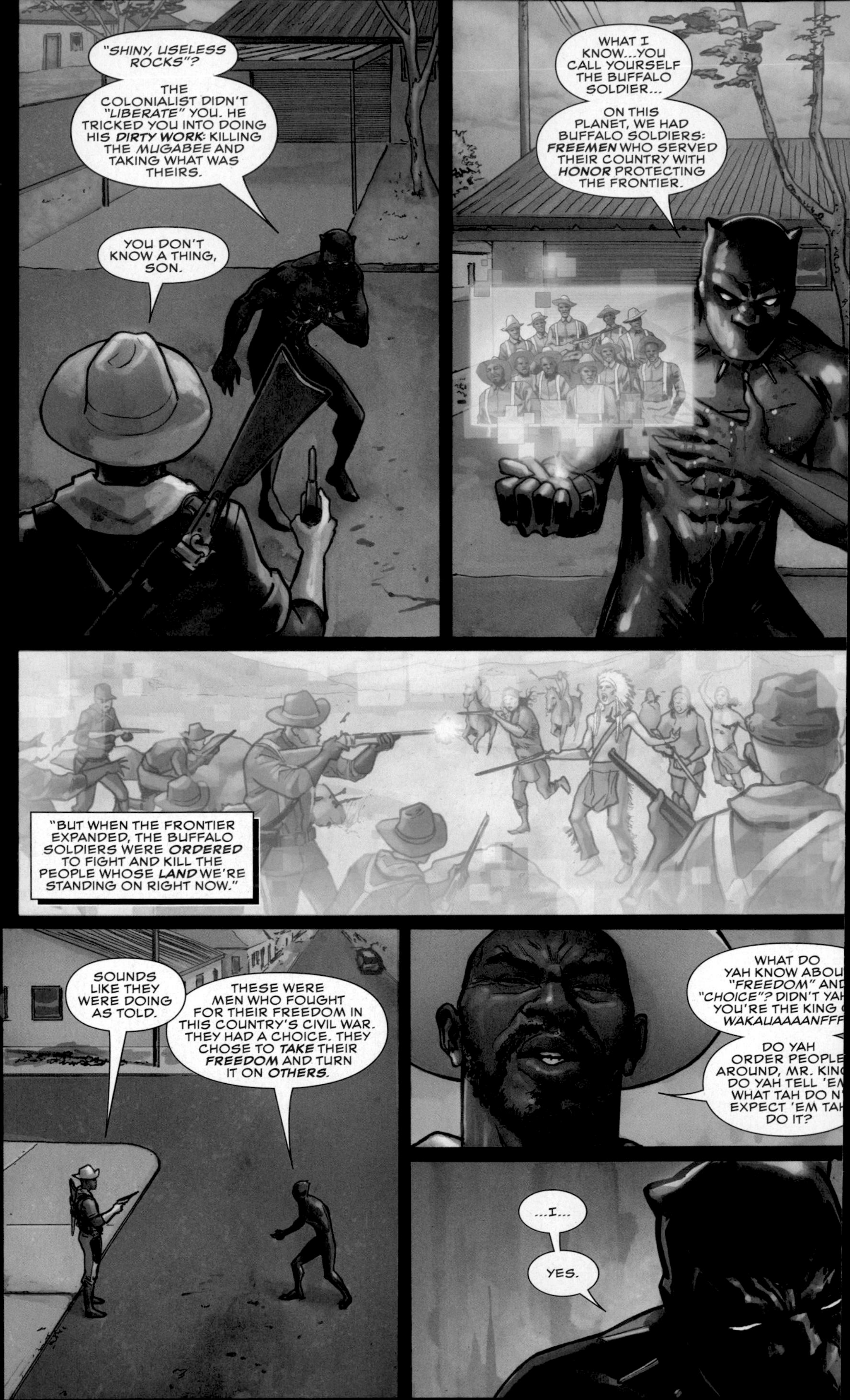
"SHINY, USELESS ROCKS"?
THE COLONIALIST DIDN'T "LIBERATE" YOU. HE TRICKED YOU INTO DOING HIS DIRTY WORK: KILLING THE MUGABEE AND TAKING WHAT WAS THEIRS.
YOU DON'T KNOW A THING, SON.
WHAT I KNOW...YOU CALL YOURSELF THE BUFFALO SOLDIER...
ON THIS PLANET, WE HAD BUFFALO SOLDIERS: FREEMEN WHO SERVED THEIR COUNTRY WITH HONOR PROTECTING THE FRONTIER.
"BUT WHEN THE FRONTIER EXPANDED, THE BUFFALO SOLDIERS WERE ORDERED TO FIGHT AND KILL THE PEOPLE WHOSE LAND WE'RE STANDING ON RIGHT NOW."
SOUNDS LIKE THEY WERE DOING AS TOLD.
THESE WERE MEN WHO FOUGHT FOR THEIR FREEDOM IN THIS COUNTRY'S CIVIL WAR. THEY HAD A CHOICE. THEY CHOSE TO TAKE THEIR FREEDOM AND TURN IT ON OTHERS.
WHAT DO YAH KNOW ABOUT "FREEDOM" AND "CHOICE"? DIDN'T YAH YOU'RE THE KING WAKAUAAAANFFF
DO YAH ORDER PEOPLE AROUND, MR. KING DO YAH TELL 'EM WHAT TAH DO N' EXPECT 'EM TAH DO IT?
...I...
YES.

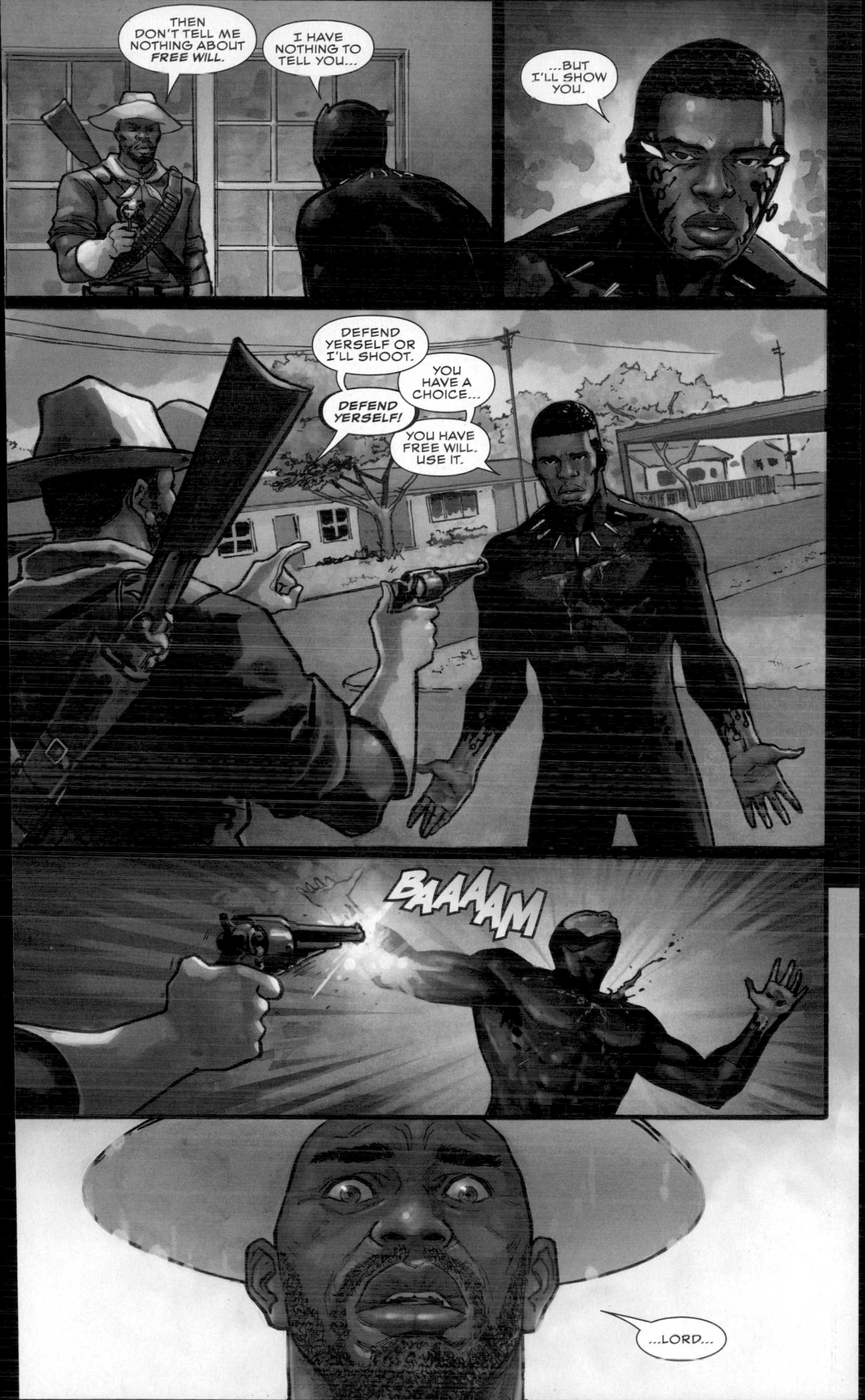
THEN DON'T TELL ME NOTHING ABOUT FREE WILL.
I HAVE NOTHING TO TELL YOU...
...BUT I'LL SHOW YOU.
DEFEND YERSELF OR I'LL SHOOT.
YOU HAVE A CHOICE...
DEFEND YERSELF!
YOU HAVE FREE WILL. USE IT.
BAAAAM
...LORD...

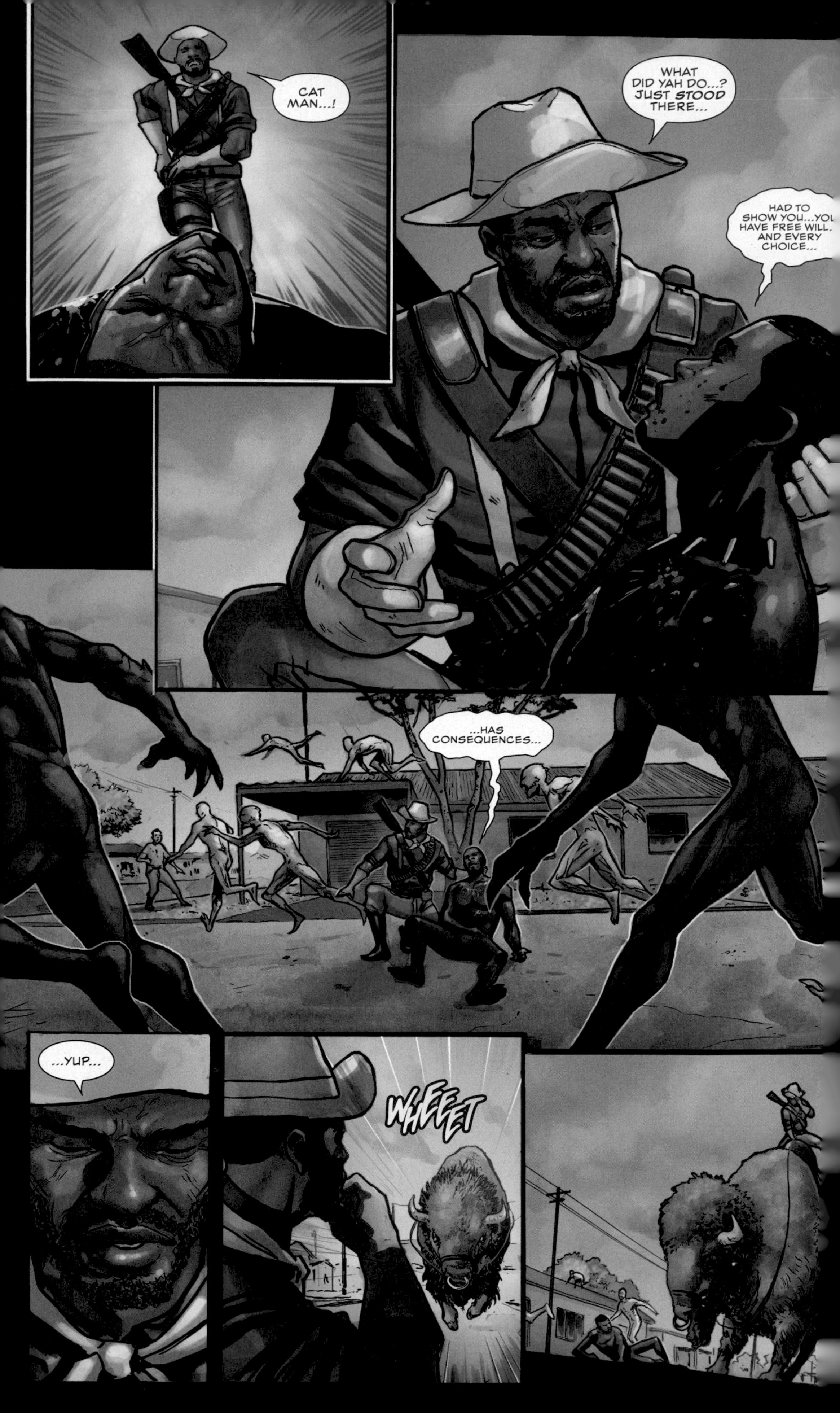
CAT MAN...!
WHAT DID YAH DO...? JUST STOOD THERE...
HAD TO SHOW YOU...YOU HAVE FREE WILL. AND EVERY CHOICE...
...HAS CONSEQUENCES...
...YUP...
WHEEET

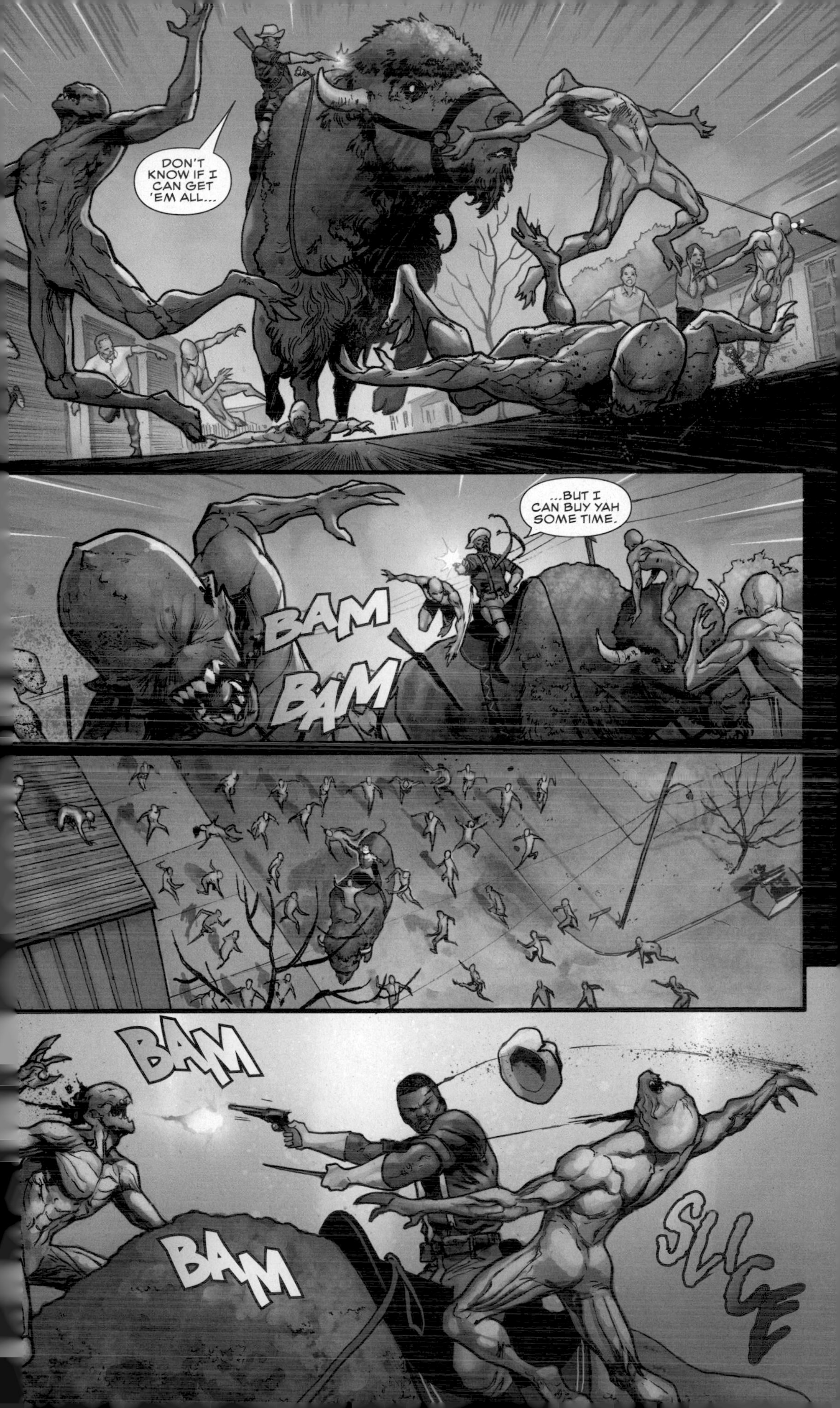
DON'T KNOW IF I CAN GET 'EM ALL...
...BUT I CAN BUY YAH SOME TIME.
BAM
BAM
BAM
BAM
SLICE

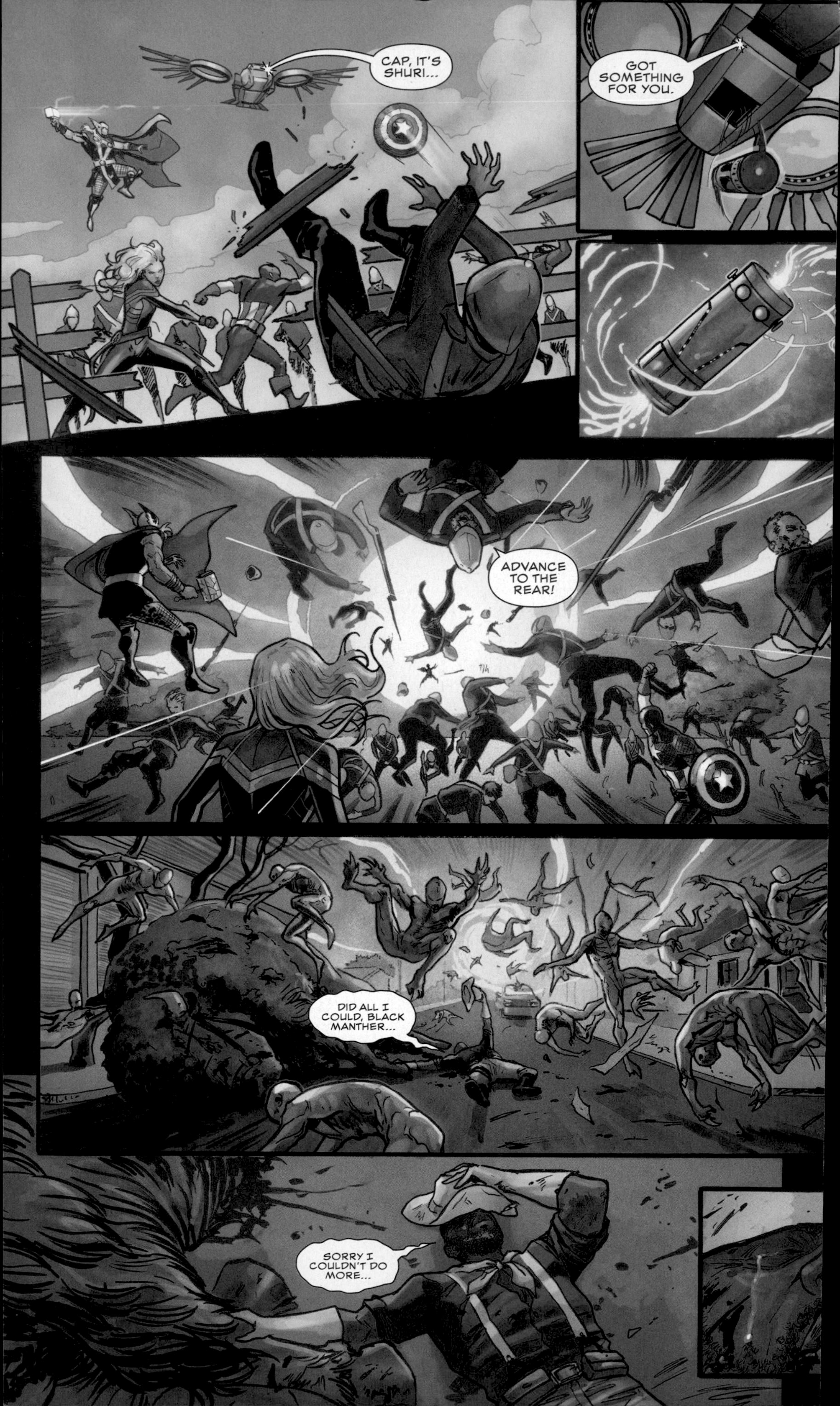
CAP, IT'S SHURI...
GOT SOMETHING FOR YOU.
ADVANCE TO THE REAR!
DID ALL I COULD, BLACK MANTHER...
SORRY I COULDN'T DO MORE...

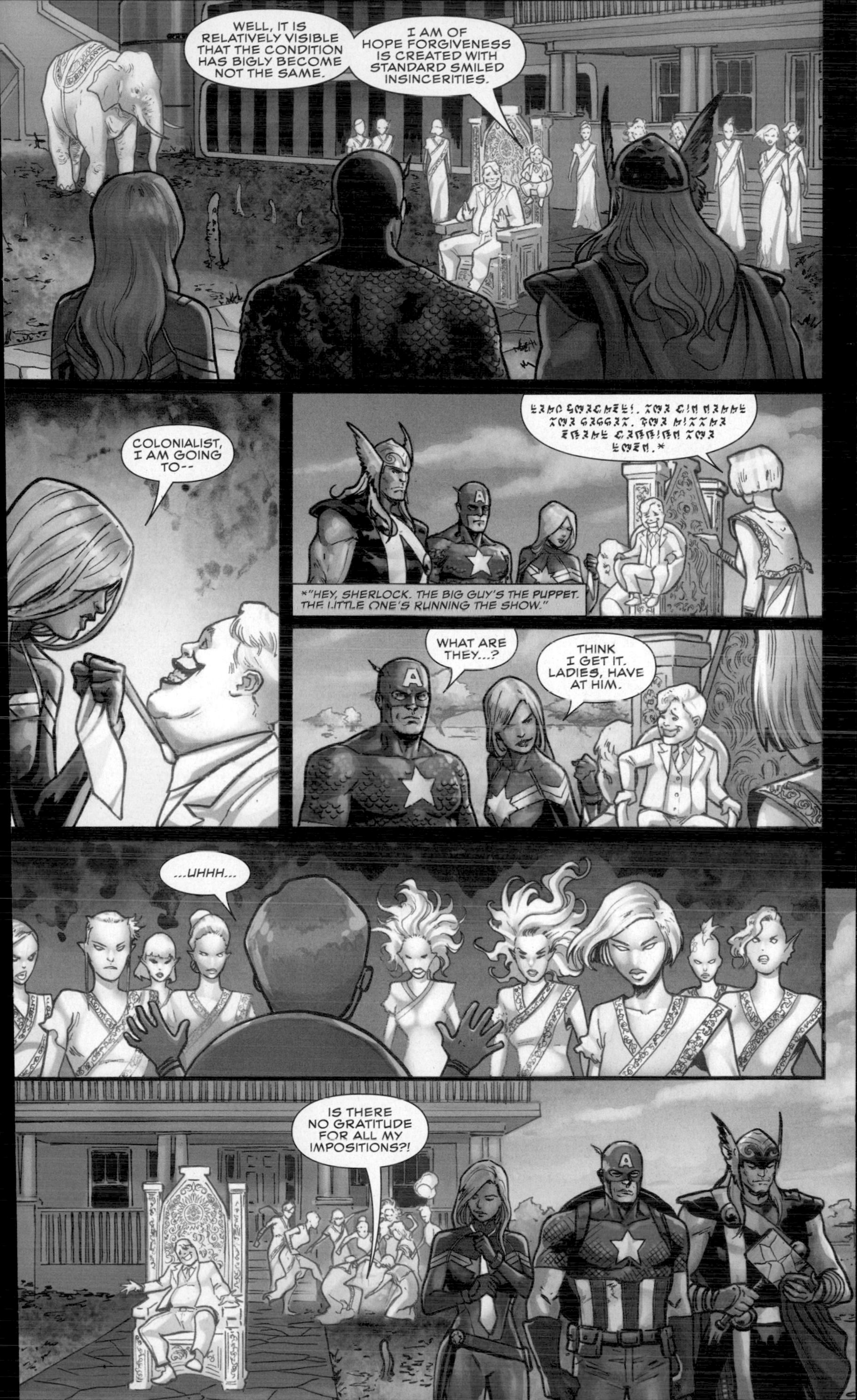
WELL, IT IS RELATIVELY VISIBLE THAT THE CONDITION HAS BIGLY BECOME NOT THE SAME.
I AM OF HOPE FORGIVENESS IS CREATED WITH STANDARD SMILED INSINCERITIES.
COLONIALIST, I AM GOING TO--
*"HEY, SHERLOCK. THE BIG GUY'S THE PUPPET. THE LITTLE ONE'S RUNNING THE SHOW."
WHAT ARE THEY...?
THINK I GET IT. LADIES, HAVE AT HIM.
...UHHH...
IS THERE NO GRATITUDE FOR ALL MY IMPOSITIONS?!

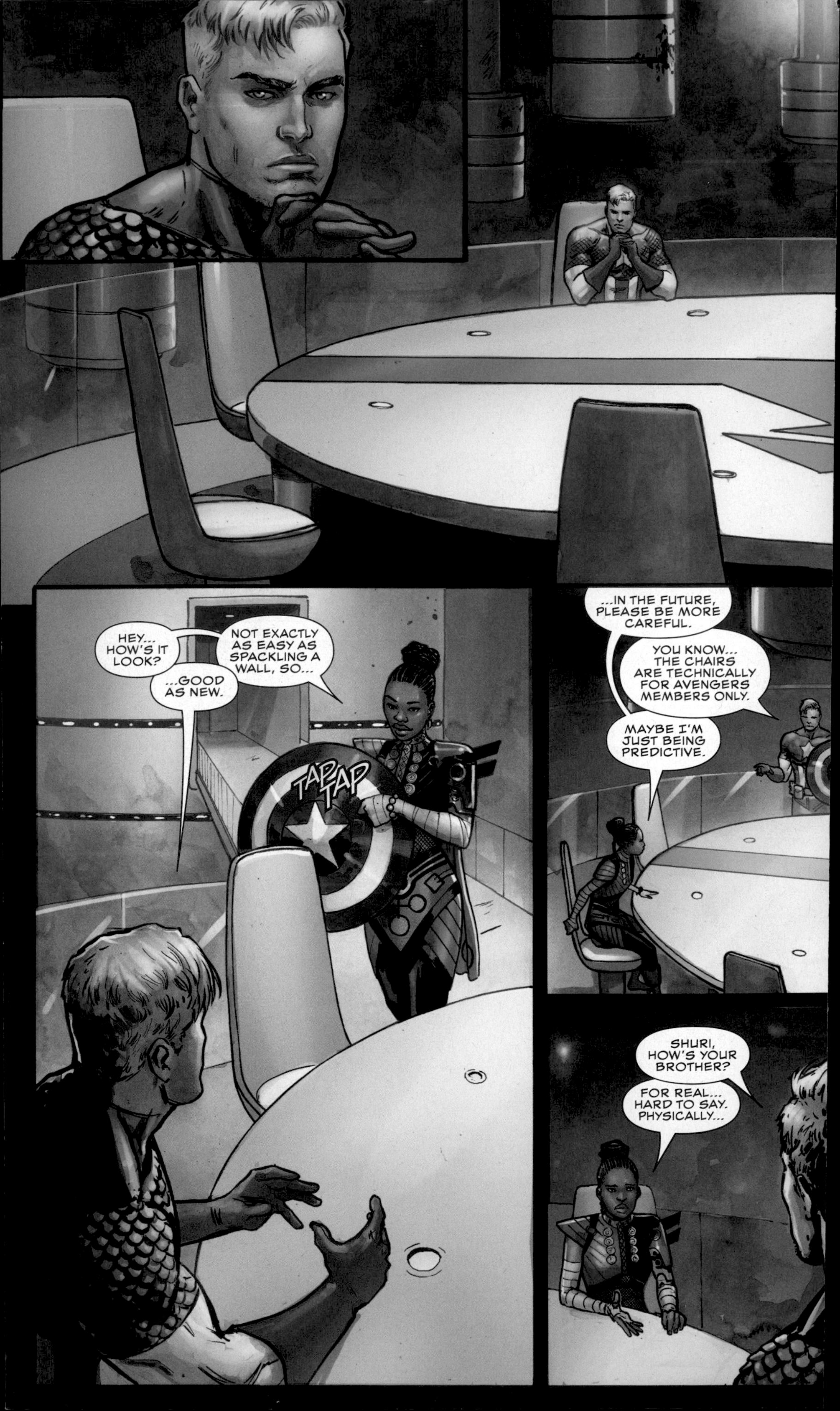
TAP TAP
HEY... HOW'S IT LOOK?
NOT EXACTLY AS EASY AS SPACKLING A WALL, SO...
...GOOD AS NEW.
...IN THE FUTURE, PLEASE BE MORE CAREFUL.
YOU KNOW... THE CHAIRS ARE TECHNICALLY FOR AVENGERS MEMBERS ONLY.
MAYBE I'M JUST BEING PREDICTIVE.
SHURI, HOW'S YOUR BROTHER?
FOR REAL... HARD TO SAY. PHYSICALLY...

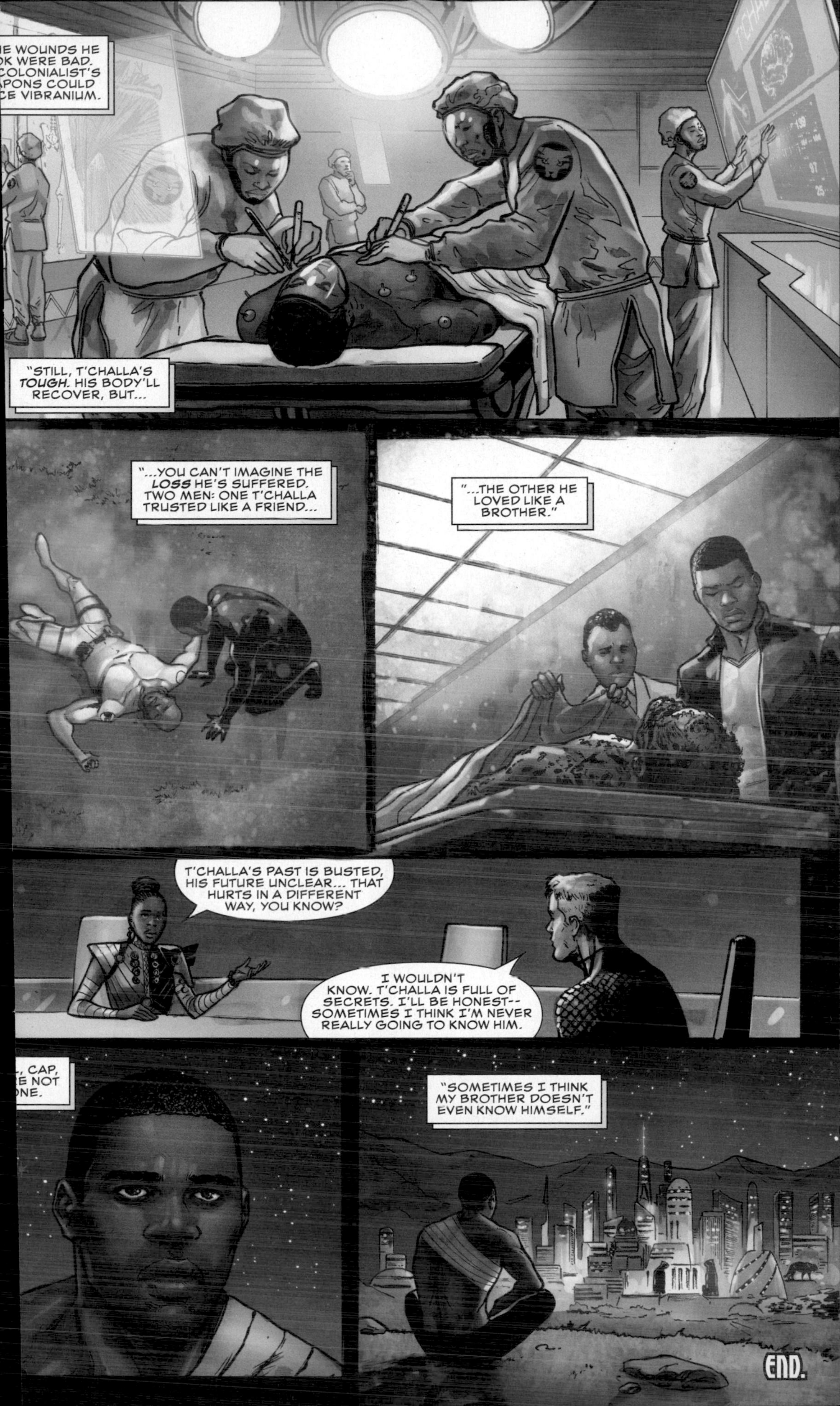
HE WOUNDS HE OK WERE BAD. COLONIALIST'S APONS COULD CE VIBRANIUM.
"STILL, T'CHALLA'S TOUGH. HIS BODY'LL RECOVER, BUT...
"...YOU CAN'T IMAGINE THE LOSS HE'S SUFFERED. TWO MEN: ONE T'CHALLA TRUSTED LIKE A FRIEND...
"...THE OTHER HE LOVED LIKE A BROTHER."
T'CHALLA'S PAST IS BUSTED, HIS FUTURE UNCLEAR... THAT HURTS IN A DIFFERENT WAY, YOU KNOW?
I WOULDN'T KNOW. T'CHALLA IS FULL OF SECRETS. I'LL BE HONEST-- SOMETIMES I THINK I'M NEVER REALLY GOING TO KNOW HIM.
, CAP, E NOT ONE.
"SOMETIMES I THINK MY BROTHER DOESN'T EVEN KNOW HIMSELF."
END.

#8 variant |||||||||||||||||||||||||||||||||||||
|||||||||||||||||||||||||| **YANICK PAQUETTE**

#9 Variant |||||||||||||||||||||||||||||||||||||||
|||||||||||||||||||||||| **MATEUS MANHANIN**

#10 Variant ||||||||||||||||||||||||||||||
||||||||||||||||||||||||||| **RAN BAZALDUA**

#10 Miracleman Variant ||||||||||||||||||
||||||||||||||||||||||||| **TAURIN CLAR**

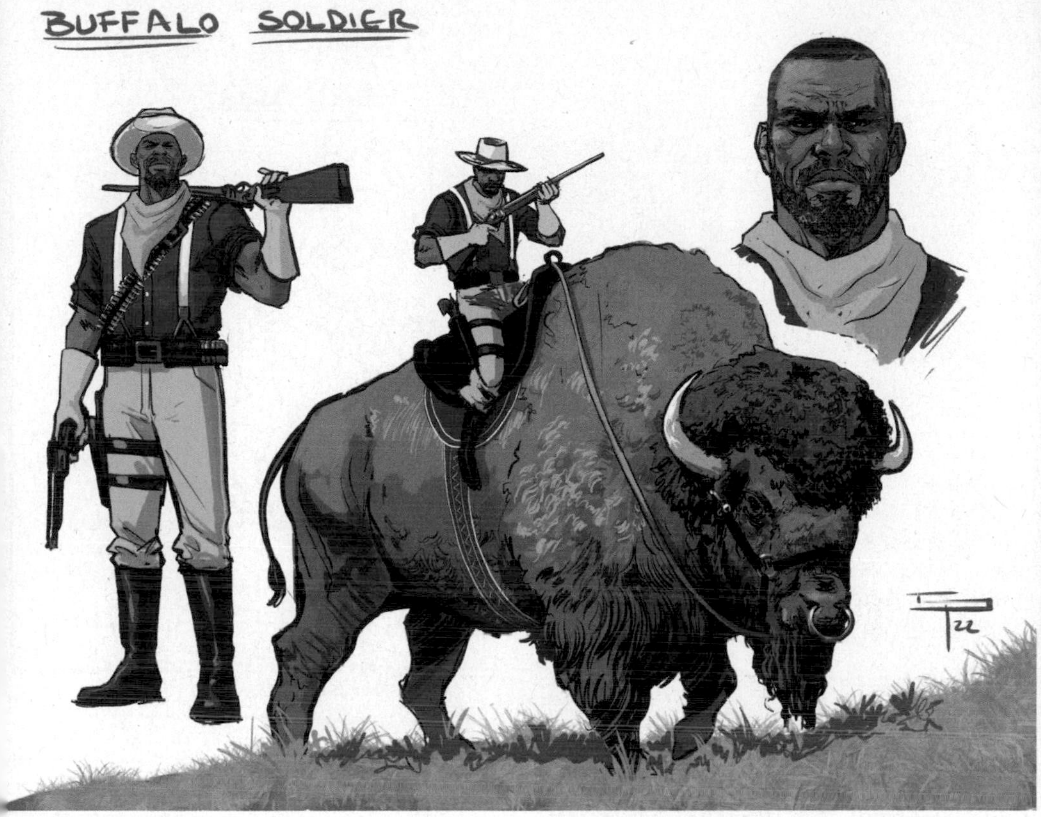
BUFFALO SOLDIER

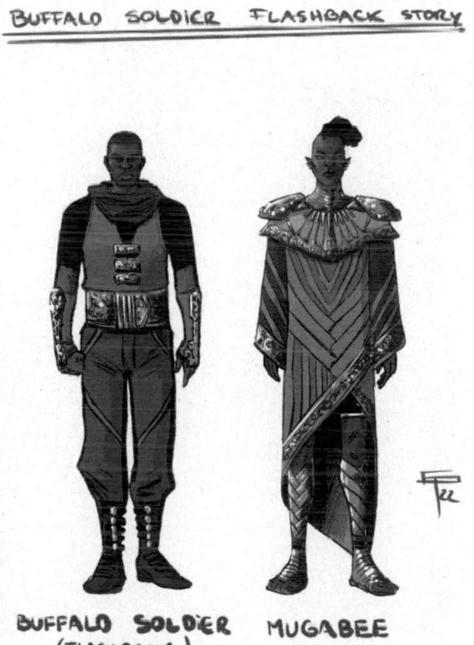
BUFFALO SOLDIER FLASHBACK STORY
BUFFALO SOLDIER
(FLASHBACK)
MUGABEE

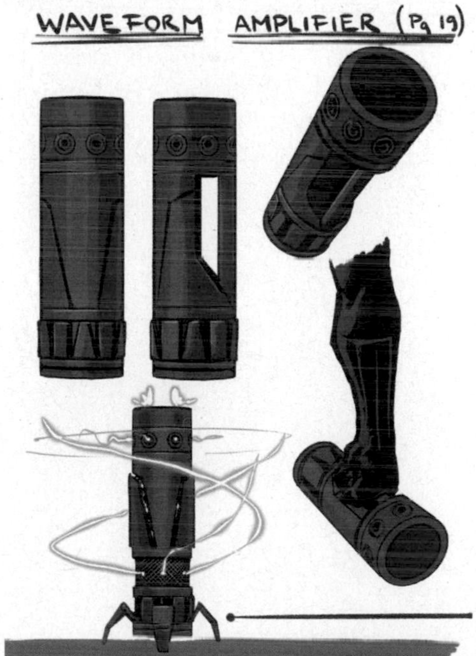
WAVEFORM AMPLIFIER (Pg 19)

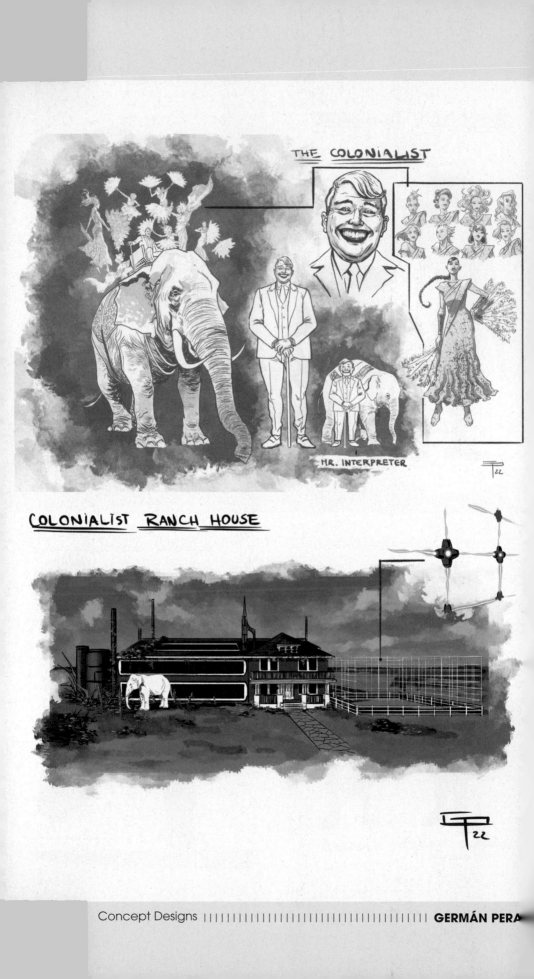

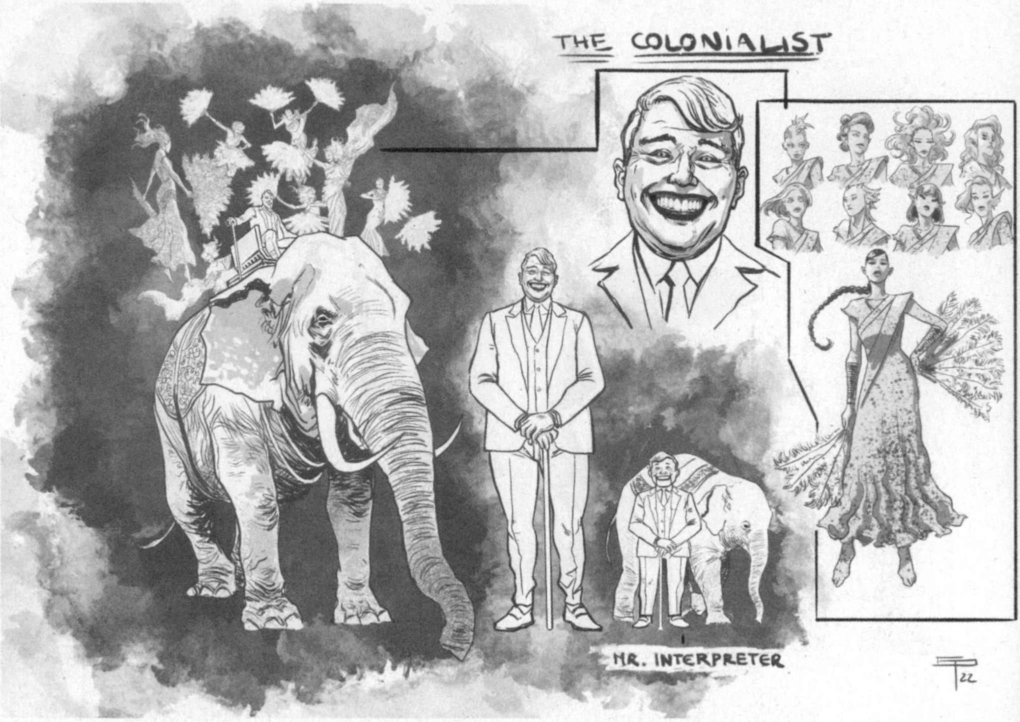
THE COLONIALIST
MR. INTERPRETER
GP 22

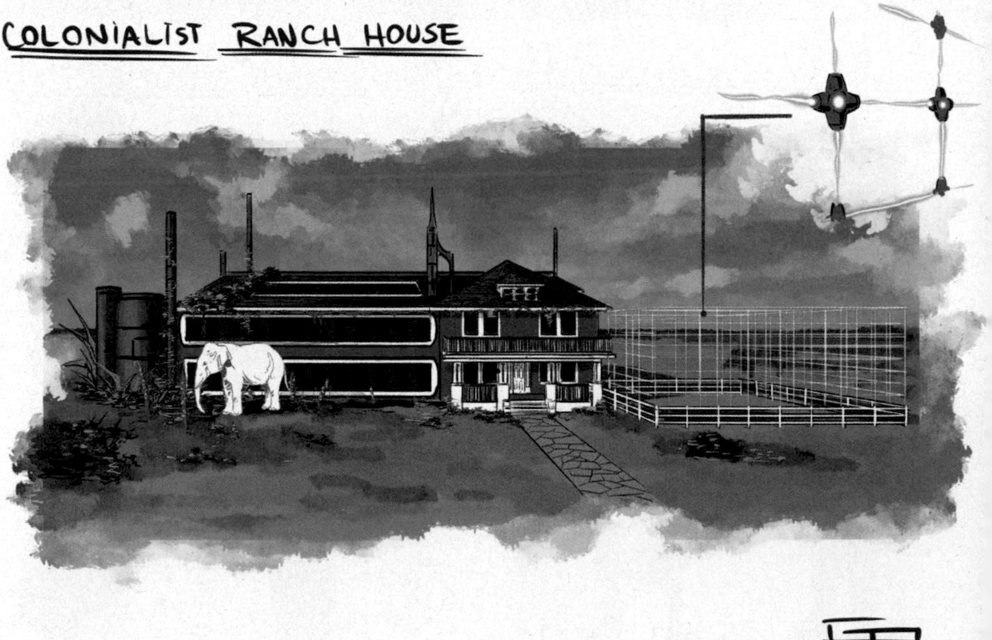
COLONIALIST RANCH HOUSE
GP 22